D1497863

Long
March
Diary

Long March Diary: CHINA EPIC

Charlotte Y. Salisbury

Walker and Company
New York

915.1
Sa3

First published in the United States of America in 1986 by the Walker Publishing Company, Inc.

Published simultaneously in Canada by John Wiley & Sons Canada, Limited, Rexdale, Ontario.

Library of Congress Cataloging-in-Publication Data

Salisbury, Charlotte Y.
   The Long March diary.

   Includes index.
   1. China—History—Long March, 1934-1935. 2. China
—Description and travel—1976-   . 3. Salisbury,
Charlotte Y.—Journeys—China. I. Title.
DS777.5134.S33   1986   915.1′0458   85-22509
ISBN 0-8027-0904-4

Book Design by Teresa M. Carboni

Printed in the United States of America

10   9   8   7   6   5   4   3   2   1

*To my companions on our Long March of 1984:
my husband, Harrison
Jack Service
General Qin Xinghan
and Zhang Yuanyuan*

FOREWORD

I cannot begin to record the tens of thousands of miles that Charlotte and I have traveled together in the back country of Asia and Russia in the past twenty years. We began these explorations in 1966, a couple of years after our marriage, and no one in the world, I would reckon, has seen as much since then of Siberia's steppes, the deserts of Gobi, the high realm of the Himalayas, the Hindu Kush, the yurts of Inner and Outer Mongolia, China's northwest Xinjiang vastness, and the trails that lead down from Lhasa to Katmandu.

None of those journeys, however, compares with the Long March that Charlotte chronicles in this book—her seventh about our distant travels. "I'm not a writer," she expostulates when confronted by a bookshelf of volumes bearing her name. "I like to garden and take care of my house."

The original Long March was the classic six-thousand-mile retreat of the Chinese Communist Red Army before the forces of Chiang Kaishek's Nationalist Army. Chiang had bottled up the Reds in the southern corner of Jiangxi. On October 16, 1934, the Red Army slipped away, and after a year of battles, evasion, deception, terrible losses, incredible sacrifices, the fleeing soldiers finally made their way to northern Shaanxi, where they found refuge.

Before the March started, Mao Zedong had been shunted aside as leader of the Communists by a Moscow-backed faction. But within two months, supported by the battle-hardened commanders, he clawed his way back into power and was never again to relinquish leadership of the Chinese Communists.

It was this agonizing epic that created the legend under which Mao and his Communists were ultimately to come to power in China. No one, until Charlotte and I retraced its route in a seventy-day journey in 1984, had

vii

made the dangerous march in fifty years. I have presented the first complete account of the march in my book, *The Long March; The Untold Story*. In Charlotte's book she tells the tale of our experiences and encounters as we journeyed in the footsteps of the Chinese Red Army.

Our journeys have never borne any relationship to pleasure trips, and this one was no exception. Once we spent four months traveling thousands of miles around the periphery of China, from the wartorn jungles of Southeast Asia to the deserts of Mongolia and the gloomy Amur River. Once we found ourselves on the Mongolia-China frontier as Soviet forces poured in, threatening Mao Zedong with nuclear war. We crisscrossed Manchuria's approaches to the Soviet Maritime provinces and inspected the underground cities that China had built in fear of Soviet nukes. We were marooned in the Himalayas by the monsoons and confined to our hotel in Ulan Bator by an unprecedented flood that left the city without light, power, water, and food.

When we returned in 1980 from a hegira that led us along the deserts of northwest China almost within eyesight of Soviet Kazakhstan, then to Lhasa and the long, arduous stone-and-gravel track that leads under the brow of Mount Everest and down to the Nepalese frontier, clambering the last miles over boulders and rocks of a landslide, Charlotte announced, "Never again!" I could not argue.

On August 17, 1983, the telephone rang. It was a Chinese official calling to tell me that if I still wanted to go on the Long March, it could be arranged. (I had first proposed the trip ten years earlier.) Of course I did. Charlotte gulped and said she would come too.

Not only did she come; she traveled beside me every foot of the 7,400 miles along mountain trails no foreigner had ever traversed. She rode her horse on the rim of Fire Mountain near Jiaopingdu as easily as she could gallop her pony over the fields of Weston, Massachusetts, as a girl. We celebrated her seventieth birthday en route, and she astonished the Chinese (as she has on every trip to China) by standing on her head, a feat she accomplishes easily and elegantly. When I fell ill, she slept beside me every night in the hospital and the Chinese proclaimed her a "model wife."

In an introduction which I wrote to one of her early diaries, I said that she saw the world with a woman's eye and a special woman's gift for observation. There were those who thought that a sexist remark, but I stand by it. Charlotte perceives the significant—the button missing from Zhou Enlai's shirt; the smog that envelops the great pagoda at Yan'an; the flash of red pumps on the feet of nimble country girls on their way to the rice paddies.

Charlotte may not, by her estimate, be a "writer," but there is no American woman who has a more intimate knowledge of Chinese life today; who better understands the long upward march from serfdom and slavery that brought China to the Communist Revolution and through the Cultural Revolution to what they now call the "new Long March."

She has met almost all of the leaders of revolutionary China and almost every surviving Long March veteran, man or woman, of consequence. She has traversed the other great Communist country, Russia, has made personal Russian friends, and can compare China not only with Russia but with India and other Asian lands as well.

No better guide to the reality of Chinese life can be found than in Charlotte's four China diaries, of which this one, the *Long March Diary*, is the most penetrating. Its panorama of off-the-map China and of that extraordinary epic from which Mao's Communists emerged to forge the power which brought them victory in 1949 makes explicit and understandable why they now lead a nation of one billion one hundred million people.

—Harrison E. Salisbury

INTRODUCTION

The Long March? Six thousand miles through China's back country along the trail Mao Zedong and his Red Army followed for a year in 1934 to 1935? You've got to be kidding, as my children would say.

That is what I told my husband, Harrison, when he shouted out the joyful (to him) news after a telephone call from the Chinese Embassy in Washington. The Chinese government had finally given him permission to make this terrible trip.

The Long March! We would never survive. Neither of us. I *knew* that. This was the word I had been dreading for years—ever since Harrison started talking about it back in the early 1970s, about what a great trip it would be. What a story! What a scoop! If he could only persuade the Chinese to let him go.

I had never believed that the Chinese would say yes. But Harrison had worked and worked on them since 1972. Now it had happened, out of the blue, and just after I had let myself relax, convinced it would never come about.

It was too crazy. Harrison was in his seventies. I was on the verge of mine. It would be the end of us, and not a very comfortable end. The Long March! How insane could he get? I wouldn't go. I wouldn't let him go. But, of course, I did, and we did.

Never in my wildest dreams as a child growing up near Boston in the 1920s had I imagined anything like this. The longest journey I can remember taking in those days was our annual expedition to Buzzards Bay. The sixty-three-mile trip from Weston, twelve miles outside Boston, to Wareham, at the head of Cape Cod, took nearly all day. It was an enormous operation with weeks of preparation. In the early morning we watched our animals loaded into a big truck—two horses, two ponies, usually a cat, a goat, several rabbits, and all their paraphernalia. Another truck was filled with trunks holding towels, bedding for fourteen beds, and other household goods we would need for the three-month stay. My uncle and two cousins spent summers with us, making a total of three adults and six children, plus a cook, a chambermaid-waitress, and a nurse.

My mother and father each drove a car. We four children were divided up for the trip, the youngest going in the car with the nurse. The maids went in the household truck, sitting high up in front with the driver. We had three dogs (I had my West Highland terrier for seventeen years, from the time I was two until I reached nineteen, just before I was married), and they came with us in the cars. For some reason they were always sick. Great piles of newspaper were essential, and I remember stopping at least two or three times to tend to an upchucking pet. On a trip of such length, there had to be numerous stops for other reasons. In those days it was usually possible to find a bush or tree not far from the road, where we could be out of sight; unattractive gas-station rest rooms were unknown to us.

The stop that sticks in my mind is the Duck Farm, not quite halfway, where we had the most luscious, greasy toasted duck sandwiches imaginable. I can still taste them, and still long for one at times.

When we were a bit older, there were longer excursions, to Putnam Camp in the Adirondacks. This really was a Long March. It took two days and a night spent along the way. No trucks, no animals. This was a three-week jaunt toward the end of August, an attempt at getting away from the ragweed that made me and my older sister miserable from mid-August to the first big frost. Our eyes were red and itchy, and we sneezed continually. Once I counted Barbara's sneezes—sixty in succession. There was no cure. But going to a little altitude did help, and we made the trip every year from the time we were the acceptable age for Putnam Camp. (I think it was ten.) It was a private camp for adults and families with well-behaved children. We had to be able to take care of ourselves.

A friend of the family, Harry Shattuck, drove my mother and the children in his big Packard touring car. My father came later by train. Mr. Shattuck picked us up in Weston. Our bags were strapped onto the running board. My mother sat in front with Mr. Shattuck, my two sisters and I in back.

We loved that drive. I especially remember the hairpin turns on the Mohawk Trail, how exciting it was when we reached the top of a peak (which probably wasn't very high but seemed so to us) to look down and see where we'd been.

Usually we stopped at Williamstown for the night, where we stayed with my mother in one inn, while Mr. Shattuck stayed in another across the street, for propriety's sake.

At the camp, we climbed mountains, even Mount Marcy, the highest mountain in the Adirondacks, and swam in the "women's pool," a natural pool in an icy brook. It was separated from the men's pool by a canvas curtain strung across the brook.

Heaven knows I had traveled since those days—all around the world with Harrison, including many remote places in China and Tibet, even jolting our way down the road from Lhasa to Nepal, as high as sixteen thousand feet. I had stayed in mud-floored barracks and cement-floored guest houses, been nearly to the Russian border where northwest China meets Kazakhstan. I had eaten mutton out of tin basins in yurts in Inner and Outer Mongolia, had bounced over the Gobi Desert in a jeep, traveled all over Siberia, and been twice to Sikkim in the Himalayas.

Yes, I had come a long way from the Duck Farm and the Mohawk Trail. But the Long March! Of course, I knew the significance of it, knew what it would mean to Harrison, realized it would be the trip of his life. But I kept thinking of what the Chinese had told us for years when we were begging to go to Tibet: "You are too old; it is too high, too hot, too cold, too difficult." In my heart I knew he would go, and I wouldn't let him go alone. I had to go too; there was no alternative. But would we come back?

Long
March
Diary

Route of Mao's Long March

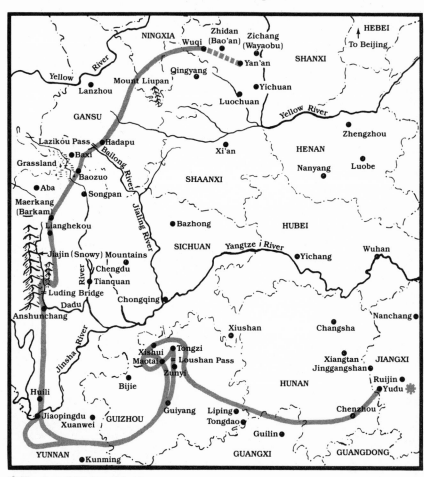

* The start of the Long March.

On the Plane to Beijing, China

It is hard to believe I am on my way to China again. We had planned to go to Italy this winter, to the American Academy in Rome. We were both going to work, but there are so many wonderful things to do and see in Italy that I don't believe I would have gotten much done. I love Italy. Once I spent six months in Florence, and I have always wanted to go back. But we never go to Florence and Rome—or London and Paris, for that matter. We go to Ulan Bator in Outer Mongolia, to remote places in Siberia, to parts of China no one has ever heard of. And now we are going back to China to retrace the Long March, the Red Army's six-thousand-mile escape from Chiang Kaishek in the 1930s.

I can't see what Harrison thinks he can find out that Ed Snow didn't back in 1936. After all, Ed talked to Mao, Zhou Enlai, and the lot, in Shaanxi, and got the dope from the horse's mouth. These men are all dead now, and I don't believe there are many survivors left. The thought of three months in China, at least two of them in very primitive areas, fills me with gloom. I wish we were on our way to Rome.

Harrison has been discussing the project regularly for years with Jack Service, who was born in China of missionary parents, went back there after school and college, and wound up as a Chinese expert in the State Department. In the McCarthy days, the 1950s, he was fired. He went to court, won his case, and was reinstated. But it took several years during which he had to work at any odd job he could find, and cost a great deal. When he was reinstated, he was sent to "Siberia," a small post in England. He has been at Berkeley since he retired.

Harrison has been sending letters to China asking permission for them to make this trip, but he never has had a favorable reply, and I was relieved and happy about it. Then last August the telephone call came. This is what I wrote in my diary last August 17 in Connecticut:

> While he was away, a man from the Chinese Mission called, wanting to talk to Harrison. When he called him back today, the man said the Chinese

were inviting us to come and make a trip covering the route of the Long March.

I just can't believe it. As long ago as 1971, Harrison had a minor operation. As he was wheeled back from the operating room, he was babbling to the doctor about going on the Long March! He has never stopped dreaming about it, and he and Jack Service have discussed it many times. Now Jack has had a heart attack and his wife won't let him go. I don't want Harrison to go either, but I can't stop him, and obviously, I'll go too.

Just a few days ago he read in *China Daily* that a seventy-one-year-old former AP man (Haldore Hanson) and his wife had gone over some of the route by bus, plane, and jeep. So Harrison sat down and wrote letters to everyone he knows in China—to the ambassador in Washington, and every other Chinese he could think of—saying that if Mr. Hanson could go, perhaps he can. There hasn't been time for these letters to even have reached Washington, so this is an amazing coincidence.

Obviously, he is on cloud nine. Is already rereading Edgar Snow and thinking of nothing else. He says he will do the second volume of his memoirs *and* the book about war on the Eastern Front *before* we go to Italy in February. It looks as if we will go there as planned, come home for two weeks, then proceed on the Long March.

Harrison said he realized I am not as enthusiastic as he is!! But he said he was going anyway, alone, if I won't go. "But," he said, "I can't think of anything more wonderful than going on the Long March with you." Not my idea of romance.

So, here we are—going halfway around the world to make a trip of more than seven thousand miles through remote places with treacherous mountains and boggy grasslands and wild river crossings. Harrison is seventy-five and has a pacemaker; I will be seventy in two weeks; Jack Service (his wife has given in but won't come herself), at seventy-four, is joining us in spite of having had a terrible heart attack several years ago. I think we are crazy and I wonder if we will survive. Mao was forty at the beginning of the Long March, almost the oldest participant, and most of the soldiers were in their teens or early twenties. Of course, we won't be walking much or sleeping outdoors or fighting battles, but still, it can't help but be a difficult trip.

Our last trip to China was in 1980 and I was sick and exhausted a lot of the time. I was allergic to the pills we had and didn't shake a bad cough until I got home. The cough came from the very dry air in northwest China. Traveling the way we do, with never a day's rest, if either of us gets sick, we have to just drag along. That, realistically, describes me on our last trip. We covered much of the Old Silk Route, saw the Buddhist caves in Dunhuang and Turpan, and went nearly to the Russian border in the heart of Asia, passing through deserts and unbelievable heat. We went

4

back to Xi'an and from there to Chengdu and Tibet and finally out to Nepal. I was so depressed about Tibet that I said I never wanted to go to China again. The deliberate destruction of a people, their way of life, their religion, their agriculture, their buildings, their art, left a very bad taste in my mouth. And feeling so lousy didn't help.

But this time I am prepared for any illness and have medicine I know I can tolerate. I have a bundle of disposable face masks to guard against smog and smoke and dust, and we are always careful about water and food. So I ought to stay healthy. Harrison is rarely sick and the only worry is his heart. He has never had a heart attack of any kind. His pulse got down too low and he had an irregular beat, so for nearly ten years he has had a pacemaker, but he is strong and vigorous. I must force myself to look on the bright side, which I don't see very clearly, and not dwell on possible, perhaps improbable, disaster.

First of all, this is *the* trip of Harrison's life. I have never seen him more excited or more fascinated by a project. Contrary to what he said last August, he did not write the second volume of his memoirs, nor the book about the war, and we canceled the trip to Italy. He has spent every waking moment reading about the Long March, and probably dreaming about it at night. Some of his enthusiasm has rubbed off on me. I know this will be the trip of my life, too, but I can't get that worked up about the Chinese Revolution. I believe it was inevitable, considering the circumstances, and I think that, with the exception of the lost years of the Cultural Revolution, the Chinese have made tremendous strides and accomplished miracles in educating millions of people, curing and eliminating drug addiction, malaria, and many other diseases, and giving the average guy a chance to have a good life.

But anticipating our Long March "doesn't thrill me at all," to quote Cole Porter. It scares me.

At least I have some idea of what to expect. No matter how difficult the intimate details of living may be, nothing could possibly equal some of my previous experiences in Mongolia and the northwest. Being prepared is half the battle. Our first trip in 1972 took us from Beijing to Xi'an, to Yan'an, Anyang, Linhsien, Wuhan, Changsha, Shaoshan (Mao's birthplace), and back to Beijing, Shanghai, and Canton (now called Guangzhou), all big cities or large towns. We stayed in hotels and up-to-date guest houses, and only when visiting selected communes or going from one place to the next were we in the countryside. We traveled mostly by train, airplane, and an occasional minibus.

The next trip, in 1977, was quite different, though it began the way all our trips to China have begun, with several days in Beijing to meet important people and make plans. After that, we went first to Daqing in the northeast to see the oil fields, then to Harbin. In Mongolia we visited Hohhot, which we used to call Huhehot, the nice big capital city with lots of trees, then to Silinhot, as near to the Russian border as the Chinese would allow us that year. To Shanghai again, to Hangzhou on beautiful West Lake, Guangzhou, and home. In rural areas and in Mongolia we got used to conditions I can only call appalling. I don't really mind any of these inconveniences; after all, the Chinese never expect us to have anything less than they have, and in all those places we were given the best there was.

Thinking of all this makes me realize how much of the world I have seen since 1966—probably more of China, the surrounding countries and the Soviet Union than any other American woman. It is a far cry from growing up in Boston when New York seemed like another world. And it was to my father. He went once to London and no more than ten times to New York in seventy years. Why go? Everything was in Boston. I don't feel like an important world traveler, which Harrison keeps telling me I am. I feel like a mother, grandmother, wife, and housewife. I love all those roles. I have never felt that I was the least bit inferior to men, or that taking care of my family wasn't just as important as working in an office or becoming a bank president. I am all for women having careers, but everyone is different. Anyway, now I have an added role, that of author. But fundamentally, I am a homebody.

We will have a month to get ready in Beijing, during which we hope to see some of the top people, and as many survivors of the Long March as possible. In the past we have dined with Zhou Enlai and counted Madame Sun Yatsen (Soong Chingling) as a dear friend. We have become close to many Chinese who have been in our country, visited us in our home and spent holidays with us.

But I am tired of traveling in China and the Soviet Union. If we are going to do all this moving around, I'd prefer to go to Italy, France, and England, and stay in fancy hotels. And to Greece, where neither of us has ever been. I don't want to leave home for three or four months. And the thought that I won't be able to plant my garden in the spring, that we will miss the daffodils we worked so hard over, and probably the peonies, is depressing.

But perhaps I will be pleasantly surprised, the way I often am when I dread going to a certain dinner party and end up having a wonderful time.

MARCH 2, 1984
At the Peking Hotel, Beijing, China

We arrived last night at about 10:30 China time and, after some worrying by me, were met by Mr. Li Huming from the Information Department of the Foreign Office. We had no bother with customs; after picking up our bags, we went directly to an English-drive Mercedes. We were driven to a

6

big new tourist hotel, the Yan Jing, which means "City of Swallows," and spent the night in a perfectly good room. Mr. Li kept apologizing and saying it was just for tourists, and that he would come in the morning and move us here, which he did. But we both slept well; I would have slept all day if Harrison hadn't waked me up. We had delicious strawberry jam on toast for breakfast, and now here we are in a lovely sunny room, all unpacked. I found my keys, which I thought I had left on the bed in New York.

So far the general atmosphere seems like that in a hotel anywhere. Everyone seems relaxed and many look happy. Chinese girls have pony tails or curly hair, some too kinky. The women workers in the other hotel had smart tan uniforms and wore brown leather shoes with one strap and heels—very pretty.

At six we were driven out to the guest-house area, where we had dinner with Qian Qichen, vice foreign minister, who is going to Moscow on the eleventh of this month for meetings. Our new Mr. Li was present—a tall young man who is a translator and is longing to come with us (Mr. Qian said everyone, young and old, wants to come)—and Mr. Qi Huaiyuan, head of the Information Department. All spoke English, but before dinner Mr. Qian spoke in Chinese with an interpreter. He said I was a very brave woman.

Dinner was exquisite; no urging to eat; no noticing if I didn't eat everything, which I couldn't. I can't eat abalone and all the jellyfish stuff. A waitress was quick and whisked plates away. As soon as we were finished eating, Mr. Qian said, "You must be tired from your journey," so we were able to go right home, to sleep again for ten hours.

SATURDAY, MARCH 3

This morning we were so late all the dining rooms were closed and we ate in the "After-Hours Dining Room," behind the huge room where we had all our meals on our last visit in 1980. Now it seems to be exclusively for Japanese. There was a buffet of Chinese breakfast goodies—dried fish, cold cooked peanuts, fermented bean curd, pickled vegetables, and the like. Every kind of egg kept warm, toast, butter, jam, and fruit.

We took a short walk, me with my nose covered because of the dust, and some Chinese friends came to see us.

SUNDAY, MARCH 4

Today we paid a visit to Madame Soong Chingling's Palace, which is now a museum. Yao Wei, who was our interpreter in 1972, came with us. It was strange to go in the big red gate, still guarded by several soldiers, with crowds of Chinese, pay for our tickets, and enter with the mob. No being driven to the door; no Mercedes parked in the driveway; no nice man with glasses to welcome us, as when we used to go there for dinner. As we walked in, we wondered about him, described him to Yao Wei, who said he was now in charge of the museum, and called for him. He greeted us effusively, took us all through the exhibits, explaining everything; took us upstairs to Madame Soong's private quarters. She had a big square bedroom with an upright piano in it. In the piano seat was some music— *The King and I;* a piece from *The White-Haired Girl.* Several bottles of perfume were still on her dressing table, one of Revlon's Charlie and others I couldn't make out. Not the bottle of Joy we brought her in 1980. I hope she used it and enjoyed it.

Her bathroom is huge, with a light green tub, toilet, and basin. Her study was on the other side of the bathroom. In her bookcase, along with other books, were *The Nine Hundred Days* and *To Peking and Beyond, Asian Diary,* and *China Diary.* I wasn't surprised at Harrison's books being there, but was amazed and thrilled to find two of mine.

We had never been upstairs before, or been there in the daytime. The emperor who built this palace surely lived well and appreciated beauty. The grounds must be gorgeous in the spring and summer. There are many ponds and bridges, rock formations and gardens for flowers.

The exhibit consists of a wonderful collection of photographs of Madame Soong's life, but there are pictures of her in bed when she was ill and dying, with tubes in her nose and other things attached to her, and I think that is awful. I don't mind so much the picture of her dead and in her coffin: a huge glass tomb, like Mao's.

We were interested there were no pictures of Yolanda and Jeanette, her two wards.

We took another short walk up the big shopping street and could hardly plow our way through the crowds. I said to Yao Wei that I couldn't get over the millions of people, and he replied, "Yes, it's a bit different from Taconic."

The Adlers, Sol and Pat, took us out for dinner tonight at their favorite hotel, the Xinqiao. Sol was born in London of Russian-Jewish parents. He attended the London School of Economics and came to the United States some time before the New Deal. He worked as an economist for the Treasury Department and during World War II was sent to Chungking (now Chongqing) to be head of the Treasury Department there. He came back to Washington after the war and was working for the Treasury at the time of McCarthy and the communist witch hunt. After being subjected to accusations and investigation he decided to return to China to live. He is one of the Foreign Friends, like George Hatem and Rewi Alley. (The

Foreign Friends are foreigners who sympathized with the revolution—some even worked for it—and stayed on in China afterward.) Pat is English. In *China Diary: After Mao* I wrote, "He is the picture of an English eccentric—tall but bent over the way very thin, hollow-chested people sometimes stand; long hair cut straight across the ends; baggy pants. He talks and gesticulates constantly." All still true.

After the big earthquake in 1976, the Adlers' house was so damaged it was uninhabitable and they lived in this hotel for many months. Now they live in half of a courtyard house out by the Drum Tower.

We had a lot of fun. He darts from one subject to another, amusing and really interesting. He has been very sick with cancer of the lung. Some was removed and the scar became infected. He said he would have died without Pat. She stayed at the hospital the entire time. She told me family members are expected to stay and take care of the patient. There is a kitchen on each floor, so she brought a blender and made special food he could eat. She complained about the nursing care, or lack of it, just the way we do. Nurses only want to manage things or give injections—no bed care. They never think of trying to make a patient comfortable, she said.

MONDAY, MARCH 5
In Our Room in the Peking Hotel

Harrison is interviewing Wang Yanjian about the Long March. He was about five at the time, born in 1929. He is a writer mainly of novels about the Long March, and film scripts. *An Ordinary Laborer* is a collection of stories, and his film *Four Times Across the Chishui River* came out several months ago.

Harrison is saying that Mao was "set aside" (something like house arrest) at the beginning of the Long March, and he is wondering why. Mr. Wang says, "That is a long story," and giggles. Harrison says, "Yes, but it is interesting." At that time, it seems, the Communist Party was under control of a young man named Wang Ming, who was in Moscow, taking orders from the Russian Comintern. The Comintern (the Communist International) was supposed to promote revolution all over the world, but Stalin had transformed it into an instrument of Soviet military and foreign policy. Young Chinese didn't understand this and it had great prestige and authority in Chinese revolutionary circles. It had helped Dr. Sun Yatsen with money, military and propaganda advice. It had a hand in setting up the Whampoa Military Academy in Canton, where, in the early days, Chiang Kaishek and Zhou Enlai worked hand in hand against China's feudal rulers. The Comintern had sent a German named Otto Braun (his Chinese name was Li De) out to direct Communist military operations in

9

China. Mao Zedong was quickly shoved aside, but for a time Zhou Enlai and Zhu De (who had been Mao's right-hand man) went along with Braun and the Comintern policy.

But, as Mr. Wang explained to Harrison, things went from bad to worse. The Red Army suffered great losses following the Comintern line. Over half the territory that Mao and Zhu De had won was lost. Still Mao's advice was ignored. He had begun to say the Red Army was like a beggar, and the Nationalists (the military branch of Chiang Kaishek's Kuomintang party) were king.

Still, Mr. Wang said, no one paid any attention to Mao, and the situation got so bad the Red Army had no alternative. It had to pull out of the central soviet area, the base in southern Jiangxi that Mao had created. Secret plans were made to do that. No one was told.

For instance, one of the great Communist generals, Chen Yi, lay wounded in a hospital. He didn't know what was going on, but he noticed there were a lot of soldiers marching about in the courtyard and called in Zhou Enlai to tell him what was up. Zhou Enlai told Chen Yi that they had to give up their base; had to retreat from Chiang Kaishek. He didn't tell him there would be a "Long March," because neither he nor anyone else knew that the retreat would last a whole year.

Zhou Enlai, Mr. Wang said, had bad news for Chen Yi. He was not to go on the march. He was to stay and take command of the rear guard in the central soviet zone. Like a good soldier, Chen Yi took on the assignment. But it didn't last long. He had to flee with a few soldiers to the mountains. Chiang's soldiers ravaged the central soviet area, killing and burning.

Only about eighty thousand men (and a few women) got away for the Long March.

Harrison asked whether Mao was actually under house arrest during this time. Mr. Wang said he was not. But a good many others had been punished just because they were supporters of Mao. One of them was Deng Xiaoping, China's present leader. He had lost his jobs, was sent to do physical labor in the countryside, had no horse when the Long March started, and had to carry his own baggage. He had been ordered to do a "self-criticism"—to confess his faults before a public meeting. He refused. I am surprised that this kind of thing happened so early on. Obviously, intrigue and jockeying for power began early and has never ceased.

After the first big battle of the Long March at the Xiang River crossing, led by Zhou Enlai in November 1934, they lost about half their men—only thirty thousand were left.

After hearing Harrison and Mr. Wang talk, I wonder if I will ever get straight the armies—First Front, Fourth Front, Third, Fifth, Ninth, Thirtieth? And the battles and river crossings? Of course, this is only the first interview—perhaps when I have heard more, read more, and actually see the battlefields and rivers and grasslands and mountains, I will have a better sense of the Long March. Harrison regards it as one of the most interesting and heroic stories in contemporary history, but so far, to me, it is a jumble of strange names and places and events.

TUESDAY, MARCH 6

Today at 8:45 A.M. we went to the Military Museum and spent the morning looking at pictures and maps and listening to three specialists on the Long March. Li Huming is busy arranging our trip, so another young man, Mr. Zheng, accompanied us. He was in Honolulu at Brigham Young University and has also been to the big Mormon tabernacle in Salt Lake City. Imagine if anyone had suggested such a thing in 1972. At that time we asked some Chinese students what countries they would like to visit and they answered they only wanted to visit their "sister socialist states," meaning North Korea, North Vietnam, and Albania.

The head of the museum is a handsome general who is one of the three specialists we talked with. There are very few records of the Long March, because the armies were too busy fighting or covering ground as fast as they could.

Here again I heard names that confuse me—Nineteenth Army (a new one); "blockhouses"; "fifth encirclement campaign." We heard more about Otto Braun, and about the Zunyi conference at which Mao regained his control. I got hopelessly lost in the battles, generals, warlords.

WEDNESDAY, MARCH 7

It is hard to write every night, but I must get into the habit. At home I put it off if I am tired, but that won't do on this trip.

Today was a "free day," as Li Huming said, and it has been lovely. In the morning I mended Harrison's socks, learned a new knitting stitch, and read Edgar Snow. We went for a walk and it was a beautiful day. Generally, when we get up at 6:30 or 7:00, the smog is ghastly. Coal is burned in factories and households, there are many more cars than previously, and the wind from the Gobi Desert blows in dust. I wear a scarf over my nose and mouth. Many Chinese wear face masks.

THURSDAY, MARCH 8

This morning our new Mr. Li met us and we walked to the Revolutionary Museum across the square and opposite the Great Hall of the People. We were there in 1980 and I remember being thoroughly bored. All these exhibits have the same pictures, the same pieces of the chain bridge over the Dadu River; the same revolutionary flags; the same examples of clothing, cooking, and eating utensils, primitive fighting instruments, guns captured from the Nationalists, etc. But because we are concentrating on the Long March, it is more interesting to me now.

After lunch we walked to the Peking Hospital and visited Rewi Alley, who is there with walking pneumonia. We thought he looked well and was very chipper. He is eighty-seven. He has been writing Harrison constantly and sending him book after book about the Long March. He is thrilled with our project. It is very close to his heart.

Rewi Alley started life as a sheep farmer in New Zealand. When the bottom fell out of the wool market in the 1920s, he went to sea. At Shanghai he went ashore for a few days to see something of China, got caught up in the China scene, and has never been home except for a visit. He is roly-poly, white-haired, and very soft-spoken. Until recently he has spent half of each year traveling and there is scarcely an inch of this huge country he has not visited. He is a poet, writes articles and takes pictures for many magazines, including *Eastern Horizon* and *China Reconstructs*. He started a school for Chinese boys, and many of his old students come to see him.

FRIDAY, MARCH 9

Plans for the big trip seem to be progressing. Jack Service arrives here March 16 and we leave for our Long March on April 3. It will take two months, so we won't be home until at least June 10. We will miss all the early flowers.

This morning we drove out to the Academy of Military Science, where Harrison talked to General Xiao Ke, another participant in the Long March. The academy is just beyond the Summer Palace in the Western Hills and is out of bounds for most people. The Foreign Office had to get special permits for us.

We were greeted by three polite soldiers, and one of them said, in English, "The general is sorry he has to be at a meeting so couldn't greet you," and I thought, Here we go, he won't appear at all. But he arrived just as we were sitting down in a freezing cold room furnished with the customary armchairs covered in tan cotton with tables beside and in front, all arranged in a rectangle.

The general is a nice simple man. He wore no insignia and his uniform was just like those of the other men, who may have been officers or ordinary soldiers. I like that. It revolts me to see American and European officers with epaulets and stripes, and medals covering half their chests.

12

He and Harrison discovered they were both born in 1908. The general said the Chinese feel there is a special relationship between people born in the same year. They talked for over two hours, and as he warmed to the subject he sent for two big maps. One was hung on a stand, the other laid on two tables in front of him. He said he was born in Hunan Province near the five ridges separating it from Guangdong Province. His family was "petty intellectual," he said. He was head of the Sixth Army in Hunan, and in August 1934, before the Long March started, he set out to meet up with He Long and the Second Army. It took him two months. At the start he had nine thousand troops, but by October, though he had broken through the Nationalist blockade and joined He Long, his army had lost five thousand to casualties, desertion, and sickness.

He said that in the beginning his army had only a small school geography map and never knew where they were. When they came to a village, men would go out and ask the villagers about the countryside, and from what they were told they made their plans for the next day. Later they found a map in a church, in French, which no one understood. General Xiao Ke stayed up all night with a French priest who knew Chinese, writing all the names in Chinese on the map. I remarked that the priest must have been sympathetic to their cause, and the general laughed and said, "You might say he was under house arrest." The priest had never heard of the Red Army.

He also said that when they were in areas inhabited by Tibetans, the people were friendly and helpful. We have heard and read other reports to the contrary; that the minority people (the non-Chinese) preyed on the Red Army and didn't like any Chinese.

General Xiao Ke wrote many poems and was known as the Scholar General. He gave us several and we will have them translated.

This general, one of the heroes of modern China's most fantastic adventure, was in bad trouble in the Cultural Revolution and was sent to the country to do labor for two years. Going home in the car, I said I couldn't understand such a thing, an army officer hero treated like that, and our interpreter said, "Probably it was because he was not on Lin Biao's side." This is the first time I have heard any Chinese mention his name since the furor over the Gang of Four.

We are just back from dinner at George Hatem's. He is an American Lebanese, born in Buffalo, New York, who came to China as a young doctor in the 1930s. Like many other non-Chinese, he got caught up in the revolution, went to Bao'an right after the Long March ended there, knew all the leaders of the Chinese Communist Party, and decided to stay and help. He married a Chinese girl, Su Fei, who is more beautiful today than when they were married, and has raised his family as Chinese.

He picked us up in his big car with a chauffeur. The Chinese government treats their Foreign Friends well, and now that they are old and have

13

been ill, like Sol Adler, Rewi Alley, and George (who has cancer but is in remission at the moment), they all have houses and cars and receive the best care when they are sick. I think this is wonderful. I can't imagine our government doing this. We provide our ex-presidents with millions of dollars and quantities of security people, but we don't do anything from the heart.

George lives in a comfortable courtyard house on the same street by the lake as Madame Soong's house, a few doors down. We went in a door that he unlocked with his key, walked through the open-to-the-sky entrance, about twenty-five feet long, and up some steps into another open narrow walk. He pointed out two small statues, one a Ming figure. Both had been damaged during the Cultural Revolution. We saw the hammer marks and places where new stone was inserted. We turned right into a big courtyard with four flower and vegetable beds and a little gray furry bunny eating greens in one of them. No pen or fence. All the rooms are off the courtyard, and George said they could sleep as many as twelve.

Su Fei, his beautiful wife, doesn't speak English. Neither do the children or the daughter-in-law, or his son, who wasn't there. He gave me some very good vodka, which reminded me that someone said Chinese vodka is the best in the world. Then we had a wonderful meal. No fish except some little fried shrimp cakes. Tasty vegetables, meat, and chicken soup made by just steaming the chicken in an earthenware pot, no water added. A little greasy, but good.

George and Harrison talked after dinner, and I looked at a book Haldore Hanson had made from his dispatches and pictures taken when he was in Yan'an as a reporter for the AP in 1938-1939. I found it fascinating. Some of the pictures are better than any I have seen in published books or museums here. It must have been an exciting, romantic time for a young newspaperman.

SATURDAY, MARCH 10

This morning a new, very serious young man from the Information Department of the Foreign Ministry escorted us to a tomb that was discovered in 1974 and excavated soon after. It is about seven or eight miles southwest of Beijing and is of the Han Dynasty, 221 B.C. to 220 A.D. Except for the tomb itself, very little is preserved. Just a few bits of metal, knives, and tips of shovels, for example.

Driving to the tomb, it was interesting to see the intensive farming right within the city. Over most of the cultivated fields—and there are no others—are plastic domes, temporary or winter greenhouses where the vegetables for the city are grown. Straw mats hold them down and are rolled up on the south so the sun gets in. They are lowered at night. The only heat is the sun. When it is time to plant outside and the winter crops are harvested, the plastic is taken away. The plots are fertilized, plowed, and planted again. Most are too small for tractors, so most of the work must still be done by hand.

Even just a little out of the city center there seem to be a lot of people on bicycles pushing or pulling big loads. Hardly any animals—no dogs, no cats, no cows; only a few chickens, one goose, and a few pigs. Cows must be somewhere else and kept in. There is a big campaign to get people to use more milk. I have the most delicious yogurt for breakfast every morning and we have hot milk with coffee. The Chinese have never drunk milk the way we do; they process it and use it for children. I wonder how far they will get with the campaign. Milk just doesn't seem to fit into the Chinese diet.

At one corner there was a big sign: *Serve the country—make the peasant rich.* In Chinese, of course.

Right after dinner Huang Hua and Madame—who is now He Liliang, not Ho, as she used to be—came to call on us. There was a lot of talk about the Long March, *our* Long March, and Harrison's interviews. I didn't follow it all. Huang Hua was interpreter for Ed Snow in Yan'an in 1936 and he told us a great story. Most people who went to Yan'an had to go through Xi'an, where the Young Marshal, though ostensibly on Chiang Kaishek's side, was sympathetic and helpful to the Communists. Even with Kuomintang soldiers and police all around, the Communists managed to get a lot of people through. Soldiers all dressed alike and it must have been impossible to tell who was who. Huang Hua was in a hostel waiting for his contact when suddenly two Kuomintang police were stationed at the front door and two more came up to his room. They demanded to see his suitcase, his papers, and made so much noise that every other guest came out into the hall to watch and listen. Huang Hua said his hostel room was his home and the police had no right to come in or to look at his belongings. He then asked the police if they knew a certain girl who was about to be married. She turned out to be a good friend of theirs, so they stopped harassing him. He then invited them into his room and said, "My bags are under the bed, look at them." But they were embarrassed, felt he was a friend, and left him alone.

Next morning he told the hostel manager he was going to do some sightseeing, left, made the contact he'd been told to, got on an army truck and was driven out of the city, and thence to Yan'an.

We talked about how the Russians had misunderstood the Chinese Revolution, how they saw it strictly in Russian terms. They couldn't conceive of a successful peasant revolution; Mao knew this was the way

15

for China. This misconception was the reason for the Red Army losses when Mao was pushed into the background and Wang Ming and the twenty-eight Bolsheviks were making policies based on Moscow's orders.

SUNDAY, MARCH 11

This morning Christopher and Jacqueline Wren (he is the *New York Times* correspondent here) picked us up and we drove out to I. M. Pei's new hotel at Fragrant Hills. So many drives could be pretty if there weren't so many wires and poles interfering with views, and so much junk along the roads. You can scarcely see the hills and mountains until you get right to them.

The hotel is spectacular and nestled—except it is too big to be nestled— at the base of a hill or mountain that has some temples and old houses barely showing through trees. I was disappointed in the hotel; Harrison was not. When you drive into the big entrance with high walls on both sides, it is impressive, combining delicacy and strength. But I object terribly to the wall on the right, which cuts off the mountain. I know this is the Chinese way, and I appreciate concentrating on a beautiful entrance. I just would like to see the mountain from the court. Sometimes I think architects are jealous of nature and try to block it out.

When you go through the big room and out to the garden, from there, of course, you can see the mountain.

Inside, the space is like the new building of the National Gallery in Washington—big, with nice proportions. But I didn't like a lot of the details, especially the light-colored wood. It is like the furnishings in many Asian hotels I have been in. It would be handsomer in dark teak or mahogany. I didn't like the brown chairs either. And the dining room upstairs I found oppressive and dark, lit only with artificial light from a low ceiling. It was a heavenly day, and it seemed ridiculous to eat lunch as if we were in a nightclub. In the ladies' room there was not even a fixture for toilet paper, or place for one, and, of course, no paper. I know the upkeep is poor and the Chinese don't use it as a hotel the way the architect envisioned, but my criticisms are directed at the plan.

MONDAY, MARCH 12

Today is my birthday, my seventieth. It is just about impossible to believe. As the mother and grandmother in *Fanny and Alexander* said as she looked back on her youth, "Where have all the years in between gone?" It is perfectly clear where they have gone, but they have gone so fast.

We went to see Rewi again this afternoon and had a nice visit. He looks fine and his only problem seems to be low blood pressure. But there are drugs for that. He hopes to go home soon. Another visitor was there when we arrived, and after he left, Rewi told us he had had a terrible time in the Cultural Revolution but that his wife had suffered more. At one time she was so desperate she tried to cut her throat with scissors, was found, and then beaten almost to death. Her torturers didn't want her to take her own way out, even such a painful one. We keep hearing stories like this, and each one makes that period harder and harder to comprehend.

We got dressed up for dinner, Harrison in his suit and I in a silk blouse and skirt, and off we went in a taxi to Maxim's. Pierre Cardin owns the famous Paris Maxim's, and last year he opened this restaurant here. As neither Harrison nor I have ever been in the Paris Maxim's, we can't tell if this one is an accurate replica, but it is supposed to be and is certainly gaudy and quite marvelous. It seemed huge and empty. The only people besides us were a lone Chinese in a gray sweater, no coat; a table of four; and another of two, a Japanese and a strange-looking Western man. The head and three captains are French; the many waiters are Chinese who have been well trained by the French. I don't know if Mr. Cardin makes money with the Paris restaurant, but he must be losing his shirt on this one. Maybe when there are more tourists it will be fuller. I understand he has eight factories in China, so perhaps he has this Maxim's as advertising and promotion, and maybe a tax write-off.

We had a lovely dinner: roast beef that was more like sliced steak, and delicious vegetables. It was a nice change from our steady diet of Chinese food, no matter how good it is. A martini costs about $7.50 (American dollars) and a half bottle of wine, the cheapest, was $18.00. A nice simple way to celebrate my birthday!!

TUESDAY, MARCH 13

We have settled into a routine here in the hotel and every day is much like the others. We have breakfast in the Western dining room, where we can have fruit, eggs and ham or bacon, pancakes, yogurt, toast and jam, butter, coffee and milk. We eat lunch in the Chinese dining room, which is so popular we have to get there before noon or wait until the first people have finished, about 12:45. We nearly always have the same dishes. Harrison likes noodles in a big bowl of broth with chicken shreds; I have chicken shreds and bean sprouts, bean-curd soup, and beer. I never drink beer at home, but I like it here. Sometimes I have chicken with garlic tips but Harrison says he smells garlic on me afterward, so I don't have it if we are going out to dinner. We have dinner also in the Chinese dining room and usually have a pork dish, rice, and vegetables. No butter, no desserts, but we go to the bar in the lobby afterward, and Harrison has an ice cream sundae. An interesting item on the menu under Special Reserved Dishes—which means you have to order it ahead—is wolfberry and ox-penis soup.

Harrison was interviewed by a young man from *China Daily* who wants to write an article about him. He studied at the East-West Institute in Hawaii, but Harrison was amazed at how little he knew about anything. He is surprised that a foreigner should want to write about the Long March—how and why could he be interested in it? This young Chinese knew practically nothing about it himself.

At 4:30 we went with the Wrens to call on a couple who are both translators. She is English, from a missionary family; he is Chinese. They met at Oxford while they were both studying; he was in England from 1934 to 1939—he left just before the blitz. They live in a big flat, actually two or three put together, just behind the Foreign Language Publishing House. It is clear they suffered a great deal during the Cultural Revolution. Two daughters are now in the United States. One is at Harvard teaching English. The other is in Chicago. These women are in their late thirties—the generation that missed out on education and just about everything else. Both have families here, living in this extended flat. Chinese couples are separated so much. We know young men who have come to the United States to study, leaving behind a wife and new baby. They are apt to stay two years. We would consider that a hardship and many marriages wouldn't survive. To the Chinese, it is an opportunity and all in the line of duty.

Soon after we had arrived, our hostess excused herself—said she hoped we wouldn't mind if she took a quick bath. Hot water is available only occasionally, so she took her bath, then ran a tubful for her husband to use after we left.

WEDNESDAY, MARCH 14

We lunched with a group of foreign correspondents at the Wrens' flat. The man I enjoyed the most was the Yugoslav correspondent, who has been here ten years. It interested me that, coming from another communist country with similar regulations, he was very critical of Chinese rules and restrictions about seeing people and other personal freedoms. There was a lot of talk about how often mail is opened, and how some people have received copies of letters to them instead of the original. Mail, evidently, goes to and comes from England in four days, but to and from every other country takes much longer.

At 3:10 we went to the Great Hall of the People and had an interview with Ji Pengfei, former foreign minister. He was on the Long March as head of medical departments and supplies. We haven't been to the Great Hall since 1980, when we had an interview with President Li Xiannian.

Mr. Ji is now seventy-three, at the time of the Long March he was twenty-three or twenty-four. He is tall and thin, beginning to get bald, but has very few gray hairs. He wore tortoiseshell glasses. He seemed reluctant to talk at first, but when he got going, he enjoyed it. He said it was easier to write about the Long March now than when Ed Snow was writing. Museums have collections, research has been done and is continuing, roads exist where there were none, places are accessible. At Bao'an Ed Snow only had interviews and what people told him. He was not able to go to or see any of the important sites.

Mr. Ji talked about the difficulties caused by the altitude—twelve thousand feet and more. Many soldiers were wounded and ill. After crossing the Golden Sands River and shaking off the enemy, they had to cross one of the Snowy Mountains. This could be done in one day. They climbed up the southern slope, but going down the north side it was all ice and snow. They held onto their horses' tails, which slowed the horses and supported the men. Most who rested at the top could not get up again. They lost a lot of comrades, mostly from the weather and lack of oxygen. Some froze to death, some couldn't breathe. They died very quickly. Many suffered broken bones from sliding down the mountain. Mr. Ji said it was impossible to apply first aid—it was too cold. They could only help people to move. A special detachment followed the army to pick up those who had been left behind. We have heard that his story is not true; that many badly wounded had to be abandoned. Occasionally some would be captured in a battle with the Nationalists. But even in the central soviet area, where there was a medical school, it was primitive. There were not many real medical doctors; there was not much equipment. Water was boiled for sterilization, barber's scissors and razors used for scalpels. They relied on herb medicines and whatever supplies were captured. If a soldier didn't die yet could not continue the march, he was left behind with peasants.

The Grasslands we hear so much about are the high boggy plains in western China (in Sichuan and Gansu Provinces), inhabited primarily, where inhabited, by Tibetans who left Tibet centuries ago for a more agreeable climate. We will go there on our Long March, and I am interested to see for myself what the area is like. Except for the marshes it sounds like Montana, only higher.

Mr. Ji said the weather on the Grasslands was weird, changeable from hour to hour. From sun to rain to snow and sleet. They were on the Grasslands for three to four days and it was difficult to find a hard, dry place to camp. No trees, only small bushes. No food. They were greatly weakened. Many died at night. They lost more on the Grasslands than on the Snowy Mountain crossing. "Every morning we counted the men," he said. Harrison asked what they ate. They carried some wheat, which they boiled or fried. But many died from inability to digest raw grain when they could not cook it. People who came after his outfit boiled their belts, drank the broth, and ate the leather.

When Harrison asked him if he was a real doctor, he laughed and replied, "Amateur turned professional." Harrison said he understood Mao had been sick and had to be carried across the mountains. Mr. Ji said no, Mao wasn't sick, but Zhou Enlai was very ill on the Grasslands. Harrison also said we had heard that Mao's wife, He Zizhen, had given birth to a baby on the Long March. Mr. Ji denied this. But he said that she was sick and spent a lot of time on stretchers.

Mr. Ji said that for him the most difficult episode in the Long March was crossing the Dadu River at Luding. He was in the vanguard at the bridge. He had walked 120 kilometers, and the head of the bridge was in flames when he crossed. The wood planks had not been replaced; it was terrifying to look down at the surging water.

Harrison asked if he had encountered Deng Xiaoping. The man on Mr. Ji's left whispered something to him, and then he answered, "I knew about him, though we didn't meet much. He was political commissar of the Third Group, known to be in charge of propaganda work."

At 6:15 we took a taxi to the Sichuan restaurant that Huang Hua and He Liliang took us to in 1977. It is a huge old warlord's palace with many buildings and courtyards. No gardens or flowers, but trees in every courtyard. They were giving a dinner in our honor and it was remarkable. We gathered in one end of a big room. A huge round table was set at the other end. Guests beside us were the Adlers, the Hatems; Yao Wei; General Qin, who is in charge of the Military Museum; the writer Wang Yanjian who spent so much time with Harrison last week; Yan Mingfu, secretary of the Standing Committee, which Huang Hua is on; and several others, including Israel Epstein and our Mr. Li Huming.

It was like a dinner party at home. Harrison sat on Madame's right and I on Huang Hua's. There was an enormous amount of food, dish after dish, and soup three times to clear the way for more. A beautiful swan carved out of a white turnip with spread wings of thinly sliced vegetables and fruits was the object of great admiration. Warm rice wine was served in little bowls over hot water, white wine, beer, orange pop, and a never-ending supply of maotai, the fiery 160-proof national drink of China.

There were lots of jokes and toasts in three languages—Chinese, English, and Russian. Mr. Yan speaks Russian well—he was Mao's interpreter in Moscow—as do Epstein and Madame He. (Many Chinese went to Moscow to study in the thirties, forties, and fifties, so many speak

Russian.) Those three and Harrison, who also speaks Russian, were referred to as the Gang of Four, Russian spies.

Many of the guests had been in jail during the Cultural Revolution. Epstein, who has been a fanatically loyal Communist sympathizer, had four and a half years of solitary confinement.

It was a lovely, affectionate evening. We can't get over it, all this friendly attention.

THURSDAY, MARCH 15

This morning at 8:15 we went to the headquarters of the Standing Committee of the People's Consultative Congress—whatever that means—and had a talk with General Yang Chengwu.

He is seventy years old but looks younger. He is a native of Fujian and joined the guerillas at seventeen and the Long March at twenty. He was twenty-one when they reached Shaanxi. It had taken one year and two days. Before our meeting I had written in my notebook: *Rose in the army under Lin Biao; led regiment during Long March; had a distinguished record fighting against Chiang Kaishek, then the Japanese. He was deputy chief of staff of the PLA in 1959; eliminated from the Red Army by Lin Biao in 1967.* Someone told Harrison that in 1967 a mass meeting was held at which Mao and Lin Biao both denounced Yang Chengwu.

Harrison said, "We have never met, but you are familiar to me; I have read your account of crossing the Dadu River on the Luding Bridge. I think this must have been the most difficult of the whole march." General Yang: "It was of major strategic importance—a key point. The position was so dangerous." Harrison: "If you had not been able to cross that bridge, you would probably have been annihilated." General Yang: "Yes. Chiang Kaishek's planes dropped leaflets over that area. The leaflets said they would wipe us out as Prince Shi Dakai, the last of the Taipings, was wiped out by the imperial forces of that time. They killed everyone." (Harrison told me that Prince Shi was taken to Chengdu and sliced like a hunk of meat until he died.) "The difficulties were beyond our wildest imagination."

General Yang's book, *Reflections on the Long March,* was published in 1982. He tried to give a true account, not just of the march, but of the peasants and life in the villages. He wrote a poem describing the night the Luding Bridge was taken.

The Luding Bridge was, and is, one of those suspension bridges high over rushing rivers in the mountains. I have been over several in North Sikkim, and one here in China at the famous irrigation works near Chengdu. The Luding Bridge had thirteen heavy chains fastened in the stones on either side of the river: nine chains on the bottom, or floor, and two on each side, serving as railings. (Ed Snow wrote there were sixteen chains, but this is wrong.) Wooden planks were put down on the bottom, but the enemy had removed most of them and set them on fire at the far end of the bridge. Twenty-two volunteers were the first to go over. They began at four o'clock in the afternoon, after having marched 120 kilometers without rest or food, racing to get there before enemy reinforcements who were marching on the other side of the river. By dusk the bridge was taken and the enemy in flight. The picture of those young soldiers (Rewi Alley says most were in their teens or very early twenties) getting across the bridge by crawling on their stomachs, or swinging hand over hand with rifles and grenades strapped to them, being fired on by the Kuomintang troops, is haunting. Only three were lost.

General Yang was head of the vanguard group and was one of the first to cross after the bridge was taken. At midnight he escorted Marshal Liu Bocheng to the site. Liu said, "Oh, Luding Bridge; now we are victorious, but we have lost so much." Mao, Zhou Enlai, and Zhu De all came to praise this regiment soon after. General Yang said he called the assault on the bridge "The Flying Leap."

Harrison asked if Chiang Kaishek used planes for bombing at that time, and General Yang said, "Quite a few enemy planes dropped bombs, but far fewer than in other places." Harrison asked about Lin Biao: "He hasn't been mentioned. I know this is a delicate question, but was he a good commander in those days?"

General Yang got to know Lin Biao in 1931. In 1932 Lin Biao was commander of the First Army Group. The general admitted that he was capable: "I cannot say he was a poor commander, but he was politically weak, wavered a lot."

Harrison asked if he encountered Deng Xiaoping. Yes, he was Yang's commanding officer. "He was a small man wrapped in gentleness." Harrison asked about Zhou Enlai—was he a good leader? Yang said he was a very wonderful leader. He contributed to the founding of the Red Army. He had rich political theories as well as experience. An educated person in many fields. Clearly General Yang admired Zhou enormously. "He had the high respect of all of us." Also, the love.

When he mentioned how Zhou treated subordinates as equals, I remembered the dinner we had with him in 1972. He said that though he was sitting at the table and the waiters were serving him, that was just their job. When they went through the door with him afterward, they were equals.

Harrison said he is surprised so little has been printed about Zhou on the Long March. He keeps saying this at every interview and I wonder if we will ever get an explanation.

General Yang said Zhou didn't have the title of chief of staff, but that he really was. He suffered liver disease (hepatitis?) during the crossing of the Grasslands. Harrison has heard somewhere that Mao was sick during the Long March. Yang said Mao didn't suffer from anything serious as far as he knew. Yang himself had typhoid and was so sick everyone came to say good-bye to him. But he recovered. He was wounded three times, twice on the Long March. He was given two washable cloths for bandages. No disinfectant.

General Yang, a real hero of the Red Army, was in jail for seven years during the Cultural Revolution. He was falsely accused of ordering the beating up of Jiang Qing. "Of course, it wasn't true," he said. Harrison replied it would have been a good idea, which provoked a lot of laughter. (Jiang Qing was Mao's last wife, and became leader of the Gang of Four, who were arrested in 1976 after Mao died and are now in prison.)

FRIDAY, MARCH 16

I have nearly finished rereading *Red Star Over China,* and have read some contemporary Chinese short stories, very touching and human. Harrison types up his notes every day or night, but I'll have to wait until I get home to type this diary in one fell swoop.

This morning we went, early again, out to Peking University to talk to Professor Xiang Qing, specialist in Communist Party history. He is a tall, good-looking man. Harrison thought he was in his thirties; I thought his fifties, and one of the Chinese with us thinks he is in his sixties. Most Chinese don't show age the way we do, and it is hard to judge.

Harrison said that next year is the fiftieth anniversary of the Long March and there is no written record of Zhou Enlai's role in it. Professor Xiang said that there were no newspapers in remote areas to keep track of details of the march, and added, "We are in the same boat." He would like some records too.

Harrison mentioned a party historian, Xu Mengqiu, whom the Snows met around 1936. He told them he had collected seven hundred documents pertaining to the Long March. But he was disgraced, and as far as Harrison knows, none of those documents have come to light. He feels somehow he will run across some of them—how, I can't imagine. Professor Xiang suggested that Mr. Xu had "betrayed the revolution" and was a traitor, so was removed, along with all his works.

Professor Xiang is going to the University of Chicago in July for six months, to study political science.

The interview was held in the house of John Leighton Stuart, who was president of Yenching University for many years before he was United

States ambassador. Yenching was the missionary university founded by Americans in 1898, but in the leaflet we were given, there is no mention of the United States. After 1949 Yenching was taken over by Peking University. Dr. Stuart served as ambassador until 1949; he was our last ambassador on Mainland China until "recognition" in 1979.

Harrison asks everyone about Deng Xiaoping—whether it is true he was in trouble because he backed Mao as early as 1934, was sent down to the countryside, refused to admit any error, stuck to his guns. Everyone has said this is true. Harrison likes that story.

After lunch we drove out again to the Headquarters of the Standing Committee of the People's Consultative Congress to have a talk with another old survivor of the Long March, General Xiao Hua. I refer to these men as "old," and most of them are about my age, some younger. But we are all old, and these people seem especially so because they have been through so much.

General Xiao Hua [he died in August 1985] is stocky and quite bald and was very friendly. He is the author of a collection of poems called *The Red Army Fears No Hardship on the Long March*. These were made into songs and are known to millions. They are played in schools and many young people have learned of the Long March from them. During the Cultural Revolution they were banned. Harrison suggested the author also was banned, and General Xiao said, "Yes." He was in prison for seven and a half years. We asked if he could sing his songs in prison and he replied, "There were guards; I could only sing in my heart." When Zhou Enlai was dying in 1976, he asked to hear these songs again, and the Gang of Four refused. Such a mean thing to do! General Xiao said of himself, "The Gang tried twenty-one ways to put me to death." He said that the Gang had not participated in the Long March. This is true, but Lin Biao, who was in cahoots with them, did.

He talked about warlords—said they had two guns, a real one and an opium pipe. His regiment went through country inhabited by Yi tribes, one of China's many minorities. They had a backward slave society, were constantly fighting among themselves, and were preyed upon and sometimes wiped out by local warlords. They hated the Chinese and knew nothing about the Red Army. The Yi thought they were warlord troops and refused to let them enter their territory. Sparsely dressed with no shoes, armed with bows and arrows, spears, knives, and rocks, they presented a formidable blockade.

Communication had to be through local Chinese traders, for no one else understood the Yi language. The Yi demanded "road money" for allowing the Red Army to even pass through their land. The army tried to explain who they were and how they would help the Yi, and gave them some silver dollars. General Liu Bocheng said, "We only want to borrow your path for a moment."

This led to a famous ceremony—the swearing of an oath of brotherhood in chicken blood between Liu Bocheng and the handsome Yi chief, Xiao Yedan. (It amuses me that the Yi chief had the same name as the general we are interviewing.) A cock was beheaded and the blood allowed to flow into two large bowls of water. Wine was supposed to be used, but there was none. The two men drank this concoction and became "Brothers." (There are pictures of this ceremony in the exhibits of the Long March.) So the Yi helped the Red Army to cross their territory, and because of the blood oath they were spared any attacks from the local people.

These four generals we have talked to were all on the Long March. They are heroes of the Red Army and so of the Chinese Communist Party. All four of them suffered in the Cultural Revolution. They are lucky to be alive. They rarely talk about anything that happened to them, just say they were put aside, or in jail, or sent to do labor. When we were in Chengdu in 1980, our host at dinner didn't say anything about himself, but he got a young man to tell us about the torture of his family and himself. What a story this will be someday. There have been books in the West by people who are not in China anymore, but nothing by army people, professors, and the like.

Jack Service is arriving tonight and Harrison is going to the airport to meet him.

SATURDAY, MARCH 17

It is nice to have Jack Service here. Although he and Harrison have been talking about this trip for years, I had never met him until this morning. He is very nice and easy, tall, thin, and healthy-looking.

This afternoon, with Jack, we went to see Rewi. We talked about Madame Soong's foundation for children and how they would like more people all over the world to know about it. There are three hundred and fifty *million* children under fourteen years of age in this country, many living in remote areas.

SUNDAY, MARCH 18

We have read in the paper that our Northeast has had the worst storm since the blizzard of 1888. All I can think of are the poor birds starving to death. Harrison and I took a walk poking around in old hutongs (ancient narrow streets), and Eppy (Israel) Epstein had supper with us. He is one of the Foreign Friends, has an English wife and is a Chinese citizen. His parents came from Polish Russia. He went to school in Tientsin with John Hersey, whose parents were missionaries. Elsie Epstein is in the hospital, in the last stages of cancer.

MONDAY, MARCH 19

This morning Harrison and I and Jack Service took a taxi to George Hatem's, where they talked for more than two hours. George went to Yan'an with Ed Snow in 1936. There he saw the arrival of the Second and the Fourth Armies from the Long March. The First had already arrived. Harrison asked him his impressions, and he said one of the very first was amazement at seeing so many pregnant women. On the march there were some births, and babies were left in villages with peasants. In fact, Mao's second wife is rumored to have been pregnant at the start and to have left the baby along the way. These babies were never found, or reunited with their parents. Supposedly the women did everything they could to prevent pregnancies, but when they arrived at Yan'an caution seems to have been forgotten. George delivered many babies, though he had imagined he would be a medical hero saving wounded soldiers.

George brought in medical supplies, such as he could. There were no antibiotics in those days, though the Swiss had discovered some kind of sulpha drug that was given by injection. The conditions were so primitive he first felt he couldn't practice medicine. At Yan'an at that time, they did have a pharmaceutical factory—one hundred people working in caves— and doctors wrote prescriptions on any old scrap of paper. George realized he was affected by outward appearances, that much could be done without the medical apparatus he was used to; that the body is tough, can take a lot. There were only ten qualified doctors who had been to medical school, and no laboratory equipment. But they had a local hospital and they taught people. They used animals to teach anatomy; once in a while they had a human body. Some men were gifted in making beautiful, accurate anatomical drawings. One doctor, Qin Xinzhong, had two tin boxes of medical books in German which he carried on the Long March, studying them all the while. He was a surgeon and taught George a lot. He watched him set a broken leg with a piece of kitchen equipment George called a flour sifter. Whatever it was, it had wooden handles that could be used as splints.

During the march, plaques with medical questions and anatomical drawings were mounted on pack animals in front, or on a man's back, so medical students could study as they walked. Morale was high in the medical group. They carried their own supplies, tended the sick and wounded. He told about a soldier who had a bad head wound who wouldn't let the medics treat him until his political adviser was sent for so he could give him his gun for another soldier to use. George hadn't realized soldiers' morale and belief in Mao and the Red Army was so strong.

Malaria in the shivering stage was treated with acupuncture. It was so successful a man could get up and continue the march or his work. In the Tibetan areas, they used scrolls of Tibetan scripture as bandages.

George and Harrison talked about the Rectification Program, which Mao launched in 1942 in Yan'an, to eliminate the Twenty-eight Bolsheviks, Russian line followers who were his enemies. They were Chinese who had been to Moscow to study and believed in the Russian idea that revolution could only be successful if based in the cities and factories. Mao, however, was convinced that if the peasants were told that the Red Army was on their side, that if they could be organized and educated, the Communists would be able to throw off the old feudal system and then defeat the Japanese with a united country. As 80 percent of the Chinese people were peasants, this made sense. And it proved to be right in the end.

A tragic event related to this was when, in 1944, Roosevelt sent Patrick Hurley to China to see if there was any possibility of Chiang Kaishek and Mao getting together to fight the Japanese. At Yan'an Hurley and Mao wrote a declaration uniting the Communists with the Nationalists to free their country from the Japanese aggressor. Mao had always wanted to be on terms with the United States, and this was a sensible move on his part. However, when Hurley presented the declaration to Chiang Kaishek, he refused to sign it. He and Madame talked Hurley into seeing only their side. Roosevelt sent him back to China, and this time Hurley went through Moscow and saw Stalin. Stalin didn't think much of the Chinese Communists. He had told Averell Harriman they were red on the outside but white inside, and he sent the message to Roosevelt that he, Stalin, favored Chiang Kaishek in the Chinese civil war.

Jack has ordered a rubber stamp of George Hatem's name and address and plans to send him a card or letter from as many places we go to as possible. He is an enthusiastic collector of stamps and postmarks. I wonder how many places will have post offices.

Harrison has had to buy more typewriter ribbons. The man who fixes our typewriters gave him some he had sealed up for Margaret Bourke-White in 1945, and insisted they would be okay. Of course they are not— they're all dried out. So Harrison bought some Chinese ribbons, and since his old Remette has smaller reels than the average typewriter, he has to cut them and rewind them on his spools.

TUESDAY, MARCH 20

Harrison and Jack went off early to talk to Hu Hua, a professor-historian at People's University. I didn't go; it was too early and I felt very tired. Somehow the door to our terrace had been left open last night and the wind came up like blazes. While the door didn't bang, there was a whistling noise and roar that kept me awake a lot. So I rested most of the day.

Wang Bingnan, who heads the China Friendship Society, gave a dinner for Jack and us. He was ambassador to Poland and was the middleman in the long negotiations in Paris between China and the United States. We met him on one of our earlier trips. We went to the old Italian Embassy, where his office is, and I remember being horrified at how grubby it looked.

He was the spirit of geniality tonight. Harrison sat on his left, Jack on his right. The dinner was seated in the old Chinese way—men all together and women next to each other. I sat between Lu Cui and Li because there were more men than women. Lu Cui is a handsome lady with pure white hair, which I haven't often seen here. In fact, I wonder if Chinese ladies don't dye their hair, as so many Italian women do.

Lu Cui speaks perfect English and I enjoyed her immensely. In 1935, during a student demonstration against Japan in Beijing, the university gates were locked so the mob of students couldn't get in. Lu Cui crawled under the gate and opened it from within. Jack Service was in Beijing at that time and he saw her. He said she was tiny and very young. Then, she told me, she was on a blacklist and wanted by the police. The Snows hid her in their apartment and Ed took her to the station himself and put her on a train for Shanghai. She was in Yan'an at one time, and during World War II was sent to the United States and met the Roosevelts.

There were twelve courses and lots of toasts. Excellent white wine called Dynasty, which is a product of a "joint venture" by France and China.

Li told me we can't go to the town of Maotai where the famous drink is made and which is an important place on the Long March, because it is not open to foreigners. And there are problems about other places. I'm sure it is mostly to do with bureaucratic local officials who have no conception of what Harrison wants to do and just go by the rules.

28

WEDNESDAY, MARCH 21

Harrison was furious about the local officials saying we can't do this and can't do that, and he has written a letter to the head of the Information Department objecting to such restrictions.

This is another day when we have no appointments. I don't understand it. We have been here three weeks already and we haven't seen half the people we asked to see. And we are sure they are here in Beijing. Harrison considers these wasted days, and they are. So we sat around in our room writing letters and reading. I have finished *Death Comes for the Archbishop* and wish I had brought all of Willa Cather's books. She is such a lovely writer.

We took a walk with the purpose of having my shoe mended. In a tiny repair shop several people were mending a variety of things. A girl who was restringing a badminton racket put it aside, took my shoe, slit the seam with a razor, put a small patch inside, sewed it up again, all in under ten minutes. It cost thirty cents, Chinese money (fifteen cents, ours). Prices have risen. In 1972 it cost two cents to mend a shoe.

In the evening we went to the Military Museum to watch a film of the Long March—episodes of the four crossings of the Red (Chishui) River and many battles. It was terribly long, three hours, but really interesting. The actor who portrayed Mao was wonderful. I thought he looked feminine, and Harrison says many writers said that about Mao when he was young.

THURSDAY, MARCH 22

This morning we met with Li Yimang, a writer, chairman of cultural exchanges, former ambassador to Prague, Vienna, and Burma. He has a big round stomach and held a pipe all the time, constantly packing down the tobacco. The woman in attendance came across the room to light his pipe, but he waved her away and lit it himself. It went out immediately and he never really smoked it, just played with it.

He gave a different picture of the Long March than we have heard from the generals. (Later we learned that some of his facts were inaccurate or, at best, questionable.) He was thirty at the time, was in the security apparatus and in a central column that did not get into combat. Commanders as well as political leaders were also in this central column, protected by soldiers. He had a horse to carry all his stuff. It doesn't seem that they rode; horses were pack animals. He had the same horse all through the march.

Harrison asked how Mao could have walked all day and worked all night. Li answered that communications were in effect only at night. As soon as they settled down to camp, the radios started working. Armies and units were in touch with each other, could report progress and make plans together. There were no directives coming from Shanghai, not enough wireless power to contact Moscow, but they could, and did, reach other armies. Jack Service referred to the "bamboo telegraph"—word spread from village to village, another means of communication. The leaders were young and strong. They got into the habit of staying up most of the night. In the morning they could snatch two or three hours of sleep while the armies got going.

Harrison asked if women were in the central column. Li said only twenty-odd started. When Harrison asked what they did, Li laughed and said, "Nothing." "Did they take care of their husbands?" "Many were not married." "Did many give birth on the Long March?" "No." Harrison said he had heard that Mao's wife was pregnant at the start. Li said he was not in a position to answer; he couldn't remember. She was injured before the march at Jinggangshan, according to him, but nothing happened to her on the march.

He said he had been with Deng Xiaoping for quite a while, had walked with him during the day and talked at night. It wasn't true, he said, that Deng Xiaoping had had to carry all his stuff. He'd had a horse too. At that time Deng was editor of the army paper and had nothing to do because putting out a paper under the circumstances was impossible.

To his knowledge, Mao was not ill. Zhou Enlai had a kind of typhoid, not malaria. His wife was with him all the time, not sick herself. He said he hadn't found the Snowy Mountain too high; people crossed it in one day (as we have been told). The Grasslands were Tibetan summer pastures and it took his outfit two and a half days to cross them. There were dry places to camp, but a lot was wet and like quicksand. Many soldiers were so weak they couldn't make it, fell and couldn't get up. Animals, too. He ate the raw grain, had to use his teeth like a grindstone.

Harrison asked Li Yimang if he had felt Zhang Guotai had wanted to take control. He said, not at first, but as Zhang began to make errors in thinking and judgment, he realized something was wrong.

We dined with a group of Chinese writers. Jack didn't come because he has bad laryngitis and can't talk. We missed him terribly; there was one interpreter, seven Chinese who didn't speak English, and us. Conversation was difficult, but Harrison kept talking and the interpreter worked hard. Dinner consisted of fifteen dishes. I don't feel like having so many different tastes one right after the other—fish, meat, vegetables, sweet, sour, soup, hot, cold, peppery—I will never get used to it.

It was a nice group of people and a very friendly gesture. There is to be a meeting of Chinese and American writers here in October and Harrison told them the names of a few people he thinks will be coming: Bill Styron, Francine Gray, Allen Ginsberg, Toni Morrison, Walker Percy, and I can't remember who else, but it may all change.

FRIDAY, MARCH 23

Harrison went up to Jack's room this morning to talk to Professor Hu Hua again. Jack is better today, but I seem to be getting the sore throat and cold that Harrison had and Jack has. I'm doing everything I know of to ward it off. The air is so dry I don't think I could ever get used to it.

We have been here three weeks and two days and it seems to me to be a terrible waste of time and money. So far Harrison has had interviews with four generals, two professor-historians, and George Hatem. We have been to museums and seen exhibits of the Long March, and to many dinners. We have met interesting people who live here, but many days go by without an interview. We have not seen one woman survivor of the Long March, though there are several prominent ones living here, including Mao's second wife and Zhou Enlai's wife.

I am discouraged and bored with this hotel life. I feel I'll scream if I have to eat any more Chinese food, no matter how good it is. I am sick of the Long March, sick of this life, sick of my clothes, sick of myself.

I wrote the above this morning at an exceptionally low moment.

Madame Ding Ling is one of the great revolutionary and literary ladies of China. She lives on the tenth floor of an apartment house near the superhighway that has replaced the old city wall. Between the building and the street there is a row of one-story garages, all with roll-up doors and heavy padlocks. A car is in every garage. By any standards, hers is a large apartment. A wide passage with two rooms on each side leads from the entry. Two doors were closed, and two were open, showing rooms filled with books and papers.

The living room is furnished with a sofa, a table in front, several armchairs, a glassed-in cabinet with books and papers neatly stacked, and an upright piano covered with a cloth. Pots of greens and flowers stood on the floor by the window. Throughout the rooms we saw, floors were of yellow vinyl tiles, about fifteen inches square. Very nice, and a blessing compared to the cement floors that are in so many apartments.

Ding Ling did not go on the Long March. She arrived in Yan'an in 1936, following the same route Ed Snow, George Hatem, and Huang Hua took—to Xi'an and thence to Yan'an, all under cover. She stayed in Shanghai with a German dentist who had fled Germany because he was being hounded for his antifascist views. He had a dog named Hitler. Not knowing much Chinese, he went out one night after curfew and was shot by Kuomintang soldiers. She herself had been held prisoner by the Kuomintang, and her husband was tortured and killed. She was released in 1936 and soon after went to Yan'an.

She said the women on the Long March were tough—they had to be or they would not have survived. There were about thirty of them who walked from Jiangxi to Yan'an or Shaanxi Province. They had a joke that mules are better than husbands; they are indispensable, husbands are not. Zhu De's wife, Kang Keqing, was a political instructor. She was a country peasant without much education. A flaming Communist, she could communicate easily with soldiers. Ding Ling called He Zizhen, Mao's wife, a petty intellectual (a teacher or writer, but not a top-ranking scholar). She said that Zhou Enlai's wife, Deng Yingchao, was well educated (she was a university graduate). Li Bozhao, wife of General Yang Shangkun, had studied in the Soviet Union, knew Russian dances and songs, which she performed and taught. (Harrison had asked to see her before we left home.) We asked what the wives did—they were not with their husbands except during rest periods. Ding Ling said they did propaganda work, organized local women to make straw shoes and other necessities for the soldiers. Sometimes they were involved in actions against landlords, distributing grain and food. Propaganda teams would go ahead of the troops, paint slogans on rocks and cliffs. Ding Ling said they were very busy, which contradicts what Li Yimang said ("They did nothing"). The women on the Long March, and those who came to Yan'an afterward, mixed easily with the masses. She said it was because of the unity and solidarity of the army and the people that the Communists were victorious.

In the Fourth Front army there was a women's regiment led by a woman, Zhang Qinqiu. They were mostly peasant girls who lived and fought like regular soldiers. This regiment was nearly wiped out by Muslim troops of the Kuomintang, and those that weren't killed were taken prisoner, raped, and butchered, the usual treatment meted out to women in war and probably worse for these women because they were soldiers.

Ding Ling said not many women had babies. We hear from other sources that quite a few did and had to leave them. So far, everyone has denied that Mao's wife was pregnant at the start, had a baby en route, and left it with some peasants, never reunited. Ding Ling told us a wonderful story about a couple who was ordered to Yan'an. They had a new baby and couldn't take it with them as they had to go near and around enemy lines and be as quiet as possible. So they left the baby with peasants. The peasants wrapped the baby like a package and were able to move it from village to village because the Kuomintang didn't watch the peasants' daily comings and goings and were not suspicious. So, in relays, the baby was brought to Yan'an and given back to the parents.

She referred to the Five Elderlies, five men who were over forty on the Long March. I am always amused at the way the Chinese constantly use numbers in describing things: the Four Pests; the Gang of Four; the Four Olds; the Four News; the Four Modernizations; eight-element pudding.

Ding Ling said women's feet were made bigger by all the walking on the Long March. Also, that they had problems going to the toilet. If they stopped, they were left behind and couldn't catch up. They had to wait until they got to the campsite—it was very painful and not good for them.

Harrison asked if there was bad feeling between Long Marchers and people who came to Yan'an to join Mao after the march was over. She said only rarely; the young recruits respected the older ones. She said that when some wives went off to the Soviet Union to study, leaving their husbands, "they left a vacancy that was soon filled." There were changes of wives quite often, it seems to me. Mao had four wives. Ding Ling said that Mao told her he hadn't wanted his wife He Zizhen to go to Russia, had even wired her at Xi'an not to go. Yet we have always understood he sent her to Russia for mental health care and that Jiang Qing took her place.

She said the spirit of Yan'an was wonderful. "We all cherish the feeling in Yan'an. There was democracy and criticism, much better than now. However, we cannot make things stable. We don't know which way the world will go." She said this spirit was the continuation of the spirit of the Long March. There was a closeness among people, no personal thinking, no thoughts of money, a great feeling of optimism. Many intellectuals had come there, many students. There was a "rich air of study—of improving oneself." They set up institutions of learning, even though they were very poor. They had no textbooks, no desks, no chairs or lamps.

It must have been wonderful—the success of the march, the determination to win out over Chiang Kaishek and the Japanese, the excitement of a new beginning, of success, optimism, youth. They had so much going for them. It must have been very romantic.

Everyone we have talked to wishes Ding Ling would write her memoirs. She has lived through so much and, miraculously, survived. In the Cultural Revolution she was in great danger from the Red Guards, and Wang Zhen, chief of staff for Xiao Ke, saved her by sending her off to a farm in the northeast, where she lived for twelve years. Her second husband, the quiet little man we met today, accompanied her voluntarily, and there she wrote a novel, which the Red Guards burned when they finally tracked her down. She returned in 1976 and is considered a living monument to the revolution.

This evening we saw two movies at the Friendship Association in the old Italian embassy compound. The first was a documentary about Rewi Alley and was adorable, just like him. There were pictures of him as a shepherd in New Zealand, and as a handsome sailor. But most were of him traveling around the country surrounded by smiling children. Second was another documentary about Mao, not just about the Long March, but the whole story from the early thirties to 1971, when China was taken into the United Nations. The bad mistakes were left out—the Great Leap Forward, communes, the Cultural Revolution. It was good, interesting, and much more sensible and honest than the former idolatry.

(The Great Leap Forward was a project launched by Mao in 1958. China was to lift herself up by her own bootstraps without any outside help. Communes were organized; backyard steel mills proliferated. These were small, inefficient handmade mills. Local ore was used and fired by any available fuel. The quality of the iron was so low that it broke, splintered, and was useless. So much manpower and energy went into these projects that the fields were neglected and there were serious famines in many provinces. Rural China was a mess; cities did not have enough food. Mao received numerous reports of these conditions, but he defended his policy and denounced those who opposed him.)

SATURDAY, MARCH 24

Again, nothing scheduled for today. We talked about plans for the trip. Harrison is dissatisfied with our itinerary. There is so much going back and forth, so much retracing steps. In each province we are to go first to the capital and then to the places that are important for us to see. We return to the capital after several days and then proceed to the capital of the next province, even if our interim trips bring us to the borders of the next province. It seems absurd. Also, he is worried that we won't have a really qualified guide, someone who is an expert on the Long March. I just hope the whole thing won't be a bust.

SUNDAY, MARCH 25

This morning at 10:30 we took a taxi with Jack to the north gate of the Forbidden City and walked in that gorgeous place for two hours. It was a heavenly day, sunny, not windy, and it was a perfect way to spend the morning. At this time of year there aren't many tourists, but lots of Chinese. Many of the new Chinese families: father, mother, and one child. The other day I asked a young Chinese father whether they had birthday parties for their children the way we do. He replied that with one child, two parents, and four grandparents, you might say every day is a birthday party for a child. It will be interesting to see how these children turn out. I have seen little children stamp their feet and cry and scream, something we never saw here before. I can't imagine a whole generation of idolized, spoiled children submitting to the iron discipline demanded of the Chinese, especially of those in important positions.

We dined with Jack and the Adlers in the dining room on the seventh floor that specializes in the Mongolian hot pot. This is a small cylindrical burner with a charcoal fire and water or broth in a section that goes around the middle. Any kind of food can be cooked in it, like a fondue, but here they serve very thin slices of mutton and vegetables cut into small pieces.

MONDAY, MARCH 26

We lunched with Chinese friends in a well-known restaurant that is being done over. The first two floors are closed and we had to go through an alley, into a little backyard, stepping over coal and old boards and general mess. I didn't mind that, but once inside we saw a man spitting in the corner of the first landing, and the stairs were piled with cement and sand, stones and wood. On the top floor there was a curtained room on each side with the doors shut, and looking ahead into the main building it seemed as if a bomb had exploded there.

We went into the room on the right. A table in the middle was set and brown plastic-covered chairs and sofas were placed against the wall. It was lovely and sunny outside and not as dusty up three flights as on the street, and the windows had been open to the warmer air. They were shut as soon as we entered. Except for a few special buildings, such as this hotel and Ding Ling's building, heat is turned off on March 15 no matter what the temperature, and not turned on again until well into the fall. It was freezing in that room and I kept longing to open the windows again but didn't dare. By the time lunch was over, I wished I had worn my long underwear and wool socks.

The food was delicious. I don't see how they managed under the circumstances of remodeling. One guest had been in the United States recently and I asked her if she liked American food. "I hated it," she said. "I cooked my own when I could." So I guess I won't worry anymore about not eating everything. I have never said to a Chinese that I hated their food, though there is some I do.

In the afternoon we went to the Music Conservatory to meet the professors and hear a concert by students. Part of the conservatory is in the remains of a palace that belonged to a Manchu prince. Only the gates and two handsome buildings are left, but they make an attractive entrance and are a big contrast to the dreary cement-inside-and-out four-story buildings that constitute the rest of the conservatory.

The ten years of the Cultural Revolution cost the conservatory dearly. Half of their classrooms were taken away; they lost much of their faculty. Nothing definite was said, but it seemed obvious that many teachers spent time doing labor. They still have not reached their former level; they need a few more years. They need more buildings and equipment, and, most important, they need teachers. There is a real generation gap here—the generation that would have been studying during the Cultural Revolution. Most of the professors are in their sixties; there are none younger. And they would like to retire, but they will have to wait until a new group has been trained.

There are eight music conservatories in China, and all are working to raise the level of appreciation of all people. Minority people are anxious to come to learn; Mongolia sends groups of about thirty who stay six years, then go back as an orchestra. We heard a smaller group play when we were in Mongolia several years ago—accomplished musicians who travel around the country entertaining and educating people who have never had such opportunities before.

Everyone at the conservatory read the article Schuyler Chapin wrote for the *New York Times* after he and Beverly Sills visited here in 1981. He wrote that the rooms were dingy and the pianos barely in tune; also, that the quality of the students was not what they had expected. The Chinese were hurt by these remarks and said they didn't feel very friendly toward him. I don't blame them. If one stops to consider the conditions just eight years ago, what has been accomplished in this conservatory is miraculous.

The concert took place in a big bright room on the top floor. First we heard two traditional Chinese instruments, an erhu and a yangqing, one like a xylophone and the other a stringed instrument held upright on the lap and played with a bow. Next, a young tenor sang a song by Richard Strauss and a Chinese song. A tall, thin, ascetic-looking eighteen-year-old pianist played a Chopin Andante and Polonaise as excitingly as I have ever heard such pieces played. As I watched him, I could hardly keep the tears back thinking of the Cultural Revolution and what must have happened to artists like him. How extraordinary it is that the teachers here have been able to start again from the havoc of that insanity, and can teach so much so quickly. Harrison said he was thinking of the young pianist whose fingers were broken by the Red Guards. We were told that he now plays again and gives concerts, and hits the piano so hard he needs a new piano for each concert. What a miracle his hands healed so he can use them.

Accompanying herself on a Chinese mandolin, a girl sang a song of the Yi people, one of the many minority groups. (We will go to that region—the Long Marchers spent a lot of time in Yi country.) A young man played the violin; another, a baritone, sang songs of Brahms and Fauré, and a tiny girl sang arias from *La Sonambula*. She was lovely and her voice was clear and true. I told her teacher that the last person I had heard singing those arias was Joan Sutherland.

It was very moving and inspiring.

An English quartet is here teaching and playing. They are going to Wuhan, then to Shanghai, to visit the conservatories there.

TUESDAY, MARCH 27

Nothing was scheduled for today. We had Takashi Oka for lunch. He was with the *New York Times* in Tokyo the last time I saw him, more than ten years ago. He is now with the *Christian Science Monitor,* where he was before the *Times*. He is very, very nice, thoughtful and intelligent, and a first-rate journalist. We talked about the "spiritual pollution" campaign that was promoted last fall and made a lot of people worry. It smacked of the Cultural Revolution in that there was criticism of Western influence. I find it scary. There must be many people with ideas like the Gang of Four's, and I hope they don't get control of this country again—ever. Everyone says they won't—"the people won't permit it." But this latest exercise scared people, foreigners and Chinese alike.

WEDNESDAY, MARCH 28

The International Club is a big building about ten minutes' drive going east on the main avenue from our hotel. It is on the edge of the diplomatic compound where most foreigners live, newspaper people as well as diplomats. Back in imperial days embassies were in the Legation Quarter, close to the Peking Hotel. These stylish buildings are now used by the Chinese, and the present embassy buildings are all in this new area with walls and gates and Chinese policemen.

The International Club is a meeting place with reception rooms, dining rooms, a theater for showing films. It is used by Chinese as well as foreigners. The room we sat in this morning was sunny and cheerful with a spotless green carpet and red-plush-covered sofas and armchairs. The lights were on all the time, hardly necessary with the bright sunlight.

We met with Wu Xiuquan, which is pronounced "Wu Shiuchuan." I can't get the pinyin system through my head at all; the other way, Wade Giles, makes much more sense to me. (Wade and Giles were two

Englishmen who invented this system of transliteration, and for years that's what was used. A few years ago the Chinese adopted the pinyin method and say it is much more accurate, much more like the Chinese words sound. But really, neither makes much sense. Take, for instance, Zhou Enlai, as it is written now. The other way was Chou En-lai. Yet his name actually, to me, is pronounced almost like "Joe.")

Mr. Wu is both a general and an ambassador, was on the Long March from the start, and was interpreter for Li De (Otto Braun).

I had never heard of Otto Braun before this trip, and now I hear Harrison asking about him every day. There are several versions of his story, and a question as to whether he was Austrian or German. One version is that he fought in World War I, was captured by the Russians and sent to Siberia. When the Russian Red Army was organized in 1918, he joined it. Later he attended Frunze Academy, the top Soviet military institution.

Another version is that he fought in the streets of Germany for the German Communist Party, was imprisoned by the Weimar Republic, escaped in 1928, and went to the Soviet Union on party orders. Whatever is true, he was trained as a revolutionary and sent to China as a representative of the Comintern. When he first came to China, he spoke German, English, and Russian, but not Chinese.

Wu Xiuquan spent five and a half years in the Soviet Union, going first in 1925 with one hundred Chinese students. He studied in Moscow and was good at the language. In 1927, with the Chiang Kaishek betrayal, he and the students were stuck in Russia. They stayed and went to military schools. But they wanted to get back to China to help. Finally Wu got permission and set off for the border. Wu was lucky. Many Chinese were stopped, interrogated, and shot, because they were sympathetic to the Communists, not to Chiang Kaishek. Wu got on a truck with some Russians and they were not stopped. He finally got to Shanghai in July 1931 and, with help from the underground, made his way to the soviet area in Jiangxi.

He has been ambassador to Yugoslavia, and in 1952, as head of China's delegation to the United Nations Conference on Korea, he criticized the United States—in twenty thousand words—as the aggressor in the Korean war.

General Wu is seventy-six, rather slow at moving and talking, but very much alive and alert. I noticed he has a hole and long scar on the left side of his face. It must have been a bullet wound. Harrison didn't notice it; he was always on General Wu's other side. He, like so many others, was in jail for eight years during the Cultural Revolution. Whenever Harrison asks about this, it is greeted with embarrassed giggles and laughs.

He gave us an elegant lunch there at the International Club, hors d'oeuvres and ten courses, including Peking duck.

In the evening Dick Young, who is director of the new Great Wall Hotel, and his wife, met us here and we had to take two taxis because we were five and the rule is no more than four passengers in a cab, just like New York. They took us to the restaurant we went to with the Wrens, but we pretended we had never been there. They told us that the park next to the restaurant is a dating bureau. It is difficult for young people to meet other young people unless they happen to be in the same office. Unlike Americans and other foreigners, the Chinese have few social events. One day a week, men and women can meet here and "socialize," as the saying goes. It is acknowledged and acceptable, but if you don't find the right person after three times, you can't go again. It's like baseball—three strikes and you're out.

The restaurant wasn't crowded and we had a good dinner. Afterward, we took taxis out to the Great Wall Hotel. It is even farther out from the center of town and I would think it's too far for a hotel. But it is right across the street from some of the embassies.

It is huge, with glass facade and red vertical trim. The architect did a hotel in Dallas and this one would be just right there. I don't know about here in China, but Mr. Young seems to think there will be enough rich Americans and other tourists who will pay $130.00 a night for a real luxury hotel managed by either American or European professional hotel personnel. The rooms are pleasant and "tasteful," the lobby is fantastic, with enormous polished steel columns, and nicely furnished with several attractive areas to sit, not just one big space. There are lots of flowering plants. The most attractive place is a bar in the six-story atrium, where we had French pastry and fruit. There will be a nightclub, a French restaurant, a ballroom that is in three parts so the size is flexible, and a coffee shop. Vegetables are being grown specially without night soil, the usual Chinese fertilizer.

The staff is Chinese. The women wear dresses designed in New York and made in Hong Kong—very pretty, in a stylish multicolored pattern. They are cheerful and polite, and if they can be trained to be efficient, fine. I guess it can be done, but it could end up like I. M. Pei's hotel, whose management is a disaster. Harrison thinks Mr. Young and his group can pull it off. It is partially open—300 rooms. There will be over 1,000 when it is completed. The correspondents who come with Reagan in April will stay there, and Dick Young said they have to set aside 550 rooms. If they are not all used, the hotel will lose money.

THURSDAY, MARCH 29

Today we went to the Temple of Heaven, three beautiful structures set in a park, not far from the middle of the city. On our previous visits we could see the big temple clearly from our hotel windows. Now we can just see a little piece in between new apartment buildings.

But once there it is a joy to behold. The big temple, or Hall of Prayer for Good Harvests, is round and built without nails or pegs. The beams and supports are fitted together. It is painted in bright colors. From the entrance at the top of stone steps, you look south to a second, smaller temple, the Imperial Heavenly Vault, and from that one to the Round Mound, a platform with three tiers of marble and carved stone balustrade. A Chinese man told me that the emperors came here to talk to the gods and tell them what had been going on, and sacrifices were made to ensure a good harvest.

The last time we were there it was being redone, and now it is lovely. The park has been planted with new trees, the pavement is smooth and clean, and there are no more revolutionary posters or signs. But there are too many tourist shops and booths right next to the buildings, inside the park walls.

This evening we attended the Peking Opera. The first was wonderful, full of action and easy to understand. It was about a girl who has a stick fight with a marshal and wins. Marvelous swordplay. In the second, a girl had been sold by her family to be a prostitute. She was sent to a county court to be tried and her ex-boyfriend was a judge. It went on and on; the theater was freezing cold as there was no heat, and we left before it was over.

FRIDAY, MARCH 30

In the morning we went to the Health Department office, which is an old Manchu palace. On this street, next to the lake, soldiers were busy cutting down old trees and planting many new cedars and pines. I wonder how evergreens can survive the dust and dryness, winter and summer. They must have to be washed off. The pines along the streets look very dried up.

We talked to Qian Xinzhong and Dai Zhengqi (pronounced "Chiang Tsinzhong" and "Dai Zhengchi"). Dr. Qian talked without stopping, but he was interesting. He was the only real doctor in his outfit—the rest were medical workers trained on the spot. In 1927, he had become a member of the Communist Youth League, at the time Chiang Kaishek was slaughtering Communists—maybe ten thousand, may one hundred thousand. There is no real count.

Back to the march. Dr. Qian told us that medical supplies, what drugs they had, and simple surgical instruments were carried on shoulder poles. No antibiotics, no X-ray equipment, no anesthesia.

40

On the battlefield the treatment was conservative. If a bullet could be found, usually it could be removed. Wounds were bandaged; no blood transfusions. The wounded were divided into three categories: (1) those with light wounds that could be treated on the spot; (2) those whose wounds would heal when treated and could either walk or had to be carried on a litter or stretcher for several days; (3) those seriously wounded or dying, who had to be left behind in the villages with the peasants. They were given money and whatever supplies could be spared.

Harrison asked about soldiers marrying. Answer: Only top officers were allowed to marry on the Long March; ordinary soldiers were forbidden to. Most of them were in their teens, which might have had something to do with that.

The medical group, consisting of a few women nurses and some young male orderlies, generally marched in the central column. Wounded were sent there from the front. Harrison asked if any of these nurses got pregnant or had any special female problems. The answer was "No. They were mostly in their teens, were healthy; none were wounded or killed, and they were too busy to get pregnant." I wonder.

Getting back to treatment in battle—bullets were hard-nosed; not like "treated" bullets, which fragment in the body. They usually went right through an arm or leg. Malaria, diarrhea, cold, ulcerated wounds, and sores on feet were the main problems. Snow blindness in the Snowy Mountains and other high regions.

Harrison always asks about babies being born on the Long March, and he puts the same questions to everyone we talk to. The answers vary considerably. Dr. Dai said the wife of the commander of the Ninth Army gave birth on the March, and that Mao's wife did have a baby, either before or after crossing the Dadu River.

Dr. Qian was twenty-three, Dr. Dai fifteen, at the time of the march. Dr. Dai was sent to the Friendship Hospital here in Beijing to study after Liberation. Since 1954 he has worked with George Hatem. During the Cultural Revolution he was criticized, "stripped of his freedom" for four months, and sent to cadre school.

Everyone we have talked to was either in prison, under house arrest, or on a pig farm, being humiliated, persecuted, tortured, during that time. I still don't understand how the whole thing got going so violently and how it got so out of control, if it did. Jack says it's impossible to get close to an accurate figure of deaths because there weren't actual executions. People were driven to suicide; there was a lot of fighting between factions, people were beaten and tortured, sometimes to death. Some say thousands died; one or two million is perhaps more accurate. The extraordinary thing is that all these old guys (no older than I) spent from four to ten to twelve years in prison, and now they are out and running the country. Are they

41

bitter? We don't see many signs of it, but there must be a huge portion of the population bitter as hell.

Dr. Dai asked if he could describe a day on the march. First, on being waked up by a loud whistle, the soldiers returned doors they had borrowed from villagers. Chinese doors are set on pins, like some of our doors, and are easy to remove. They can serve as beds. Returning the doors, washing, and brushing teeth took fifteen minutes. In another fifteen minutes breakfast was eaten—rice, or sometimes sweet potatoes. As a medical orderly and member of the propaganda team, Dr. Dai then made rounds to see if there were any problems.

At lunchtime they often had nothing to eat. The scouts, or vanguards, got to the villages first, so there wasn't always much left for the troops following. They would have ten- or twenty-minute breaks during the day. Soldiers learned how to take rests; they dozed when walking if not going too fast. But Dr. Dai had no rest. He had to go around to see that everyone was camouflaged against enemy planes, which flew very low.

We talked about the Grasslands, and he said conditions there were the worst of the march. First of all, everyone was exhausted from marching, from battles, from crossing the Snowy Mountains. Lack of salt was a big problem. Soldiers were so weak. "We would see a soldier walking and suddenly collapse. We would go to him, he would tell us his home village, say to please tell his family, and die." Also he spoke of psychological problems. There were no villages, no peasants, not even animals, in the Grasslands. Chinese aren't used to this. There is a saying that a Chinese is never out of earshot of another person. The soldiers felt isolated and lonely.

The Kuomintang raided the villages, took what they wanted, were terrible to the peasants, tied them together and dragged them away to fight for the Nationalists. The Red Army paid for what they took, spent time and effort explaining their mission, enlisted peasants, understood if they wanted to leave the army after a while and return home. All pretty idealized, but on the whole this must be true or their revolution would not have succeeded.

In the afternoon we drove again to the Headquarters of the Standing Committee of the People's Consultative Congress (what a mouthful) to talk to Cheng Zihua. He was commander of the Twenty-fifth Army. He has a nice face. (At the end of our trip we heard things about him that made me wonder about his nice face.) He read from written notes and it was hard for Harrison to ask questions. It was a complicated tale of armies and strategies and I couldn't follow it all.

Both Cheng's hands and arms are badly misshapen. The left hand was wounded first, then the right. Bullets went right through both wrists. The wounds became infected and the diseased area was cut out with a knife.

Herb medicine was the only treatment. He was confined to a stretcher for eleven months. His deputy commander also was wounded, and later the third officer was killed. Cheng gave orders from the stretcher.

He said they had no communication with any of their fellow armies; they learned their whereabouts from Nationalist newspapers in the villages.

This man, like the others we have talked to, was in prison for five years during the Cultural Revolution.

SATURDAY, MARCH 31

This morning we went back to the International Club and met with Dr. Du Tanjin and Dr. Sun Yizhi (no relation to Dr. Sun Yatsen), both of whom had worked on the Long March.

Dr. Du did most of the talking. He said medical health and knowledge was a political task. People had to be educated. There was a medical group in every battalion and regiment. They put up slogans such as *Be careful and wear your shoes*; *Don't take off your clothes or you will get cold*; *Drink only boiled water—fill up your canteen with boiled water. If not possible, drink only flowing water, never still.* Scouts were sent out to mobilize the peasants to boil water for the soldiers. When it was available, they used alum to purify water. Jack said he used it in Chungking during World War II.

Harrison asked what they did about going to the toilet. Dr. Du said they had rules; a deep pit should be dug thirty to fifty meters away from the campsite. It should be covered up on leaving. This sounds unlikely; the local farmers would have appreciated the contents.

Feet were a big problem. Many soldiers had blisters and bad sores. Harrison asked if the stories we have heard of soldiers washing their feet in maotai are true. Dr. Du said he doesn't know about the stories, but it was customary for people to reduce pain and swelling by bathing their feet in maotai and camphor spirits. However, Dr. Sun joined in here and said the stories are true. He saw soldiers opening bottles, swabbing and rubbing their feet with the liquor. Lots spilled on the ground and the whole town was fragrant with the smell. He enjoyed telling us this. They said that soldiers learned the warlord method of binding up their feet and legs with cloth puttees. This helped prevent cuts and scratches from grasses and briars.

Besides battle wounds and ulcerated sores, there were wounds from falling and stumbling during night marches. Men and horses were tired and drowsy, would fall asleep while they were walking.

They tried to look after everyone, wounded and stragglers. Otherwise they would be captured by the enemy. Dr. Du said they had special groups to round them up, and a medical man had to be in each group. Often "ideological work" had to be done before the peasants would accept the wounded. The Red Army and its motives were explained, and money and supplies were left to help with the care.

Snow blindness and mountain sickness were common. Snow blindness diminished with time. Injections of camphor and smelling salts helped restore breathing, but many did not recover, fell, and lay forever where they died. Nothing was known about the effects of high altitude, and it is interesting that every Chinese we have encountered worries about going where it's high. In Tibet in 1980 our companions were constantly ill with vomiting, dizziness, and respiratory problems. Maybe it stems from these ghastly stories about the Long March.

On the Grasslands the losses were heavy. Dr. Du said they told the soldiers which wild grasses were edible and which were not, but some soldiers didn't realize and ate the wrong kind. Parched barley and roasted wheat were the basis of their diet.

Dr. Sun said he had been with the Kuomintang but was captured by the Red Army in 1933 during the fourth encirclement campaign. Harrison asked how he happened to change sides; was he "reformed"? He answered that the Red Army treated him well. They hoped the professionally trained captives—doctors, medics, telephone and wireless operators—would be reformed and join them. But they could go home if they wished. He, Dr. Sun, was "educated" by the revolutionary spirit and turned from being against the revolution to joining it. He worked in the Battalion Cadre Recovery medical clinic and took care of important cadres, including Deng Yingchao, Zhou Enlai's wife. Harrison asked if she had TB. No, the one who had TB was He Zizhen, Mao's wife. In Guizhou Province she had a baby. He did not deliver it, but heard it was a boy and was given to peasants.

Harrison asked what he treated Deng Yingchao for. Dr. Sun said he didn't treat her; she was weak and couldn't move easily. Harrison asked, "Didn't she go to Zhou Enlai when he was ill on the Grasslands, and take care of him?" Yes, when they were in the Tibetan area, the Snowy Mountains and the Grasslands, Zhou was sick with hepatitis. In answer to whether Mao had malaria, Dr. Sun said no.

SUNDAY APRIL 1

Today we went with Jack to two Buddhist temples about thirty or more miles out to the west, and a little bit south, of Beijing. Ordination Terrace Temple, or Jie Taisi (according to Nagel's guide), is huge and hugs the side of a wonderful hill, or mountain. It seems to face Beijing, but smoke from factories in the valley and the dusty atmosphere made it impossible to see any distance. The Temple of the Pool and the Zhe Tree, Tan Zhesi, is more intimate, nestled in a crevasse in the hills and facing south. It is prettier and more compact. Both temples were dreadfully damaged in the Cultural Revolution, and much has been restored. But there's a lot more to do. These temples, and those in Tibet and Sikkim, need to be painted constantly because of the weather.

MONDAY, APRIL 2

Today at four o'clock we met with General Yang Shangkun at the Great Hall of the People. We sat in one of the big meeting rooms that had a tan carpet and chairs covered in red, placed in the usual semicircle. Also present were Huang Hua, General Wu (who gave us the nice lunch on the 28th), General Qin, the director of the Military Museum, Eppy (Israel Epstein), several aides of General Yang, and Mr. Li.

General Yang greeted Jack effusively and said he hadn't seen him for forty years, not since he was with the Dixie Mission in Yan'an. Jack said that the last time he, Jack, was in the Great Hall, General Yang had been in jail. "At least I wasn't locked up," said Jack. References to the injustices done to so many people by their government always provoke a self-conscious laughter, while I feel like screaming at the stupidity, bigotry, and cruelty.

General Yang is short and has a round face, receding hairline, and a wonderful smile. He was born in Fukien into a peasant family and joined the guerillas at seventeen. He was educated mainly by the Communist Party and the army and served under Lin Biao before, during, and after the Long March. He was arrested on July 1, 1966, the birthday of the Chinese Communist Party, and not released until December 1978—he was in jail for thirteen years; "Longer than anyone," he said. He was accused of having illegal connections with foreign countries, of being too friendly with Americans in the Dixie Mission, and of being a "black" general. He said he suffered in this period but came to look on it as a "forced rest."

Harrison said that General Wu had been accused of being a Russian and Yugoslavian spy. General Yang said he was accused of being a Russian and American spy. Then Harrison said something very interesting. "There is a common thread here—Mr. Service gets into trouble in the United States for too close connections with the Chinese, and you get into trouble for being too close to the United States. I hope that in the future, friendships between Americans and Chinese can be regarded as a positive, not a negative."

General Yang said, "I believe the time has come for this, and we will not let such a thing happen again. I believe the Cultural Revolution will not be repeated, and that what happened in the United States will not happen again." Jack agreed.

The General said, "There are three members of the Dixie Mission present: Huang Hua, Jack, and myself. Our ambassador to the United Nations, Mr. Ling, is another, and so is George Hatem." He suggested they should have a reunion, that they got along very well in spite of political difficulties.

Harrison asked about his wife and family. His wife, Madame Li Bozhao, was director of the art school in Yan'an and is a well-known playwright. She wrote the first play to be produced in which Mao is portrayed onstage. The title is *The Long March.* Recently she wrote one called *Going North,* about the meeting of the First and Fourth Front Armies and the struggle between Zhu De and Zhang Guotao. It has been shown by the army theater group on TV. In the Cultural Revolution she was "under supervision," was made to scrub the floors and toilets of an entire four-story building. She suffered from hypertension and developed a blood clot that led to partial paralysis of one leg. At present she is in the hospital, but when we return from our trip she will be out, and we hope we can see her.

Like so many others, she studied in Moscow and knew Russian songs and dances, which she performed and taught in the central soviet area and later at Yan'an.

General Yang said he was lucky; his children were subjected to forced labor but were not injured or killed. Many were; he mentioned Deng Xiaoping's son, who was maimed so badly that he is paralyzed and confined to a wheelchair. General Yang had no word from his family for nine years! I don't see how these people stood it.

Jack asked if his children had any education. The oldest son is a military man and he had graduated by the time of the Cultural Revolution. The next son was about to graduate from college, but his daughter was a middle-school student and her education stopped.

They began talking about the route we will take—to Jiangxi, Guizhou, Yunnan, Sichuan, Gansu, and Shaanxi—what we well see and what we will skip. He said it will take us two months and asked if we are in good health. I felt like saying, "We are now, but who knows what we will be like at the end of such a trip?" He said he had arranged for General Qin to come with us. He is expert on the details of the Long March and has been over some of the route. He will be an enormous help to Harrison. He will also be a good liaison with the military along the way and make things easier with provincial authorities who may not be enthusiastic or understanding about our mission. So, with Mr. Zhang Yuanyuan as interpreter, we will be a nucleus of five.

There was a long discussion about the debate between Mao and Zhang Guotao as to which direction the Red Army should go after the joining of the First and Fourth Front Armies. Mao wanted to go north to Gansu Province; Zhang Guotao wanted to go west or south. This debate continued for two months until finally Zhang reluctantly agreed to go along with Mao, though he quickly reneged. I couldn't possibly follow it all.

After the discussion, a big round table was rolled into the end of the room, all set for dinner, with flowers in the middle of the lazy susan. Madame Huang Hua and Huang Bing joined us, but Eppy left. As always, there was an enormous amount of food, but I skipped many courses and ate little of others. I notice most Chinese do this.

TUESDAY, APRIL 3, 8:00 P.M.
At the Airport Hotel, Beijing

This is the last place I expected to be tonight. We packed yesterday, got up at quarter of six this morning, and came out to the airport only to wait until 1:30, when our plane was canceled until tomorrow. It was very foggy at first, but cleared up by about 10:00, and many other flights took off. But not ours. It was raining in Nanchang, our destination. So here we are in this revolting motel-hotel with no nightclothes or slippers. Thank heaven I have my toilet case and the vitamin pills I need. From now on a nightgown comes too, no matter where I am. It was freezing waiting at the airport and my feet got very cold. Here I have been in bed most of the time and am finally warm. We have had supper and are scheduled for departure at 1:30 tomorrow. If we don't leave, I'll insist on having my suitcase.

WEDNESDAY, APRIL 4, 8:00 P.M.
At the Airport Hotel

We went to bed last night at 9:15 in our clothes, and got up at 6:00 this morning. Even though the bathroom was disgusting and filthy, we were able to wash in it. Harrison took a shower, but I didn't want to put my feet in the tub. So I washed in the basin and put on the clothes I had slept in. We had a nice breakfast and delicious strawberry jam. It's odd that the Peking Hotel never has anything but that plum or apple-plum jam. For three hours we sat on our beds under the quilts, me with my coat on, and returned to the airport at noon. We waited until 2:30, when the flight was canceled again. It was raining in Foochow, which is the ultimate destination of that plane, though it was clear in Nanchang. We sat in the dreary waiting room and I showed a Chinese woman how to do the lacy knitting stitch I'm doing. She had shown great interest in it yesterday, so I wrote the directions for it in English. Today I gave her a paper and pen and knitted while she wrote down in Chinese what I was doing. She has teeny-weeny needles and the stitch would look like nothing if she used them. I pointed to my needles and she shook her head. I guess big needles can't be bought, but she could make some out of wood, or chopsticks. I would like to give her mine, but then what would I do for two months? I'll probably go crazy even with knitting.

We insisted on getting our bags, and after endless fussing and more waiting, they were located. Taxi drivers can refuse to take a passenger if they don't want to go where the passenger wishes. No driver wanted to take us just down the street to the hotel; they all wanted to go back to the city. So we had more waiting until one man was persuaded to oblige.

For tonight we have a cleaner room with a double bed. I took a hot shower, washed my clothes, put on clean ones, and felt much better. Before supper we watched a hysterically funny English-language program on TV. Many Chinese are learning English, and other languages, this way. In this one an English lady librarian was explaining to an English man about another man who was dressed like Sherlock Holmes. He had given a book to the library and came in every day with a magnifying glass to see if it was there. It was always out, and he would say, very slowly, "Ah, someone is reading it." The librarian had it under the counter so he would think it was out. There were examples of English accents: two Cockney mechanics working on a car; a man and woman in an office; some scenes from the movie *Jane Eyre* in which George C. Scott plays Rochester. And a few phrases to be memorized: "I don't know if he is married"; "What is he doing now?" The librarian and the two men spoke in nice, clear British accents, as did an English teacher who appeared now and then, and a Chinese man who explained everything in both languages.

We have had a rather revolting supper, but I am thankful for my nightgown and slippers. There are always slippers in every hotel room, but I don't like to use them. Who knows what feet have been in them? I guess it's too dry for athlete's foot, but still.

THURSDAY, APRIL 5
Nanchang

This morning there was talk about what to do if the plane was canceled for a third time. If we had taken the train in the first place, we would have been there on Wednesday. Harrison is sore because we are already two days behind our schedule, which is pretty tight for such a long trip (which, in the end, turned out to be 7,400 miles, not counting miles covered by trains and planes). But, thankfully, we got off at 12:30 and arrived here around 2:00.

General Qin and Mr. Zhang were able to go home both nights and didn't have to stay in the airport hotel. We were amazed when the CAAC (the Chinese government airline) reimbursed us for the cost of the rooms. Of course they are supposed to, but sometimes don't. They wouldn't pay for Jack's first night because he didn't have his receipt. He had thrown it away, which surprised us. Usually he is so meticulous about everything. I wrote a stinging complaint about the hotel having no heat and being so filthy. Jack said he had wiped the dust off his window with a towel, and it was so dirty he washed out the towel so the hotel people wouldn't think he had cleaned his shoes with it. Incidentally, the rooms cost us fifty Chinese dollars a night; the same rooms would cost a Chinese twelve dollars. That is the sort of thing that makes me furious. Other countries don't treat their guests that way. At least we got a lot of reading done. I finished rereading *To Kill a Mockingbird* and have gone back to *The Red Badge of Courage*, which is not my cup of tea, but I have never read it. I brought mostly books I can leave here, books I would be proud to have represent American writers.

The flight was uneventful. As we came down to earth, we saw bright green and yellow fields and water everywhere—the river, ponds, irrigation ditches. What the Chinese call rape and use for oil is very like our wild mustard, which few Americans eat or use, and most regard as a weed. At this time of year the green in most plots is fodder. It has a small purple flower and looks as if it is related to alfalfa. It is used for animal feed and also turned under as fertilizer.

About fifteen minutes after we arrived, we went to the August First 1927 Uprising Museum. This uprising, led by Zhou Enlai, though unsuccessful, established the Communist Red Army as an independent force and is celebrated as the birthday of the People's Liberation Army. The Communists took over Nanchang but held it for only two days. To give a little background, early in 1927 the revolutionaries were both Nationalists and Communists—Chiang Kaishek, Zhou Enlai, Zhu De, and other now-famous individuals—all united in a program to overthrow the feudal system and foreign concessions. They were marching north from Guangzhou (Canton), and Zhou Enlai went on ahead to get Shanghai ready for an uprising. It was successful, and the workers were waiting for Chiang Kaishek and the Red Army.

He kept them waiting for two weeks while he connived with foreigners and gangsters. After being welcomed by the victorious workers, Chiang turned on them, slaughtering them by the hundreds. This was in April 1927. Zhou Enlai was arrested but escaped, and from then on the two factions engaged in a civil war.

49

The museum used to be the Jiangxi Hotel, built in 1923. It probably was elegant in 1927 when the Communists made it their headquarters. It is four stories high and built around a courtyard. The rooms are large and could be light and airy, but closed doors and windows keep out sun and light. Now it is musty and dark and dirty, and the display is not very interesting. There are pictures we have already seen many times and copies of newspaper articles, along with pictures of this hotel and other buildings and the countryside. The head of the museum couldn't answer any of Harrison's questions and nervously paced up and down making an irritating tap-tap noise, while the girl guide did her best. No one seemed to have any idea of the number of casualties in the Nanchang Uprising, on either side. Jack said the Communists lost a lot but never admit it. If every place we visit is as lacking in knowledge and historical documents as this one is, I don't see how Harrison can get enough accurate information to write a book. For over an hour it was Dullsville.

We were met at the airport by our local interpreter and another man who manages the details, with two sedans. The Chinese feel these cars are appropriate for our status, but it means we five have to be separated, and however we divide ourselves up, it is unsatisfactory. Harrison needs to be near Jack to talk to him—he is invaluable—and he needs the General for his knowledge. We can't move without Mr. Zhang, and there are these two new men from this province. Harrison said it will be a disaster if we aren't all together.

In this hotel we have a huge bedroom and sitting room and an enormous bathroom, very Russian in design except for the wallpaper and wood latticework. Supper wasn't very good and I had rice and vegetables.

We have our schedule and it seems pretty strenuous to me. Almost every night in a different place until back here on the 14th.

FRIDAY, APRIL 6
Near Jinggangshan

We set off this morning soon after 7:30. Disaster has been averted; we are all in a minibus. It makes it very jolly; one can talk or not; there is room to move around and plenty of room for all the luggage.

It was raining when we left Nanchang and it rained all day, sometimes heavily. The fog is thick up here in this village and we must be fairly high. We climbed a great deal and hardly went down at all. In the middle of last night there was a lot of thunder and lightning, and we are now having more. We drove all day through the most well-used fertile land, with no big fields. You couldn't possibly use even a hand, or walking, tractor in the small plots. It is too wet. The water buffalo seem to be almost up to their chests in mud. Looking at a man and his buffalo in a rice paddy today must be about the same as looking at the same scene three thousand years ago. Most of the vegetable and grain patches are the same as they have been for years, often curved in shape and all nestling together, separate but part of a huge whole. The water runs in ditches next to vegetable plots and drops down to other plots a little lower, and so on. Lots of yellow rape brightens up the landscape, and there are many fruit trees, orange and grapefruit, peaches in blossom. No lemons; they say you have to go farther south for them. Beautiful red azaleas cling to a hillside.

In the smaller towns pigs are everywhere, as are hens, ducks and geese, and a great many sad-looking dogs. They wander all over and I wonder if they ever get fed. They act like scavengers, picking up what they can. Most are thin and look as if they were a mixture of cat, coyote, chow, and just plain dog. I believe they are eaten, but none I saw had any flesh to speak of.

Very pretty white-flowered trees that Zhang says are parasol trees. They have flowers like our horse chestnuts, but these flowers are out before the leaves. Also many camphor trees. We went through Camphor Town, the home of herb medicine.

We stopped for lunch at a guest house that was freezing cold. We were shown to a suite that consisted of a bedroom with two double beds, a sitting room with the usual sofas and chairs, and a bathroom that boasted a Chinese toilet, a western toilet, a urinal, tub and basin, and there was water. After lunch we rested on the beds under all the available covers.

All along the highway are signs, reminding us of the Burma Shave ads of our childhood, advising drivers (in Chinese, naturally):

Pay Attention to Safety
Don't Try to be a Heroic Driver
Don't Drive a Sick Car
Drive in a Civilized Way
Don't Hang Onto a Truck [for bicyclists]
Intoxicated Driving is Forbidden
Drive With Caution
Don't Chat With the Driver
Don't Mix People and Freight
Observe Traffic Regulations
Don't Forget Safety
Wishing You a Safe Journey
Be Careful of Slippery Asphalt

No Careless Parking
Better to Wait Three Minutes Than Try to Save a Second
Don't Be in a Hurry

Written on houses are still a few slogans stemming from the Cultural Revolution—*Put Agriculture First* and *Long Live the People's Commune* (this one is very outdated, because most communes have been turned back into villages; they still have work teams, but each family has a plot of its own and can grow what they want and sell it in the open market after they have fulfilled their quota for the village or government).

Another sign said, *Support the Army—the Army Loves the People*. This is a post–Cultural Revolution sign attempting to undo any bad feeling there might have been against the army.

We have a very good, careful driver, not at all like some we've had. He is especially careful of his vehicle, goes very slowly over bumps and holes. It is a rule that if he hits a chicken, it's just an accident. But if he hits a duck or goose, or other animal, he has to pay for it.

We got here around 5:00 and it's really depressing. After the dryness of Beijing, here it is so wet my clothes feel damp and cold and I am freezing no matter how much I put on. It is worse than I remember in Sikkim. There they did have fireplaces, but nothing is heated here—it's too expensive and there isn't any fuel.

Not long after we arrived, we were given a banquet by the magistrate of the area, a historian, and other representatives of the county or town. The magistrate is forty-six and has five children. He is old enough to have missed the new edict limiting children to one per family. There were quite a lot of jokes about that. There must have been twenty courses. The hors d'oeuvre dish looked lovely, with a turnip carved into a chicken head and thin slices of vegetables and meat making the body and wings. As many toasts as courses were proposed—to China, to the United States, to our Chinese friends, to our American friends, to Chinese-American friendship, to the future, on and on. The best thing about Chinese banquets is that they begin early and end early. We got back to this room at 8:00.

SATURDAY, APRIL 7
Jinggangshan

At breakfast we had nice hot milk and coffee. In this area the sugar is coarse, which I like. In Beijing it is now refined, just like ours.

Right after breakfast we set off in the bus and drove up and down mountains in thick fog to several outposts that Mao had used when he was on this mountain for two years and five months. It was the period after the Autumn Harvest and Nanchang Uprisings in 1927. While the Nanchang Uprising was going on, Mao was in the Changsha region hard at work organizing another revolt. This, the Autumn Harvest Uprising, was also unsuccessful. Mao was captured but, like Zhou Enlai, escaped. Temporarily stopped by their former allies, the Nationalists, what was left of the Red Army retreated to this high, inaccessible mountain area.

It was raining cats and dogs and so foggy we could hardly see. Once in a while the clouds parted, or blew away, and we could see other mountain peaks for a few minutes. We had on our rain suits and got out to walk to the lookouts, but most of the time we were in the bus. We stopped for lunch in another dreary guest house at Maoping.

We made two stops to see buildings that are structurally very handsome. Both were built as schools and each had a nice central courtyard and rooms around it. Mao had his bed and desk on the top floor of the second building and it had a wonderful roof with decorations and paintings on the ends of the curves on the roofs—pictures of pigs and geese, trees and flowers. Really lovely.

We visited an ancestral hall that was part of a very nice compound. Ancestral halls were used by clans for meetings, to gather to pay respects to their ancestors, to put up tablets to honor their dead. A clan is an extended family, generally several hundred people, seventy or eighty households. I wondered why these buildings weren't destroyed, either by the Kuomintang or the Red Guards. The answer is that the Kuomintang would not destroy an ancestral hall. In other words, no Chinese would have in those days. The Red Guards worshiped Mao and this special area, and because he had slept and worked in these two buildings, they wouldn't touch them. Mao, Zhou Enlai, Zhu De, and the lot always took the best accommodations, and I imagine many fine houses still stand because of that, though they may be run-down and shabby.

On the road today we came to a barrier that had to be raised to let us through. It is a checkpoint to be sure no one takes wood illegally from the mountain.

Jack told us something interesting about the Catholic Church in China. The Catholics came to China after the Portuguese took Macao in 1557, and they disagreed over whether the church could accept ancestor worship. The Dominicans were against it—said it was idol worship, and convinced the pope. The Jesuits accepted it as a continuation of respect for elders, realized it was not a form of worship such as worshiping God. The argument set the church in China back two hundred years. The emperor's court, which, while not being converted, had had many cultural and intellectual dealings with the church, got fed up and severed relations with both groups.

Ganzhou

We had a "seminar" this morning at Jinggangshan with several experts, including the museum director. In other words, a lot of talk trying to get some facts straight. In the museum, to which I did not go, there were pictures of the two bandits Ed Snow wrote about—Wang Zuo and Yuan Wencai. They are shown as members of the Communist Party and great guys. Ed Snow wrote that they had joined Mao and been part of the Red Army at Jinggangshan but that when Mao left in 1929, both Wang and Yuan returned to their bandit ways. What came out of Harrison's intensive questioning was that in the beginning when Mao first went to Jinggangshan, both Wang and Yuan were wary of him. Mao met with Yuan and made a deal; one hundred rifles for money and the promise that Yuan would set up a hospital for the Red Army (the first school building we saw yesterday). Evidently both these men had rifles and about two hundred men each. They preyed on villages, taking what they wanted, and that's how they lived.

Wang was reluctant to join Mao. He said, "If you will give me the head of my chief rival, Ying Daoyi [whose headquarters were in Ganzhou], I'll realize you're being serious." Mao sent an adviser to work with Wang, to try to convert him, and he made some progress. But Wang kept raising the question of his old enemy. Finally, the Red Army, led by He Changgong, the adviser, attacked Ying's headquarters and captured him alive. When Wang's men saw him, they were "so happy" they chopped off his head and gave it to Wang. This convinced him of the Red Army's sincerity and military capability; "He took it deep into his heart and went over to the Red Army."

The two bandit tribes fought for the Communists until Mao moved to Ruijin in January 1929. Then they went back to their bandit ways. Some of the surviving Communists invited them to a meeting, ambushed them, and killed Yuan. Wang escaped through a window, jumped on his horse, and somehow fell into a stream and drowned. Wang's brother, Wang Yunlong, took control of the mountain and held it until 1949, when the Communists were victorious in the whole country. Quite a story, and not a pretty one. In the beginning of the meeting, before I had heard any of this and was listening to the director insisting that the bandits were good guys, I wrote in my notebook: *Perhaps they are writing their history to eliminate the idea of bandits at such a late date and are trying to make them heroes.* The museum director had said it was not right to call them bandits, because they had done many good things. Harrison asked, "Then why did Mao refer to them as bandits? Didn't he know about all their good works?" No answer.

Harrison asked about conditions before, and at the time, Mao came—in 1927. There was a doctor and there were private schools. Well-off families would get together and build schools and hire teachers for their children. Poor children had no schooling. People were superstitious. They believed in devils, the goddess of mercy, and the dragon king.

At the General's suggestion we had lunch at 11:30. We had a long way to go and the road was bad, he said. Much was under construction and was bumpy and full of stones and rocks. In the mountains pale purple and a few red azaleas grow right out of the rocks.

We went through many villages and I wrote in my notebook, *No one who has not seen what we have seen today can begin to realize what the poverty must have been in the past, and the miracle of what Mao did.* The destitution and squalor of today are appalling to me, and I can't imagine what life was like before. I don't see how people living in conditions that we see all day can be free from disease. And yet they are; free from malaria, from schistosomiasis (the disease caused by snails in rice paddies); from the diseases children used to die from—TB, diphtheria, cholera, typhoid. They are taught to boil all water, and there are barefoot doctors (paramedics) in every community to give inoculations and care for minor sickness. They are healthy no matter how primitive everything looks to my Western eye.

Way out here in the countryside there are still many revolutionary slogans that have gone out of style in more sophisticated areas:

Long live Chairman Mao.
Study Chairman Mao's works.
Long live the Chinese Communist Party.
March forward.
Prepare against war, prepare against natural disaster, do everything for the
    people [a quote from Mao].
Serve the people.
Destroy the 4 olds.
Establish the 4 news.
Down with the old—up with the new.
Nothing for yourself—everything for the Chinese people.
Long live invincible Mao's thought.
Long live people's communes.
Firmly push forward the revolution of the dictatorship of the Proletariat.
Liberate Taiwan.

On the mountain road we saw many buses and trucks, among them a refrigerated truck carrying meat. Big yellow steamrollers were on the side of the road every few miles, to help with the constant repairing and upkeep, most of which is done by hand. In one paddy a man was plowing with his yellow cow (as the Chinese refer to most work cows; in reality, they are brown). She had a plastic cover over her back to protect her from the rain, though she was up to her knees in mud. Jack said this was a real proof of individual peasant ownership. If the cow belonged to the commune, he wouldn't be taking such good care of her. A woman was doing her washing in the stream, but under a bridge, to keep the rain off herself.

We were supposed to go to Xingguo but the river is so high the ferry can't go across it safely, so we are here in Ganzhou in the local guest house. These guest houses are all over China in remote places. They have been built since Liberation, not for tourists, but for Chinese party officials and dignitaries. A wall or fence surrounds the compound. You enter through a gate, which is always locked at night, and the houses we have stayed in have been one, two, or three stories. In Beijing, the big guesthouse area is a beautifully landscaped park with many houses scattered among gardens, with bridges over little canals and wonderful trees and shrubs. President Reagan will stay there when he comes to China later this month.

Generally there is a central staircase with a landing halfway up to the next floor. Sometimes the WC is there, either with running water or without. Men's and women's are always separate, but often right next-door to each other, with partitions that don't reach the ceiling. A corridor runs the length of the building with rooms off each side. Most rooms do not have bathrooms or running water in this area, or in most of the areas we will go through. We have been privileged and given the best, even if there hasn't any water. There is always boiled water in a thermos, undoubtedly the biggest luxury to a traveler. You can have bouillon, tea, or coffee at any hour. Tea is always provided.

So far on this trip we have had a suite—living room, bedroom, and bath. The ceilings are about fifteen feet or higher. In the bedroom there are two big beds or a double and a single. A heavy cloth that looks like a tablecloth covers the mattress (mattresses vary in thickness). A quilt inside a silk or cotton cover is rolled up on the bed along with heavy blankets. Pillows are apt to be hard, with pretty embroidered cases and a towel over them. Except for most hotels in big cities, bath towels are the size of our dish towels, and very thin. When Chinese travel, they roll up their towel and carry it in a tin cup. Here we are in cuspidor country—four in the sitting room and two in the bedroom. They are half-filled with water and fill me with horror. I have hidden them all.

I don't believe the Chinese pay for these accommodations, but for us the prices differ. Sometimes we pay twenty-five Chinese dollars for one, sometimes thirty-two for both of us. Sometimes it's fifty. It never seems to have anything to do with the quality of the rooms; it is just random pricing.

Xingguo

We drove here this morning, mostly along the river. It wasn't spectacular like yesterday, and to me looks primitive, poor, and squalid. In the villages pigs, chickens, dogs, people, children—all squatting suspiciously in the rice paddies, though it's said they don't. In every field there is an outhouse, so it's raw fertilizer no matter what. Everything is green and growing like mad. Lots of water—the river has flooded some fields.

This is sugar-cane country. After the cane is harvested, the roots are dug up and dried by the side of the road and used for fuel. Short stalks are sold to chew; several of our party buy some when they can.

Mao traveled around this countryside to find out about conditions. In a population of 240,000 he found that landlords and rich peasants made up 6 percent and owned 80 percent of the land. They charged 50 to 60 percent interest a year on land the poor peasants worked; 30 percent on money; 50 percent on grain; 75 percent on oxen; 150 percent on salt; and 20 to 200 percent on oil. (And we think our interest rates are high!) There were no newspapers then, and no good landlords. Eighty thousand people joined the Communist Party, including some rich peasants.

Mao established laws that were the basis of reforms, and made rules for the peasants to live by. Land was to be distributed to peasants, and even to beggars, prostitutes, and thieves. The blind and cripples would have their land worked for them. All people were to remit their debts and to have political power. They were not to take opium, not to steal. Doors could be left unlocked. Here they mentioned the "Four Frees": to be self-supporting; to have self-respect; to have self-love; to have self-decorum.

We had a nice lunch but far too much. Here, Jack, Harrison, and I sit curtained off from our Chinese companions and eat by ourselves. Jack has made it clear that we want only three dishes and rice, but we always have at least six and a soup, plus steamed bread and fruit. There seems to be nothing to do about it, and we pay for it all whether we eat it or not. We were given a bottle of the local fiery drink, something like maotai, but it is too strong for us.

In the afternoon we went to a freezing-cold room in the museum where there are still pictures of Marx, Engels, Lenin, and Stalin, as there used to be in Tien Anmen Square, and everywhere. We talked to a tiny old guy who was here in the twenties and thirties. It is obvious he has told his story many times and enjoys it. He is seventy-nine years old, came from a poor peasant family, and worked as a mason. His wife is seventy-two. They have five children, eight grandchildren, six great-grandchildren. The family consists of twenty-seven members.

In 1929 he joined the party. There was an underground for which he ran errands, mailed letters, put up slogans. When the Long March started and the Red Army left, the Kuomintang came in. Anyone who was known to have been connected to the Communist Party was executed, so it was wise to deny any relationship and to band together with friends and protect each other. A few people were turned in by personal enemies; some fled to the mountains, but most stayed. Of nine thousand people left in the country, about two thousand were executed, he said.

After supper a little woman carried in two huge buckets of hot water on a shoulder pole, staggering under the weight, for us to wash with. Thank heaven for my hot-water bottle. It's not as dripping wet and freezing as in Jinggangshan, but it is very damp and cold and the bed is awful until it is warmed up. The lights have gone off and on, but Harrison is still banging away on his typewriter by candlelight.

TUESDAY, APRIL 10
Ruijin

We left Xingguo at about 8:00 this morning. I was glad to leave. Everything we own smells damp, old, musty—it's horrible. But here it is better. We have a huge living room, a huge bedroom, and a revolting bathroom, but at least a WC. We were told there would be hot water after supper and a girl came in and turned it on in the tub—very rusty at first. I washed my hair and myself, so did Harrison, and when we pulled the plug in the bathtub, the water ran out all over the floor. This must be intentional, because there is a hole on the side at the bottom of the tub, and there is always a drain in the floor in Chinese bathrooms.

These bathrooms look like old cow or horse barns with cement floors and walls, a tub set on huge cement blocks and the toilet propped up by another cement block. The fixtures are enamel in this bathroom, granite or dark stone in others, and this one is much cleaner than in most places. But overall they are so unattractive people in the United States would be shocked. We asked for more towels to dry my hair and afterward had to use them to mop up the floor. However, this is a much airier and more cheerful place than any so far since Beijing.

We drove through some wonderful scenery this morning—big, black menacing rocky hills and mountains, something like the pictures of Queilin. The earth, for the most part, is very red, and has been heavily reforested. The Kuomintang burned much of this country, and the Chinese people had been cutting down trees and using underbrush for fuel and fodder for years until the mountains were—and some still are—bare. In a few places the trees have had time to get established, and if they were tended carefully, real forests could grow here. Much of the planting is new—trees only about two feet high at the most.

We saw many footpaths, which the Long Marchers traveled on—there were no real roads in those days—and some lovely old footbridges of all sizes, shaped and built the same; they are made of stone and arch over the stream. Steps lead from each end. On some bridges the steps have been smoothed over to make it easier for bicycles and carts, but they are not half as pretty this way.

We gave the liquor the local people gave us to our Chinese companions and one bottle spilt in the bus. The smell is nearly as bad as our clothes.

We had lunch at Yudu, which is where Mao started out on the Long March on October 18, 1934, when the Kuomintang surrounded the area. We saw the house he left from, and we went to the river where he crossed on a bridge made of boats tied together. The entire army—approximately eighty thousand men—was able to cross over in a week. In some places, where the water was not so deep, they could walk.

We also visited Stone Cloud Temple, a pretty building up on a hill, still another house where Mao lived for a while. He moved around so much because it was safer to go from place to place than to stay in any one for very long.

On the way home we stopped at a magnificent old ancestral hall and had a typically boring briefing. More driving, then here. The windows were open in our "suite," and in spite of the leaking tub and a toilet that doesn't flush, we are at last clean.

WEDNESDAY, APRIL 11
Ruijin

Today we spent visiting places Mao slept in or had meetings in or started investigations in. He liked the fancy places, so nearly all his headquarters were in landlords' houses, ancestral halls, and temples. All that we have seen look terrible, however—dirty whitewashed walls, hard dirt floors, sometimes stone; nothing to see except a bed, often with mosquito netting, a rough table and benches where the great man sat and either organized something or wrote a poem. These buildings were once brightly painted and polished. Some of the woodwork is heavenly, with little carved scenes of animals, birds, flowers. The Communists took over the landlords' houses for themselves in 1929–1930.

The Kuomintang moved in about one month after the Communists left. Landlords who hadn't been executed took back their property. These houses are probably the only ones that weren't destroyed by the Kuomintang, and they weren't damaged in the Cultural Revolution because Mao had stayed in them and he was sacred to the Red Guards. Heaven knows what happened to the people. Many were killed by Chiang Kaishek's soldiers—including one hundred buried alive at Dabodi, not far from Ruijin—and all benefits were taken from the survivors.

While I get hideously bored with repetitive descriptions of meetings and uprisings and am baffled by all the armies, the more I think about what one man did—how he "mobilized" the peasants, as we hear every hour, and created a social system with ignorant, uneducated, misused, and abused people with no obvious ability except to continue to live their lives the way they had for centuries, and to do this while he was putting together an army, struggling to have and keep control, and trying to defeat Chiang Kaishek, and then the Japanese—it's inspiring and very moving.

Time magazine told Harrison they want to do a bit about him making this trip, and they wondered if they could send a photographer down here to photograph the start. All these places we have been are off limits to foreigners, so that was out of the question. We have all been taking pictures and will send them to Beijing when we get back to Nanchang on the fourteenth, and hope some are suitable.

The market here is full of individuals selling their wares—private enterprise, or the "responsibility system" we hear so much about. There are lots of vegetables, many pears, oranges, and sugar cane, and little stalls selling "fast food" Chinese-style, steaming bowls of noodles and other quickly cooked dishes.

Along the roads there are privately owned public toilets. The owners get the contents for their vegetable plots. Often there are three in a row, and we were wondering who would use the middle one?

We were given a banquet by our local hosts. The General made a toast to Mao—"Without him, none of us would be sitting around this table together." An interesting thought.

THURSDAY, APRIL 12
Ningdu

This morning at Ruijin we had a "seminar" that lasted from 8:30 until noon. We sat in a room filled with big sofas and chairs all upholstered in bright orange flowery-patterned brocade. Not very suitable for this kind of climate. It gets smelly and grimy and seems always to be damp.

The poor man who is the "leading historical archivist" of the museum had a hard time with many of Harrison's questions, and often he had to say he didn't know. It makes it difficult for Harrison, because while he doesn't want anyone to lose face, there's not much point in coming all the way over here and spending what is going to be close to four months on this trip if he can't get answers to his questions. The men in Beijing were more helpful. Perhaps they know more.

Harrison said he wanted to get a picture in his mind of how the countryside looked, what crops were harvested, what still in the fields, and what the weather was like when Mao left in October 1934. The weather was (and is) generally good at that time of year; the second crop of rice was not yet harvested; soybeans had been pulled up—they pull the whole plant—and put on fences and roofs to dry. Red peppers had been strung and were hanging in houses; some melons had been harvested, but watermelons were still in the fields, as well as other types of beans and sweet potatoes. Sugar cane was not grown then as it is now, just a bit for eating. Now it is widely used in granulated form. There were chickens, ducks, geese; water buffalo and yellow cows. The Red Army left at night and probably there was moonlight. A vanguard went ahead to figure out the route and stationed themselves along the way to guide the soldiers. They marched at night and hid by day.

As we have been told, the army crossed the river on boats and bamboo rafts lashed together with planks, wide enough for two or three men to walk abreast. Again we heard it took about a week for eighty thousand men to cross.

Harrison said he had read that a house had been built for Li De, and here they say he lived in a temple. It seems a temple was remodeled for him. Jack said they probably just moved out some idols, and a Chinese man said, "And moved another in," which caused a laugh.

At lunch, our last meal in the nicest place so far, we had the best food we have had since we've been in China. Stuffed bean curd, chicken bits with little pea pods, cabbage hearts, noodles, soup, and tangerines.

We left soon after lunch and came here to Ningdu. When we arrived at the city limits, we were met by the chief of police in a jeep. He led us through the maze of narrow streets, trucks, people, babies, pigs, piles of evergreen boughs, bamboo, you name it, waving a red flag ferociously at anyone who didn't get out of the way. This guest house is up on a hill overlooking the town. We have one small room, which suits us fine; the bed is just a board, but we have a toilet that works. In Jack's room is a list of 1982 House Rules:

1. If husband and wife want to stay in the same room, you must have a marriage certificate or a letter from your unit.
2. You must recognize the authority of the people in charge and show that you are authorized to go on to the next place.
3. You are absolutely prohibited from gambling, from practices that are unlawful, from corrupt practices and other unlawful activities.

4. These rules should be adhered to in a conscientious way by the traveler, and the traveler should help the people in authority.
5. If people disobey, they may be criticized, subject to education, or asked to leave. Especially bad violators may be subject to penalties as ascribed by law.

Fuzhou

In 1931 at Ningdu, a division of the Kuomintang went over to join the Communists. This morning we visited the former residence of the German Lutheran missionary, the scene of this event. It is built in the typical warlord style of the 1920s, like a southern mansion with balconies on every side and big airy rooms, huge and luxurious compared to ordinary Chinese houses. It is odd that men of God were so materially minded; I would think that by living simply it would have been easier to spread the Word.

This Nationalist division had ensconced itself in the best building in town, and when they joined the Communists, the house became headquarters for the Red Army. It is now a museum.

I hadn't realized there were so many missionaries in China—thousands, evidently—or that every county seat had at least one big Christian church. Mao liked churches as much as he liked the big houses, and he held many meetings in them. The first missionaries were Italians, who became advisers to the emperors even before Marco Polo, and brought science, mathematics, and medicine to China. Later, French, German, English, and American missionaries came, mostly the latter two.

During the Boxer Rebellion, in 1900, the aim of which was to rid China of all foreigners and Western influence, many missionaries were killed. In the 1930s the Communists regarded them as "agents of foreign imperialism." Many fled to the big cities; some were captured and held for ransom; others were killed.

I have never been much in favor of any missionary movement. When I was a child, I remember collections being taken in church for the "heathen Chinese." It seemed then, and it certainly does now in retrospect, self-righteous and absurd for us, a country not even three hundred years old, to be telling anyone, especially an old society like the Chinese, what to do and how to think. But in China missionaries were helpful in several ways. Schools, universities, and hospitals were established, and in many cases these institutions were the basis of friendship between the United States and China. Jack Service comes from a missionary family; so does our ambassador in Beijing. Both speak Chinese and understand

62

this country far better than most people, because of their background. John Hersey is another, and the Luce family—too many to mention.

That evening in 1931, the Nationalist division officers were having dinner on the second floor of the big house. The commander announced that they were going to join the Communists. Two officers didn't concur, ran out of the dinner, and jumped off the balcony, but were caught by the Red Army soldiers who had been surrounding the building. As a museum, it is the same as most we have seen, with moldy pictures and pieces of flags and fabric, many framed pictures of orders and letters, and occasionally an oil painting of Mao or Zhu De or Zhou Enlai greeting soldiers or having a meeting. These pictures are rarely signed; they are done by a "group of comrade artists."

After an early lunch we left Ningdu and drove here to Fuzhou. It was a long, bumpy drive. We don't do anything here; it is just a break in the long drive back to Nanchang.

SATURDAY, APRIL 14
Nanchang

The drive from Fuzhou was about two and a half hours through wonderfully fertile land with spectacular-looking vegetables growing. There are large mountains to the west and some hills that must have been barren for years and are now being reforested. Large stands of pine and a kind of spruce show that tree planting has been going on for a long time. Some trees must be twenty years old, and others are newly planted. Red azaleas are everywhere and Harrison thinks they are wild, as do our Chinese companions. I don't see how they can be, because they grow where trees are just starting. Also, I saw a nursery garden of azaleas. I know it is a naturally wild plant here, but in these denuded areas it must need a big push to get going.

We have seen four small tractors in the wet fields and I would think a water buffalo or a cow is superior. They can get close to the edges; they don't get stuck; they make fertilizer; and the cost is about the same.

There are graves everywhere, including new ones. I thought burying in the ground was forbidden, that every body had to be cremated, but it's clear this is not enforced. Graves use up good land; some are right in the middle of the vegetable plots. Huge round paper wreaths are on some of the new graves, and up on a hill we saw a grave with a three-part wreath, a sort of triptych. They are really vulgar, made of garish painted paper, like a dreadful candy box.

When we arrived, the sun was shining. We are in the same hotel as before. After a nice lunch, we met with two professors who were pleasant but don't know as much as Harrison and Jack. Harrison is trying to find out what was going on here in the city when Mao left the base area. The outer bases of the Red Army had already fallen, so people probably were speculating that Chiang Kaishek would wipe out the Red Army. No one could have contemplated the Long March, not even Mao. He might have thought they would win some battles and return to the Red base area.

After the last few days, traveling in the old Communist base area and hearing so much about the encirclements and blockhouses, I have finally begun to get a good picture of what happened. Starting about 1931, Chiang Kaishek mounted big military campaigns to wipe out the Communists. The Communists' main base was in Jiangxi Province, in Ruijin, Yudu, and the surrounding mountains, the places we have just been. In the first, second, and third encirclement campaigns, the Nationalists tried to surround the mountains and squeeze the Red Army into being slaughtered or surrendering. Mao was in charge during these attempts, and his tactics of attacking and retreating and thoroughly confusing the enemy were successful. The Communists won all three campaigns, gained many new followers from prisoners captured, and took a lot of guns and ammunition.

The fourth encirclement came in 1933 at the time Mao's leadership was in question. As he did many more times in the future, Zhou Enlai was trying to hold things together, but in this struggle, though the Communists managed to hold on and to win overall, they suffered serious losses.

The fifth and last encirclement came after Mao was out. Bo Gu and Li De were running things, and they believed that standing fast and facing the enemy was the best strategy. It was a disaster, the final blow. The Communists realized they had to move on.

The basic tactic of the Nationalists was to build blockhouses, big cement-and-steel structures with machine guns on every side. They put these at every place they thought the Red Army would try to sneak through. The Communists could only attack these with grenades, and most of the time had to figure out how to go around them.

Curiously, Li De was calling the shots for the Communists, while another German, General von Seeckt, was advising Chiang Kaishek. It was he who suggested blockhouses, and this was what, in the end, did the Communists in. Li De had the same kind of German approach, but of course it couldn't work for the Red Army, which was made up of peasant soldiers with not enough weapons to face the better-equipped Nationalist Army.

Another problem for the Communists was the difficulty of getting food and supplies. There were markets and shops in the villages, but never enough for everyone. Salt, cotton clothing, and matches were rationed. Flashlight batteries were in great demand. Conditions encouraged smugglers, but anyone who managed to get past the blockhouses demanded a very high price for goods. Many ways of smuggling were used; boats had false bottoms; night-soil buckets had only a thin layer of dry feces on top. Peddlers were the best source. They managed to go in and out of the Kuomintang blockade, paying a little bribe here and there.

We had a banquet given by the local politicos. The food was lovely and the "firewater" drink quite good.

SUNDAY, APRIL 15
Nanchang

In the morning we met with some survivors of the Long March. The star was a tiny little woman, no more than four feet five (if that), Mrs. Wei Xiu-ying. She wore a blue-gray Mao suit and cap and fabric shoes with one-inch heels. She carried a bag, handmade of blue and white cotton. She is now seventy-four years old. She said she felt shy and wanted someone else to talk first, but once she began, there was no stopping her. She came from a peasant family and, at age five or six, was sold to a small-town merchant's family. She was expected to work as a slave and eventually marry one of the sons, if he so wished. At the designated time, the merchant sent a male member of his family to fetch her. This man put her on his back, but she put up such a fuss, kicked, screamed, bit his ear, that he could not handle her, and her own family had to take her.

She was with this family for ten years, doing everything she was told. She took oxen to graze, worked in the vegetable plots, and gathered firewood. She was maltreated and beaten. She didn't know anything about revolution but knew about the Red Army, and to show her sympathy, she cut off her hair. The family regarded her as a bandit woman. She ran away when she was sixteen and joined the Red Army. With other women, she took care of the sick and wounded men. They carried guns because they often had to use them. She was in a battle at Ji'an and said she wasn't frightened: "You are not afraid when you want to make revolution."

We were told that she is one of the thirty women who made the Long March with the First Front Army, and one of the few survivors. She and the other women started the march from Ruijin. Her duty was taking care of the injured. It was a clear night when they left. By day they camou-flaged themselves with leaves and branches. If there were no enemy planes, they would walk day and night. She didn't mention sleep. She talked about breaking through the first encirclement, before the Long March, and about getting sick from eating wild vegetables. She said the soldiers were so young and innocent that they thought women were shot or injured if they were menstruating and blood got onto the roads or into the rivers.

She didn't learn to read and write until they arrived at Yan'an, where she went to the Red Army School. She said Chairman Mao used to visit the classes and look at their work. If he thought they needed more help, he would sit, with the students all around him, using their knees as desks, and teach them. No wonder they loved him.

There is a picture in one of the museums of five young girl soldiers on the top of a rocky cliff. They were being pursued by Kuomintang soldiers, so they held them off until all their ammunition was used up, then threw themselves over the cliff—girls in their teens. Not many Americans can imagine life being so terrible that they would prefer to die rather than subject themselves to the Kuomintang soldiers, or live the way those Chinese girls had to under the feudal landlord system. Slogging around where the revolution got going has made me understand all this much better than I ever did before.

Another survivor we spoke to was Wu Jiqing, who had been bodyguard to Mao for six years from 1931 to 1937. He told us some remarkable things about He Zizhen, Mao's wife, and I don't know if they are true or not. He said she and Mao were married in 1928 or '29 in Jinggangshan. In 1929, when they left the mountain, He Zizhen gave birth to her first daughter, in Fujian Province. The child was left with villagers, and in 1932, when Mao was in that region again, he looked for the child but couldn't find her. "He was in a hurry," Wu said. In 1932, in Ruijin, she had a boy, Xiao Mao. Her sister, He Yi, was married to Mao's brother, Mao Zetan, and they were among the group that stayed when the Long March began. He Zizhen left this boy of two with her sister and a nurse. When the Kuomintang came, He Yi gave the baby to peasants and she and Mao Zetan tried to escape. He was killed, but she got away and ended up in Yan'an. After Liberation, He Yi located the nurse, who knew where the child was. But they were killed in a car accident and the child was never found. In 1933 He Zizhen had a premature baby boy. This child died. When the Long March started, He Zizhen was pregnant again, Wu said. This baby, a girl, was left with peasants, who were given some silver dollars. Later, she was never found.

At Yan'an this poor lady had another girl, Li Ming, who is still alive. (We learned later she had another baby, a boy, when she went to Moscow after the Long March had ended. This child died after becoming ill in a nursery school.)

As if all these pregnancies weren't enough, He Zizhen was wounded trying to protect a man who was being carried on a stretcher. His guard had already been killed. For most of the march she, too, had to be carried.

It is an appalling story. It is interesting to remember that several of the people we talked to in Beijing said that to their knowledge, she never had a baby on the Long March.

Wu said she was a brave and courageous woman.

In the afternoon we went to the Provincial Library, which is in an old building near a lake in the middle of the city. It had been headquarters for Chiang Kaishek off and on for about three years. From here he directed the operations of the five encirclement campaigns that eventually drove the Communists out of this area. Harrison wants to know what the news was at that time, what was going on in China. He looked at some copies of the Nationalist daily, *Minguo Ribao,* for October–November 1934. He wrote in his notes, *It is a fat paper of ten or twelve pages with lots of ads, mostly patent medicines featuring women's ailments and men's sex tonics.*

The main theme of most of the articles was the defeat and retreat of the "Red Bandits," the cruelty they displayed to their soldiers, their lack of food, the many who defected to the Nationalists; how the Nationalists were advancing steadily and the Red Army running away or joining them, how happy all the people were—the things every army says about the enemy. On October 28, 1934, the lead story was of the Kuomintang capturing Ningdu, where we just were.

MONDAY, APRIL 16
On the Train to Guiyang

We got up at 4:00 this morning and drove for about an hour in our minibus with the nice driver and our two companions from the Jiangxi Provincial Foreign Office, to a place out in the sticks where this train stopped, not a real station. We were early and the train was late, and we waited about forty-five minutes, standing and walking around and doing exercises. The General is very good at *taiji,* the slow movements that take a lot of control. I am good at stretching and putting my hands flat on the ground without bending my knees, which surprised everyone.

There was a full moon and it was beautiful as it was getting light. Quite a few people were heading toward the city, on bicycles laden with heavy bags of grain for the market.

We have a compartment with Jack and it is not boiling hot. In this next province, Guizhou, it will be wet all the time, we're told. Harrison has been typing all day; I have finished *Theophilus North,* which I loved, and will start on the short stories of Willa Cather.

At about 8:30 we went through Guilin and could faintly see those extraordinarily shaped rock formations. I don't know what they're called. Jack says they are eroded limestone. Harrison thinks they look like giant stalactite cave forms upside down. They have some green on them, according to Jack, they are not just solid rock. Anyway, at least we have an idea of the strange beauty of Guilin—I never thought we'd get anywhere near it.

TUESDAY, APRIL 17
Guiyang

We went to bed early, right after Guilin, with Jack in the upper berth. At 11:30 the new conductor for the night shift, who was very disagreeable, unlocked our door without knocking, and pointed out our extra berth to a tall Western-looking young man. It had all our bags and clothes on it. Jack and Harrison had to wake up and move everything down to the floor, or to our berths. The young man never came to join us, thank goodness. Spending the night with three old Americans probably wasn't very appealing, but I give him credit for being nicer than the conductor and not wanting to disturb us any further.

This morning at first we were still in country that had black rock mounds and crags, like Guilin, and I was amazed to see so much green growing out of them. Once in a while a really big tree was growing in a barely discernible crevice. That scenery lasted about one hour; everything flattened out for a while, then became mountainous with many tunnels. Quite poor-looking very small villages—no electricity, no new houses, no chimneys. Smoke goes out through the roofs.

A sad group was in our car. A beautiful young man of twenty-one has a tumor on his brain and is in a coma. He lay on a berth with glucose or some other liquid dripping into the veins in his ankles. He was accompanied by his mother and father, who is an engineer in a factory; a representative from the factory; and a strong man to carry him. He has been taken to doctors in Shanghai and Guangzhou, and all say it's inoperable, so he is being taken home to die. The factory pays for all the expenses.

A year ago the tumor was the size of a grape and now it is killing him. At least he is unconscious; he didn't move or make any sound. Only his parents are suffering. He is the only boy and has three sisters. Whenever a comment like that is made, I realize that girls are still not as desirable as boys in many parts of the world.

Also on the train were about ten Westerners; an American ex-navy officer and several young people from Vancouver. Some very blond Scandinavians, and a Chinese young woman from overseas who didn't speak Chinese. She couldn't communicate with the waiters in the dining car, but she ate noodles with chopsticks for breakfast.

Jack says this is the poorest province, the Appalachia of China. As we saw out of the windows, houses have thatched roofs, and there is terracing on what looks like poor soil up high on hills and mountains.

But we are in the first really lovely place we've been so far. This guest house is on the side of a hill; a river flows beside a winding road below. There is a waterfall and, on a hill opposite, terraced garden plots, graves, trees, rocks; willows beside the road and river, and mountains in the background. A perfect Chinese picture. Big pink peonies are blooming outside the front door.

We have a mammoth, well-furnished sitting room; a small room with a single bed and desk, which Harrison refers to as his study; and a bedroom with two oversize double beds. The bathroom is enormous and has everything necessary with a choice of toilets, Chinese or Western. There is hot water in the tap.

We are about ten kilometers from the station. We didn't see anything of the city—we just went by many factories in the midst of awful pollution. There is a cement factory, a cigarette factory, a tobacco-drying plant, and an electric power plant. Miss Yang, who is pretty and young, will accompany us as interpreter, and a man who doesn't speak English is the arranger of travel details.

After washing ourselves and our clothes, we were given a banquet by the provincial governor. This is the first time we've been honored by a governor. He is not Han Chinese, but a Miao, and the first of any minority to be a governor. He is full of energy, charm, ideas, and humor, and hardly stopped talking all through dinner. There were hundreds of toasts, to our Chinese friends, to their American friends, to Chinese-American friendship, to Harrison's book, to the heroes of the Long March, on and on. Sometimes I make a toast, but not tonight.

The governor is determined to pull his province up out of poverty. He says there are untapped minerals; they need experts for industrial development. He wants to plant trees everywhere and to establish animal husbandry. Sheep, he says, but I think goats would do well on the stony hills. He is going to get advice and help from New Zealand. We liked him because he was so honest about the poverty and lack of industrial expertise, as well as the lack of any attraction for tourists, which is such a good source of money for other provinces.

I sat on the governor's left, Harrison on his right. Miss Yang sat on my other side. I told her I was delighted she was sitting by me and hoped she didn't mind. She said, "I will be by your side." Very comforting, especially as she didn't want to eat any more than I did.

Dinner was nicely done and served, starting with a platter of hors d'oeuvres in the shape of a rooster. Hundreds of dishes followed, lovely fresh mushrooms, duck with the head on, bowl after bowl of peculiar mixtures, and the pièce de résistance—salamander soup. They told us that salamanders can't live in polluted water, which proves how pure they are. But even that recommendation couldn't overcome my automatic resistance.

WEDNESDAY, APRIL 18
Guiyang

Today is our twentieth wedding anniversary and this is a pretty odd place to be, not much like Boston, where we spent our wedding night.

We slept well and had breakfast at 8:00—gruel, three jiaozi (Chinese dumplings) in soup (Jack's had red pepper, but ours didn't—preferential treatment because he grew up in China, and they probably think we don't like hot food), garlic cloves, fermented bean curd to eat with the gruel, two fried eggs, cake, pastry, hot milk and coffee. Afterward Harrison met with a military research man and the head of the local museum. I didn't go right away; stayed in our pleasant room and wrote letters. There were several waiting for us here and it is comforting to have news of home. We have never received letters on any of our previous trips to China, and we have had them regularly so far on this trip.

When I joined the group, they were talking about the Liping meeting and the Zunyi conference. In November and early December of 1934, the Red Army broke through the last of Chiang Kaishek's blockhouse lines. It cost them dearly, and by the time they got to the Guizhou border, what was left was in bad shape. Clearly the tactics of Li De and Bo Gu were not working. Officers and soldiers were worried. They agreed to have a meeting at the first possible opportunity to discuss further plans. Li De and Bo Gu wanted to go straight north to meet Xiao Ke (whom we talked to in Beijing), who headed the Sixth Army, and He Long, commander of the Second. These two armies were merged into the Second Front Army, but each general kept his own command. They were friends and with each other all during the Long March. Mao wanted to go west to get farther away from Chiang Kaishek's armies and eventually join the others. In December a meeting was held at Liping. It was the first step toward Mao's taking control.

Not long after, in January 1935, the Red Army captured the town of Zunyi, in this province. There was time for a big meeting and long discussions of aims and strategy, and after a few days Mao and his ideas won out. This spelled the end of Li De and Bo Gu's leadership, and was the beginning of Mao's ascendancy to head of the Communist Party, and eventually head man in China. Zhou Enlai changed his allegiance and became chief of staff to Mao, a position he kept all his life.

At all these talks we have there are Harrison, Jack, me, the General,

Mr. Zhang, our local provincial companions, and the special people we question—survivors, museum directors, historical experts. Almost everyone takes notes. They continued talking about why Mao and the army had considered having a base in this province. Chiang Kaishek was thought to be weak in this area. However, once the Red army got here, warlords who were on Chiang's side attacked them, so the Red Army had to keep moving. They never found a place to establish a base until northern Shaanxi.

These men talked about the terrible poverty peasants lived in. They were always in debt to the landlord and there was no way to pay. Landlords demanded too much. According to these men, peasants didn't sell their children; they disposed of newborn babies.

But then, in the afternoon, we talked to two survivors of the Long March, and one of them said he had been sold for five yuan, about $2.50, when he was five years old. The overwhelming majority of the people were illiterate, he said. Life expectancy was around thirty; now it's near seventy. Forty to 50 percent of babies died. There were no roads linking counties.

These two men can't remember what the weather was like when they started what turned out to be the Long March. Also, they had no idea they were embarking on such a long trip—no idea they were really retreating from the Kuomintang. They said their senior officers knew, but they themselves thought it was just a tactical movement and that they would return to the base area. It seems to us now that even Mao may have thought this, or thought he could set up another base in the next province—Hunan.

One of the survivors looked like a thin, disagreeable Khrushchev. He was twenty-four at the time of the march and his work was with the masses, he said. He had to find out if landlords were bad, or if they were members of the Kuomintang or sympathetic to it, before any action could be taken against them. Rich and middle peasants were not to be troubled or have their land confiscated. He had to be very sure before he authorized any action. I wouldn't have liked being a landlord and having him in charge of confiscating my land and belongings, not to mention my children or myself. I imagine most were shot or decapitated. Grain could be confiscated, but silver, gold, and jewelry had to be turned in to Red Army headquarters. The way he talked, everything was lovely between the Red Army and the ordinary people. The army paid for everything, he said, and they undoubtedly did when they could. After all, they were trying to recruit soldiers and sympathizers all the way.

Guizhou was an opium-growing province and all men over age fifteen smoked it, so this was not a good area for recruiting soldiers. No one ever says anything about women smoking, and I wonder about that. After Liberation the supply and/or source was eliminated. Anyone connected with production and selling opium was executed; there were programs and medical help for addicts and neighbors helped each other. In these remote parts of China I don't believe there were any medical facilities; most people must have just sweated it out. But it remains one of the extraordinary achievements of the Chinese Communist Party—ridding the whole country of addiction. What a sorry role the Western nations have played in China. It is hard for me to believe that I belong to a group of human beings that, for the purpose of making money, deliberately imported or had grown, then sold to poor and rich alike, an addicting drug that ruined their lives. I guess I am naive; it's what many people are doing now in the United States. Jack told us the countryside looked beautiful when the poppies were in bloom. The flowers were white and pale pink. There are none now.

This man said they had orders to respect minority customs, to try and recruit as many soldiers as they could, and not to confiscate minority landlords' possessions. He said that when they came to a minority village, the people had usually run off to the mountains and had locked their houses. "We left the houses alone," he said, "and if we took any vegetables from the gardens, we left money and a note by the door." Sometimes they left an IOU and it was paid later on—even after Liberation. Since he'd just said almost everyone was illiterate, I wonder how they made out what the letter said and what the money was for.

The second survivor was a much nicer man. He joined the Red Army when he was eighteen, in 1933 (he's sixty-nine now). He said life under the Kuomintang was wretched. His father died when he was two; his mother married again and moved to another village. We think she must have moved and then remarried. I don't believe widows did marry again in their village. They were slaves of the mother-in-law even when the husband died. This man was brought up by his grandparents and lived with them, three uncles, and an aunt, not in a village, but by themselves on a mountain.

Harrison had arranged an anniversary party, and these two men stayed for dinner. A big cake with the characters meaning "Double Happiness" was in the middle of the table, and we had Chinese champagne that tasted like ginger ale. I don't think it had any alcohol in it, but it was good and sparkly. The man who looks like Khrushchev got drinking too much maotai and kept ordering the girl who was waiting on us to fill up his glass until our local host told her, No more. The other man was very nice and made a toast to my "long life and happiness." It was a funny group for our wedding anniversary dinner. There were lots of toasts, and Jack took a Polaroid picture of us cutting the cake. It cost one Chinese dollar, or about 50¢. Three bottles of champagne cost $3.98, or about $2.00 American. It was a nice friendly celebration.

THURSDAY, APRIL 19

Kaili

We left this morning in our Guizhou minibus, with Miss Yang and the man who is in charge of arrangements. As we drove through the town we saw that one of the movies playing is *The Legend of the Lone Ranger,* in English with Chinese subtitles.

The country looked poor—no new buildings, scanty-looking gardens. We stopped at the post office at Longli for Jack to mail one of his envelopes that have nothing in them to George Hatem, for his collection.

We didn't get here until 3:00. In the bus we have music constantly, from cassettes that belong to Miss Yang. On one we have *Carmen,* selections from *The Nutcracker,* Beethoven's Ninth, Mendelssohn's Recessional, Brahms Lullaby, "O Solo Mio," the tune to "Passengers will please refrain . . . ," all played with great vigor by capable musicians. Another has American songs: "Ole Black Joe," "Swanee River," "Home on the Range," "Red River Valley," and the like, sung first in Chinese, then in English.

We walked through the town for a bit, to a big market. We felt like the Pied Piper of Hamlen; people saw us, fell in behind us, and soon there must have been more than one hundred men, women and children following.

The prefect of this prefecture, which is made up of sixteen counties, gave us a banquet. He is of the Miao minority. The two big minority groups here are Dong and Miao. It is hard for us to tell them apart. The women can be gorgeous, and Mr. Xiao, a Dong man who was at dinner, is handsome. There is some intermarriage, and we understand some Chinese marry minority people so they can have more than one child (minorities are allowed to have two). Mr. Xiao is married to a Han, and the man who makes arrangements is a Han married to a Miao. The Chinese insist they want to preserve the native languages and customs of the minorities, but with schooling in Chinese and the chance of intermarriage, it seems that eventually they will be absorbed into the Han Chinese, and their dances, songs, dress, and customs will be just for show.

FRIDAY, APRIL 20

Jinping

We drove through some perfectly beautiful country that looked much more prosperous than yesterday. Lots of cedars, some old, some newly planted. In several places it looked like Italy. Wonderful terraced gardens, cabbage and other green vegetables. A flower like our wild phlox is in bloom in many fields. It will be plowed in for fertilizer. Holes are dug in the hillsides next to the gardens, for shelter from the rain, and for storing sweet potatoes and root vegetables, like root cellars.

One flowering tree is, we are told, a tung-oil tree. Its blossoms are white with a red-orange center. The mountains are covered with a white flowering shrub that looks like spirea. A big bird with brown body and head and white wings flies around the fields that are filled with water. It is called a crane, but it doesn't seem to have long legs.

In the morning we went by a paper factory and I saw, for the first time anywhere, the effluent, or refuse, being discharged into a beautiful clear mountain river. Huge mounds of white stuff that didn't disintegrate visibly for two or three miles. After that, the water is still polluted even if it doesn't show. I had been told that no factory was permitted to operate unless the pollution problem had been solved, yet I have never seen such dirty smoke and smelled such smells as from the factories here, and that stuff in the river was horrifying. People can't drink the water, and I don't see how it is safe to use it on crops. I know we are just as guilty, though some places have been cleaned up. Fishermen on the Housatonic River in Connecticut are told to throw back the fish they catch, and in some states they are advised to eat fish they catch no more than once a week. I have always blamed the selfish greed of business people for not wanting to spend the necessary money to clean up the filth they pour into our atmosphere and waters, but here the Chinese Communists are just as guilty. No wonder so many people all over the world are dying of cancer. Everything is being poisoned.

Our Dong friend, Mr. Xiao, came along today and told us a lot about the Dongs and Miaos (Miao is pronounced like a cat's *meow*). Dong people prefer to live down by the rivers. Miaos prefer the tops of hills, though in many places they, too, live by the river. Some Miao women wear pants, some skirts. And they have different hairstyles. Some Dong women twist their long, thick black hair on top of their heads in a beautiful way with a flower or comb, and wear skimpy bangs on their foreheads. Others wear towels or turbans or some kind of draped or wrapped headdress.

Both Dongs and Miaos have bull fights, using water buffalo. Fighting is between animals; there is no matador as in Spanish or Mexican bullfights. A man is present only to spur the buffalo on if they become uninterested. That means pricking them with spikes, I believe. He said the Dong fights were the most exciting. They let the bulls fight to the death. Miao people separate them when it is clear who is the winner. Both Dongs and Miaos raise fighting cocks and enjoy those fights, too.

Harrison and I have been talking about cruelty to animals, of which we see so much here. We decided farmers and country people are the same the world over. A pig is a pig, a chicken a chicken, on the whole not thought to have any feelings. We have seen pigs and goats trussed up, being held upside down, being taken to market, and hens and ducks tied so they can't move. They are sold alive or butchered at the market. Geese are stuffed into a big basket so that only those on top can breathe. The others are squashed down under several layers of smothering birds. I guess none of it is any worse than my eating meat. Sometimes, like now, I wonder how I can. But, to get back to the Dong people.

They used to be hunting people but were persuaded by the Chinese, around 1949, to adopt Chinese ways of farming. Now, with the new attitude of the government, minorities are being allowed to go back to their original way of life. We have seen about five men with long guns, obviously hunters. I have not seen anything anyone has shot, but one day everyone else saw a man with three very small deer slung over his bicycle. So much of this area has been denuded that I don't see how there are any animals to hunt. Our Mr. Xiao says there are wild monkeys, tigers, and bears, but they aren't for food. There must be rabbits and smaller animals. Out of sixteen counties in this prefect, eight prohibit hunting. I don't know how this is controlled, but in China everyone seems to know what the next guy is doing, whether it's going to the toilet or reading a book.

On a hill we stopped to take pictures, and coming toward us were several Dong girls, an old lady, and four men. Mr. Xiao suggested the girls sing for us, and they said they would if I would sing first. I sang, "They Say True Love Is a Blessing," and they sang to us—not exactly a melody, but unmusical guttural sounds. Our companion said he didn't understand the words; they are southern Dongs and he is northern. But there were sly glances and a lot of giggling among our Chinese companions and I think the girls must have sung something quite off-color.

Another group we met on the way was a bride walking to her wedding with about ten girls in attendance. They wore pretty blue clothes and elaborate headdresses. The bride had a gorgeous silver medallion around her neck. She was walking to meet her bridegroom. He meets her halfway and they walk back to his family's house for the marriage ceremony. The bride stops at the door and has a drink or two. Mr. Xiao told us that if you visit a Dong family you have to have at least two drinks before you enter the house, and once inside you must keep drinking. Their idea of hospitality is to get the guest as drunk as possible.

The house is decorated with banners and flowers for the wedding. The couple bows (they used to kowtow) to their parents, thanking them for bringing them up; then to their grandparents; then to each other. Usually the new couple have their own room in his parents' house unless they can afford their own. Mr. Xiao said some marriages are still arranged, but the majority are by choice. Formerly there was a matchmaker who helped with arranging marriages. He said girls usually marry at eighteen, nine-teen, or twenty, and that is younger than the government regulation for Chinese girls, which is twenty-two or older. The minorities receive special treatment in many ways (one being that they can have two children). But from what we see here, they must have more. Babies and small children are everywhere. I often see a young woman with a child in her arms, one on her back, and one by her side, all under four.

Mr. Xiao said opium smoking had not been heavy around here before 1949; people had to work too hard. It was more prevalent with Han Chinese than with the minorities, he said.

This man is an opera singer and his wife is an actress. He was persecuted in the Cultural Revolution, though he didn't say how. He was in an opera company that split into factions, but he was allowed to go out and give concerts.

We had a nice dinner—no banquet, thank goodness—and afterward Harrison went right to his typewriter and I took a walk with Jack and Zhang.

On sidewalks in Chinese cities and towns, newspapers and public notices are displayed in glass-front cases. At an important intersection we stopped to look at a large notice of recent crimes with pictures of the criminals. Almost all were young men convicted of rape. The punishment was three to five years' imprisonment. I am amazed. I thought it was death. We are told the penalty would be much more severe in Beijing.

SATURDAY, APRIL 21
Jinping

In the middle of last night two young men were playing a noisy game of badminton in the hall, but fled into their room when they saw me. We slept very well in a hard double bed. I put one quilt down to use as a mattress and the other over us, and it was just right.

We had a beautiful drive to Liping, the town where the important meeting took place in December 1934. We drove up and down mountains covered with white flowering shrubs, and saw hills of tea, planted closely in rows like a hedge.

Along the roads people were selling handmade washboards for the equivalent of sixty to ninety cents (our money), depending on the size, and chopping blocks for eighty to ninety cents. Little chairs were $1.50. The same things cost three times as much in Beijing and everyone wanted to buy something. But they were either too heavy or bulky and couldn't be carted around on our long trip. So just the local Guizhou people bought chopping blocks—big, thick rounds from tree trunks—and put them under their seats.

When they cut wood in these mountains, it is clear-cut; then the ground is burned. New trees are planted and millet sown at the same time.

In the villages we saw children playing hopscotch, jumping rope, and walking on stilts. Girls in doorways were knitting and sewing. The young men all seem to smoke cigarettes; older men, small pipes.

We drove through the old town of Jinping, where some of the Red Army stayed, and saw the old gate through which they passed. We had lunch in Liping, in a building that is normally used for local government offices, but they had expected us for the night and had transformed the offices into bedrooms with new furniture. We felt badly about this, but we are not in control of these arrangements. A bathroom was also installed just for us—off the landing on the stairs. It had a bathtub, basin, Western toilet, and about two inches of water on the floor. The pipe from the tank wasn't put together very well and water spurted out in a steady stream. I had to get my boots from the car.

We sat in a nice airy room with two long tables covered with pink, blue, and white oilcloth. Orange and pink bath towels were draped on the furniture—very sensible and dry feeling instead of velvet or plastic. The General brought in a lovely bunch of red azaleas. I wrote in my notebook: *. . . four cameras are pointing at us; I feel as if I were about to be executed.* There must be five hundred pictures of the three of us in this part of China by now—three tall gray-blond freaks.

The cultural chief of the county, a tiny Dong man, didn't really talk to us; he read out of a book, story after story about the kindness and generosity of the Red Army and how the people loved them so much. They gave clothes to children who had none; money to people who needed it; saved an old lady from a burning house. Landlords were struggled with at the people's request, he read, and their goods distributed. Bandits were executed, also at the people's request. Yet we have been told that when the Red Army was approaching, the people fled to the mountains. And that when they did come back, the army wasn't able to persuade any to come with them to help with other Dong villages. Soldiers didn't speak or understand minority languages, yet they had to go through their territory.

After lunch and a rest in one of the brightly painted and newly furnished rooms, we went fifty kilometers out of the way on a crazy drive over a terrible road, to a Buddhist pagoda on which there were supposed to be characters and slogans written by the Red Army. We crossed a river on a handmade, hand-propelled ferry, just a platform with side rails. I can't describe how it works. Harrison says the current helps. I don't understand that because the ferry goes directly across the current. Cables are pulled by three or four men on one side of the ferry, and crossing the narrow swift river takes about four minutes. Our bus and three jeeps just fit. So many people wanted to come on this outing, we had extra passengers in the bus and three jeeps full of photographers, officials of every level, and many hangers-on.

After crossing the river, the drive down the valley was lovely. The white pagoda appeared and disappeared as we went around curves. But seeing it close-up was a disappointment. It is very pretty, but it isn't old; it was built in 1912. Most of the walls and everything except the central structure have collapsed or been destroyed, and the plaster on which the slogans were written fell off this winter because of the heavy snow. Everyone (except us) knew this, so it was an absurd detour, if pleasant. It was a long way home, mostly in the dark, which is scary on the mountain roads. I had told Miss Yang I was unhappy about the window in the WC, which looked out to the hall, and when we got back to the guest house, paper had been glued over the glass.

SUNDAY, APRIL 22
Shibing

Today is Easter Sunday and this is a pretty faraway place to be. I keep thinking of all our other Easters with children and grandchildren, egg hunts and big ham lunches. The countryside continues to be lovely, and in the afternoon we stopped at Zhenyuan, a town the Red Army went through. It is also famous for a beautiful five-hundred-year-old bridge and a sixteenth-century Buddhist temple, the Black Dragon Temple, which, over the years, has been almost completely destroyed. During the Ching Dynasty the Miaos rebelled, and the emperor's armies were sent down to squash them. The temple was damaged and rebuilt twice during this dynasty. The Cultural Revolution didn't help either. All the statues and artwork were wrecked. I was reminded of the temple at Chengdu by the river near the two-thousand-year-old irrigation system. Like that temple, the Black Dragon is built right into the rocks on the hillside. We climbed up many winding steps through rooms, balconies, and lookouts to the top pagoda. Strangely, the bridge has remained intact; only a tower at one end was burned by the Kuomintang to delay the Red Army, and two of the arches were removed later, for some inexplicable reason.

Along the way I wrote in my notebook, *We saw many trucks loaded with big logs. Oil trucks have bumper stickers—"Drive politely"—but we saw three terrible accidents. One truck was upside down in a rice paddy. The cab was underwater and we felt the driver must still be in there. A*

78

small crowd was sitting by. Another truck went right through a big stone and cement barrier, breaking it and turning over. And in another place a truck had turned over and burned. All on corners. Harrison thinks their brakes give out, but I think they simply drive too fast.

On a river we saw fourteen huge, high water wheels, about ten feet apart. And lots of bamboo troughs tied together above the roads to carry mountain water to the fields, just like the ones we used to see in Cambodia. Many banana trees, but we have yet to have a banana. Small mills for grinding grain are built over or next to waterfalls on small streams and rivers.

There have been markets in many of the towns we have gone through and the roads are crowded. People walk from all directions, carrying goods to sell, and carting home what they bought. I can't get over the variety and amount of consumer goods. Plastic sandals of every color, straw sandals, Chinese shoes, Western-looking shoes with heels. Hats—big straw ones to wear in the fields—babies' bonnets and caps. There are blouses of every color, pants the same. Always lots of wool for knitting, very thin compared to most of ours, and small-size metal needles. Yard goods of cotton, synthetics, and wool. Cotton was rationed for many years, but since April 1 coupons are no longer needed to purchase it—surely a sign of an improving economy.

Girls and young women look much the same, whether in Beijing or in the vegetable fields. They wear bright-colored jackets (orange and pink are popular here, lavender was in Beijing). Many wear leather or plastic shoes with a little heel, and almost all have curly hair. Permanent waves are available at "the barber's," I am told. One of our companions thinks this is ridiculous and says he will be furious if his wife curls her hair.

They told us about a song that was popular in 1949—"One, two, three, four, five, we go to the mountain to hunt the tiger. The tiger doesn't eat people—he just eats Truman. Truman got so mad he drank a glass of DDT."

President Truman wasn't very popular with the Chinese. When the Communists came to power in October 1949, Britain, France, and many other countries recognized their government, but for complicated political reasons, the United States did not. The Chinese believed that Truman had been on the side of the Kuomintang. I understand that Truman had been planning to recognize Mao's government as soon as he felt it was politically feasible. But when the Korean War began, that put an end to any such plans.

One wall in the dining room here is covered with Chinese newspapers. Jack says that in the past, old American newspapers were shipped to China and used as wallpaper in houses, to cover the cracks.

In the men's room down at the end of the corridor, there is a light. In the newly installed women's WC right next to it, there is none. Harrison says this is evidence of male chauvinism.

MONDAY, APRIL 23
Zunyi

We left Shibing early and had a long drive here, the town where the famous conference took place, when Li De and Bo Gu were ousted from leadership and Mao, Zhou Enlai, and Zhu De prevailed. We stopped at Yuqing to pick up a picnic lunch that had been ordered for us. We were early and it wasn't ready, so we hung around the square and soon were surrounded. No one like us has ever been there, although one man said that before Liberation they had one American visitor. They were friendly and curious, which is natural, but the women always try to follow me into the public outdoor toilets. Miss Yang stands guard for me, thank goodness.

Many women in this area wear turbans, white or black. Some men do too, or those little hats that seem more Muslim than Chinese. The women have a variety of outfits and it's impossible for me to tell what minority they belong to. The minorities in this province include Dong, Shui, Buyi, and Yi, and though they say they are not mixed up, I think they must be.

Xi Zichang, a town we passed through, was having market day. Jack wanted to mail one of his letters to George Hatem, but it was impossible to get to the post office in our bus. I have never seen such crowds, even in Italy on Easter. People were packed almost solid on the streets. Our detail man went off to mail the letter and we waited, in the bus, in the square. In less than a minute we were surrounded, and if there hadn't been people on both sides, the bus could easily have been pushed over. It makes me very uncomfortable to be stared at so—animals in zoos must feel this way. Zhang opened the window and said, "Go away, there is nothing to see." But Jack said to the crowd, "Take a look and then move on so everyone can see."

One man had a cat trussed up in a basket, for sale. Not to eat but to kill rats. For some reason I haven't thought of rats, and we haven't seen any. But with fruit peels and melon seeds, so many chickens and grain, it must be ideal for rats. We saw big banner ads for rat poison at two markets.

We stopped by the side of the road for our picnic lunch and had hard-boiled eggs; corn muffins, big steamed buns that the Chinese slit and stuff with pickled cabbage; pieces of chicken; orange pop; and pomelo fruit, which Harrison and I have never seen before. It is like a grapefruit but much bigger and has a very thick skin and thick white lining. It is divided into sections, and just the fruit inside the membrane case is eaten. There are lots of seeds. It is good, slightly tangy. Jack says they get them in California sometimes.

We left the empty bottles and the mess and were assured that peasants would take the bottles within the hour, and that all the garbage would be consumed by animals before too long.

I now have a real feeling for what the Red Army went through and the miracle of their achievement. To have been able to unify so many different elements in such an enormous country is a feat no one would have believed possible. It is clear that Mao's strategy of winning over peasants in the countryside, and not attempting to take the cities, was the main reason for success. I used to be bored with all the talk about "mobilizing the peasants," "Arming the people," "Creating revolution," and so on, but it was what worked. Of course, the climate was right. The warlords and landlords were cruel beyond belief, and the Kuomintang didn't treat the peasants as people, just ran roughshod over them, taking what they wanted. An army made up of boys and young men and women, led by an idealist, was bound to be successful. The Red Army would go through villages and say, "Do you want to live like this the rest of your life? Join us." The army took care of them as well as it could, taught them to read and write when there was time. The Kuomintang would force young men to join their forces by tying them together and leading them away. Jack said he had seen this, so it isn't just propaganda. They were terrible to their troops, didn't feed them adequately, didn't take care of them, so no wonder the Communists had such appeal. Mao was clever. It's just too bad he lived so long. If he had died before the Hundred Flowers Campaign*, the Great Leap Forward, and all the insanity of the Cultural Revolution and the Gang of Four, he would have been a flawless hero. As it is, I believe he was one of the greatest men of our time, maybe the greatest.

The Red Army was in this province (Guizhou) from December 1934 to April 1935, zigzagging back and forth, up and around these sharp high mountains, crossing and recrossing rivers, trying to get out of the box they were in. They had left Jiangxi in October with the Kuomintang always threatening them. The weather was terrible—wet and cold. They never seemed to have enough clothes. They walked twenty to thirty miles a day on average, each person carrying fifty to sixty pounds of equipment—a bag of rice, any blanket or clothes he wasn't wearing, a gun and some kind of knife, cup and bowl. The cooks carried the woks, big enough to cook rice for fifty people. The sick and injured were carried on litters, and some in a kind of chair. In the beginning they carried printing presses

---

*In 1957, intellectuals were encouraged to come forward and freely criticize the government; but when they did, they were in serious trouble.

81

and X-ray equipment, but these were discarded early on. They were heavy and difficult to carry and held the army back when it needed to move fast.

We saw the River Wu, where the Red Army made three crossings. The current is very strong; it must have been terribly difficult. We were taking pictures from the bridge when a guard with a submachine gun approached us. It is good to have the General with us at such times. We also had a glimpse of the Meitan River from a point that seemed like the top of the world.

TUESDAY, APRIL 24
Zunyi

This morning we went to the house where the conference was held. It is a substantial residence, built in the early thirties by Bai Huizhang, a merchant, warlord, and division commander. Mr. Bai first built a smaller house, though luxurious in comparison to any ordinary person's house, then added this large structure. It is like the missionary's house we saw in Ningdu—two stories, columns and porches all around. This style was popular with rich Chinese in the first part of this century. I can't imagine, even if I were rich, building myself a house that is like a palace compared to the ordinary person's house. This big house is right in town in a street with poor, run-down wooden houses, so the contrast is extreme. Some of the missionaries were just as guilty; they also built big, fancy houses for themselves in the midst of poverty.

This house must have been very attractive. The rooms are large and airy. The woodwork is pretty, and in back is a big courtyard, now paved over, but which did have fruit trees and gardens. In 1964 the government proclaimed it a national site and has appropriated money to restore it.

I continue to be surprised that the Red Army leaders always took over and occupied the biggest and most imposing houses. I imagine the owners must have fled, so the houses were empty, and it would be appropriate and symbolic to usurp the best the enemy had. However, I still think it would have been more in keeping with the revolution for them to stay in more modest places. But Harrison says he has noticed that army generals take the very best quarters available, no matter what side they're on. Anyway, it means these buildings will be kept, and otherwise they would undoubtedly have been wrecked or burned.

From there we went to the Catholic church where the leaders told the cadres the result of the Zunyi meeting—that Mao had triumphed over Li De and Bo Gu. The church is a startling mixture of architectural styles,

82

with a Chinese roof, tall Gothic windows, and a big round window that might have been stained glass. It is at one end of the grounds, and the remains of several one-story structures line the street, enclosing what must have been a garden. This was built by French missionaries—most of the Catholics in this area were French, according to Jack. The shells of the original buildings look as if they were single rooms, and each one had a fireplace and chimney. Two mantelpieces are left, and I could hardly believe my eyes. I have seen blocked-up fireplaces in the old embassy buildings in Beijing that are now used by the Chinese, but I have never seen any other fireplaces in China until these. They must have burned coal, maybe had a little stove or grate. They looked very attractive. This whole compound is being restored to its original state.

Across the street is the house where Li De and Bo Gu lived. It, too, will be restored, but at present several families are living in it, so we couldn't see the inside. It is a simple, unostentatious, two-story house. An addition on the street side spoils the house and will be removed. When all this work is finished, Zunyi will be an important tourist site, especially for the Chinese.

A banner in the street says, *Emancipate our minds—Dare to create new situations*. In simpler language: *Think for yourself*. Very unlike earlier maxims that advised following the approved line and doing everything together.

We had an informal pleasant dinner given us by the secretary of the prefecture. We helped ourselves, no one piled uneatables on my plate, and it was very friendly. I toasted Miss Yang and thanked her for all her kindness and help, and she toasted me, saying she would never forget this week.

WEDNESDAY, APRIL 25
Xishui

We left Zunyi this morning and drove to the Loushan Pass. After the conference, and with Mao in charge, the Red Army left Zunyi to continue its flight from the Kuomintang. Almost immediately, Chiang Kaishek's troops occupied Zunyi and were on the Red Army's tail. Zigzagging back and forth, and finally facing them at the Loushan Pass, Mao won his first real military victory. If he had lost, the Red Army would have been in serious trouble. A big plaque at the site preserves the poem Mao wrote after the battle. Today the pass looks peaceful, with high mountains on each side, and the thought of soldiers fighting a bloody battle here seems incongruous.

For lunch we stopped at Tongzi, at another former warlord's house that had three stories and a balcony all around the second floor. Tongzi is a coal town and it's not necessary to be told that. Everything is black, and the biggest hunks of coal I've ever seen are piled on the side of the road or being hauled in carts pulled by little horses. Most buildings are gray brick and wood; the warlord's houses are plaster.

We drove up and around wonderful pyramid mountains, like the mountains at the pass. Terraces are very narrow and in many places the soil looked poor. Women work at the same jobs as men, doing roadwork, bricklaying, hauling carts, and, of course, working in the fields. They also do the cooking and the laundry. It is true we often see men of all ages carrying babies, on their backs or in their arms, but I have yet to see one cooking or washing (with the exception of two young men who were washing themselves in a river and may have washed some of their clothes, but I didn't see them do it). I saw a woman looking for lice in a child's hair, and others spinning what Jack says is palm fiber—reddish brown stuff. It is used for making rain capes that men wear when plowing. Noodles were drying everywhere, and at one house there were about fifty boxes of bees. Many kilns for bricks and tiles, and quite a few sewing machines placed in doorways to take advantage of the light. Women use a door, horizontal on sawhorses, as a washboard for large pieces, such as quilt covers. One old man had a basket of used paper and cardboard, and several men and women were collecting ashes and any kind of trash, putting it in wagons. They said they take it to the countryside. Children no more than three have baskets on their backs and seem to know which weeds and grasses to pick. Peas have purple and pink flowers as well as white. There were lots of new trucks on the road to Tongzi. The shops were full of goods.

This is a big, sprawling guest house with many Chinese either living or staying temporarily on the ground floor. We are on the second, in the same room the Hansons had when they were following some of the Long March route last year. (He is the former AP correspondent who was in Yan'an in the late 1930s.) When I turned on the twenty-five-watt bulb in the lamp, I noticed HANSON embroidered on the lampshade.

The only trouble with this room is that it is on the same side of the house as the bathrooms and the waste slides down an open trough right into a little field. The smell is ghastly. I don't see how people ever get used to it. Jack calls it the national air of China, and it is pretty constant everywhere. People carry buckets of human waste out to the fields. They carry wet, runny manure in baskets on their backs. Children squat wherever they are, pigs and dogs do the same, and everything smells all the time to me. Harrison isn't as conscious of this as I am.

THURSDAY, APRIL 26
Xishui

Well, I have seen a rat. Here, the WC is on the landing halfway up the stairs, and last night, as no lights were on in the hall, I took my flashlight. Obviously someone saw me, for almost as soon as I closed the door, the lights came on. The window, with no screen, was open, and I was terrified of bats flying in. But instead, a dark, hairy creature sprang out of the wall, streaked over my feet, and vanished. I screamed, but no one could have heard me or the entire population of Xishui would have been in there in jig time. They could use that poor cat we saw in the market the other day.

This episode reminds me of my other experiences with rats, and some of the stories I've been told. The worst are city rats, and we had a siege of them when we lived in a house in New York. The buildings next to and near us were torn down, and for some reason that means rats. They never got inside our house, but would circle around the entrance so it was scary to go out. I complained to the health department, in vain, and finally caught most of them in traps. When I asked the sanitation department to please come and take the bodies away, they said, "Just throw them in the garbage."

In the early 1900s my mother-in-law, who was an artist, had a studio in Gramercy Park. Her Irish maid once told me there were so many rats, "Be gorry, they came around the corner like a pack of hounds." In either the same, or another, studio, there was one huge rat that defied all efforts to destroy him. A friend had an equally huge cat that was a famous ratter, so it was borrowed and put in the studio for the night. Next morning there was no sign of the cat, no sign of the rat, and neither was ever seen again.

All this doesn't have much to do with the Long March. I was simply reminded.

This morning we saw the hill from which Mao directed the battle of Qinggangpo. One reason I am confused about these battles and river crossings is that we are not seeing places in the proper order. After leaving Zunyi, Mao started north. Lin Biao was sent up toward Maotai to find a good place to cross the Chishui River, which would bring the Red Army nearer to the Yangtze, which it was vital to get over. Mao was being trailed by some Sichuan regiments, which he mistakenly thought were opium-laden warlord troops that would be easy to get rid of. Instead, there was this terrible battle at Qinggangpo, near Tucheng, and the Red Army suffered heavy losses. This was psychologically bad for Mao, as he had just taken charge of strategy and tactics. Lin Biao was ordered back and they escaped across the Chishui River, through a bit of Sichuan Province, and into Yunnan. There they rested a few days, licked their wounds, regrouped, and went back and forth across the river four times in all, probably to confuse the enemy, who couldn't figure out what Mao was doing. Some of his generals couldn't figure this out either. Headed back toward Zunyi again, they met the enemy at the Loushan Pass and won their first big victory.

The battle of Qinggangpo has never been reported or written about, and neither Harrison nor Jack had ever heard of it. Things were going so badly for the Red Army that Zhu De went to the battlefield himself—very unusual for a general.

We had lunch in another landlord's house in Tucheng.

In Tucheng an order has just gone out to dispose of all dogs; just in the city, not in the countryside. They say there is rabies. In one more day, if anyone still has a dog, the dog will be taken away and the owner fined three yuan. I wonder how many people are eating their dogs. The other day, at one of the big markets, Jack said he saw four little puppies for sale. I said, "Oh dear," and he said, "Yes, I think you're right. They are very fat."

We learned today that He Zizhen, Mao's second wife, died on April 19 in Shanghai. Harrison had been hoping to see her. I wonder if he will be able to see any of the remaining ladies of the Long March. He has asked and asked, but to no avail, at least so far.

Every day the grandeur of the Red Army's achievements is rubbed in a little more. And every day the stupidity of the United States becomes more apparent—backing Chiang Kaishek and the feudal system of warlords, landlords, bandits, and opium. Even as recently as the 1940s.

Miraculously a TV had been brought in and hooked up so we could watch Reagan, who is in Beijing. The pictures were so small it was hard to tell much, but we thought he looked ill at ease. (Later, when we got to Xi'an, we were told that Reagan had made a huge hit everywhere he went. The Chinese liked "his cowboy smile." And they admire him for being so fit and spry at age seventy-three.)

FRIDAY, APRIL 27
Renhuai, Near Maotai

This morning we left Xishui in the rain. We drove to Maotai, where the famous booze is made, and where the Red Army crossed the Chishui River twice. (Before leaving Beijing, Harrison had persuaded the authorities to let us go there after all.) Along the way were many mulberry trees, rape cut and drying, wheat almost ready to be harvested, rice, corn, sorghum, and sugar cane. A coffin outside a house means that someone inside is very ill and the family is prepared. A child's corpse, all wrapped up, was being pulled in a wagon.

In 1935, when the Red Army came through Maotai, the population was three to four thousand. There were several distilleries, none of them large. Merchants got rich trading in liquor, salt, and opium, and the Red Army benefited by appropriating goods and silver dollars. Today there are about eight thousand people living in Maotai. The big liquor factory looks about a mile long from the other side of the river, and there are some smaller distilleries.

We crossed the river at the same place the Red Army crossed, in a one-man ferry that is probably like boats they used, except this boat has a small outboard motor. It could hold twenty-five people comfortably. We climbed up the high bank to a memorial and got a good look at the river and the layout of the town, and could see just where and how these crossings were accomplished.

Walking in the town, we remembered Dr. Sun, to whom we talked in Beijing, telling us that he had seen soldiers swabbing their feet with maotai, spilling it all over the ground, and how fragrant the town became. Today, unfortunately, no one was dousing his feet with liquor. It wasn't fragrant; instead the smell of fermenting mash hung over the town.

Harrison was livid because we were not allowed to visit the one real maotai factory. They said no foreigners had ever seen it and they weren't about to let us be the first. I don't understand; the Foreign Office in Beijing said we could; here, the local bosses say no. Who's in charge? Perhaps it is because the process is rather revolting and it's better people don't see what goes into the fiery drink. We know the river water is used, and that is pretty brown. We did see a small distillery, full of big vats of dark stuff and smelling terrible. Probably the big factory is just like it, only smellier.

We have tonight here, tomorrow night on the train, and then two or three days in a real hotel in Kunming.

SATURDAY, APRIL 28
On the Train to Kunming

Today we had a long drive from Renhuai to Guiyang, stopping at Zunyi for lunch. Before boarding this train, we had supper in an enormous restaurant that looked like Grand Central Station, with a rounded ceiling several stories high. Three wedding parties were celebrating with more noise and more food and drink than I have ever heard or seen. Families with babies and children, grandparents, aunts and uncles, sat at big round tables, talking, eating, and drinking all at once. The three brides and grooms, distinguished only by flowers on their jackets, went to every table of their well-wishers and drank a toast. There must have been at least ten tables per wedding and everyone was getting tipsy. As a group left a table, plates and glasses were cleared away, bones and crumbs and pieces of food swept onto the floor, and a new group happily sat down amid the garbage, not noticing it at all. The bride's family doesn't have to foot the bill for wedding parties like these; every guest pays his own way.

While waiting in the station, I taped Miss Yang singing "Red River Valley," a big favorite of hers. It was sad to leave our Guizhou friends, and especially so to leave Miss Yang. She was a lovely companion, always "by my side" (as she said she would be at our first dinner) when I needed her, never intrusive. The twelve days seemed to bring our group closer, and somehow the ordeals and triumphs of the Red Army became more real.

SUNDAY, APRIL 29
Kunming

Everyone had a good night on the train. The berths were wider and more comfortable than those on the previous train, and except for the fact we were late and didn't get here until nearly three o'clock, when we were supposed to arrive right after breakfast, the train ride was very pleasant. It gave us time to catch up a bit, and to try to digest what we have seen and heard.

Many Chinese trains are run by coal, or steam. In stations we often see women sitting underneath the cars, picking up pieces of coal that have dropped down between the tracks. At first, I couldn't imagine what they were doing.

We were greeted with the news that there would be a banquet tonight and we will leave at 8:00 A.M. tomorrow for a week's barreling around the Red Army route. I was fit to be tied. I had been counting on at least two days here. Harrison and Jack are furious because the arrangements don't suit them, either.

Miss Li, from the Yunnan Provincial Foreign Office, will be with us in this province. She is very young and pretty. She went with Harrison and Jack to the Friendship Store to buy film and managed to find us a huge jar of Nescafé and some insect coils.

Harrison has just come back from the banquet, which he said was nice and informal, the food delicious and elegantly served. A new dish was fried bees, which were delightfully crispy and crunchy. He brought me some fruit and watermelon, which ripens here in February, and both were heavenly.

MONDAY, APRIL 30
Xiaguan, Near Dali

It was nice to sleep in a real bed with sheets and pillowcases. We had toast for breakfast—first time since Nanchang—and jam and butter. These details aren't important, but at times they take on great significance.

Kunming is an attractive city and I am glad we will be coming back at the end of this week. The flowers are lovely—oleander in bloom; wonderful double hollyhocks, not as tall as ours; yellow gladiola with a red center, also smaller. Just at the edge of the city there are vegetable gardens; rice in seed beds being transplanted by many people the way they used to work in the communes. We were told that every family owns and works its own piece of land. But when it's time to transplant rice, which has to be done quickly, other families pitch in and help, the way farmers at home help each other get in the hay while the weather is good. We saw lots of chemical fertilizer in plastic bags. I hope the Chinese don't give up the ideal farming methods that they have practiced for several thousand years (using natural fertilizer, putting the straw back on the fields and turning it under, plowing in cover crops), just for the quick rewards of chemical fertilizer. In the long run it destroys the natural balance and burns up the soil. A Wisconsin farmer told me it's like putting LSD in the ground.

There is so much pollution around Kunming that the big West Mountain was obscured, and farther on a mountain stream was black from a factory that makes some substances out of coal.

We drove all day up and down mountains on the Burma Road, made famous in World War II. It runs from Burma to Kunming. We saw many trucks carting big logs, but except for eucalyptus trees that have been planted on the sides of the road, there weren't any big trees; only red, bare, sandy hills in spite of obvious efforts at reforestation. Eucalyptus trees are not native to China (nor to the United States); they were brought from Australia and have thrived here, as they have in California.

There are many minorities in this province—Yi, Bai, Nashi, Zhuang, Tibetan, Miao, and others I have never heard of, such as Jingpo, Yao, Hani, Lahu, and Bulang. They keep more animals than the Chinese; goats, cows, water buffalo, besides the usual pigs, are everywhere. Wheat is being harvested and, as we have seen before, is put in the road for trucks and cars to do the separating by running over the stalks. Then it is swept up and winnowed. Amazing it doesn't all get squashed. Big green beans were being treated the same way. Much hard human labor—women as well as men, for instance, pushing huge barrels up hills. Occasionally we see two water buffalo pulling a plow. A harrow has a board big enough for several rocks and a man to stand on, to weight it down and push the harrow farther into the soggy ground.

Yi women wear headcloths; in fact, all minority women put something on their heads. They wear dangly silver earrings and tunics over pants.

Remains of temples are up in the hills; the earth is very dark red.

The reason we are following this route is because Xiao Ke, the first general we met in Beijing, went through the area in 1936. Before that, in 1934, he had led the Sixth Army to join He Long and the Second Front Army. Individually they had established other soviet areas on the borders of Hunan and Guizhou Provinces, but from their meeting in 1934 they remained together and became fast friends. They married beautiful women who were sisters, and each wife had a child on their Long March. General Xiao Ke told Harrison that his wife had her baby in an enclosure the soldiers built for her on the Grasslands. It was an uncomplicated delivery; she was young and strong, and continued with the march in two days. This baby was a boy and called the "Grasslands Baby." Sometime after reaching Yan'an, the child was sent to his grandmother in Hunan Province, and there he died, one of thousands of victims of Japanese germ warfare.

Xiao Ke and He Long did not leave this area until Mao's Long March ended in northern Shaanxi. Then they went north to join the Fourth Front Army and, with them, went to Shaanxi.

Xiao Ke was in jail in the Cultural Revolution, as were most of the generals we've talked to, but they lived. The story of He Long is terrible. His wife left him, and later, in Yan'an, he married again (a much younger woman whom we met at the end of our Long March). At the time of the Cultural Revolution, He Long was in critical condition because of diabetes and needed insulin in regular doses. At first he was struggled with, but then it was decided he was too difficult and a "medical approach" was proposed. Staying in a courtyard house, guarded by soldiers, he was not given any water; he and his wife caught a little off the roof. He was given large doses of glucose (which has the opposite effect of insulin), and this is what killed him.

This guest house is a lovely surprise. We have beds with white organdy spreads, and a real bathroom with green toilet and pink basin, plus a clean tub and hot water. And the food is nice and simple.

TUESDAY, MAY 1
Lijiang

This morning in Xiaguan it was clear as a bell, like Colorado Springs. It is about the same altitude (6,600 feet). We had a long drive here, from 8:00 until after 1:00. We saw Lake Er Hai, where the Chinese hope to create a big tourist resort, and many Bai women wearing their pretty native clothes. These consist of any kind of pants, a light-colored shirt with embroidered cuffs on the long sleeves, a bright red or blue vest, a short white apron with blue trimming, and an elaborate headdress of embroidery and braided wool. Many minority people (but never the Han) carry baskets supported by a strap around their forehead, the way the Sikkimese do. There are signs on trees that read *Protect the environment,* because people still strip them of leaves and branches if not stopped or educated not to. This area is dry now; the rainy season is in summer. There are many dams, much irrigation.

We got here for a late lunch. The air is heavenly and the mountains menacing. The highest is eighteen thousand feet and has snow on top.

Harrison interviewed an old soldier, who told him an interesting story. The magistrate who was boss of the Town of Lijiang had a talk with a Jinshi scholar (a Hanlin scholar is the top-ranking scholar, Jinshi is second) before Xiao Ke's Red Army came, but when they knew it was on the way. They decided not to fight the Red Army. The warlords of the area were antagonistic to Chiang Kaishek—in fact, the warlords of Hunan and Yunnan Provinces had been having a lively correspondence about what to do. They hated Chiang Kaishek and were afraid he would do to them what he had done in Guizhou—drive the warlords out and put his own gang in. The magistrate called a meeting, instructed the people to welcome the soldiers, and he went off to the hills. The people lined the streets, gave food and supplies as they could, and the Red Army went through with only a show of resistance. There were a few fake battles, no one was killed, and after the army had passed through, the magistrate returned and the warlords continued their life-style. There was no recrimination against the peasants for their actions and the atmosphere was Live and Let Live. The magistrate continued as magistrate even after Liberation, and is still alive at eighty-four.

Today is the big worldwide Communist holiday, but here it wasn't any different from any other day.

WEDNESDAY, MAY 2
Still at Lijiang

This morning we drove to Shigu on the Golden Sands River, which is the upper Yangtze, to the place where the Second Front Army, led by Xiao Ke and He Long, crossed the river and went on into Sichuan Province. The river is wide there and has a sandspit in the middle. This crossing was the crucial place to hold. There are several others up the river, but no enemy could get at them if this first crossing was held. In 1936 more trees grew beside the river, enough so the eighteen thousand men could hide from airplanes. When it was safe, a bugle signaled, and fifty men came out to cross the river. They continued with this system until all were across. No soldiers were killed by the enemy, but seventeen drowned when horses and mules became panicky and turned over a boat.

On the way, scrubby crooked pines reminded me of Cape Cod. Masses of white azalea are here and there, and a pretty, fragile-looking pale purple shrub grows right out of the rocks. The two big crops are wheat and rice. Wheat is planted in the fall, and in most places is being harvested now.

There are Bai and Nashi people here and they have big herds of black goats, black sheep, and even some black cows. The pigs are black too. New orchards are being set out. Pears are the best fruit crop in this area. Next to the orchards are boxes, or hives, of bees.

Above the river is a little pagoda erected over a big stone gong, a memorial to the victory of the Nashi people over the Tibetans in 1548. We walked down to the river on a steep, stony path through an old settlement. Looking down from the pagoda, the roofs were so close it looked like one twisting turning roof over all the houses. We had a picnic lunch in the pagoda and afterward called on some people who had their few hours of glory when the Red Army came through this town.

The first was a woman, sixty-two, who was in her early teens at the time of the Long March. When we got to her house, she was just coming in from the fields with a huge pack on her back, of greens, wheat, and sesame. She put it down in a corner of the courtyard and greeted us cordially. Her claim to fame is that a wounded soldier lived in her courtyard, and when he was well enough, she led him, on her horse, to the river at night. He gave her his bamboo rain cloak and it is now in the Provincial Museum.

In Dali, a town nearby, we went to the house of a Nashi woman who cooked one meal for sixty soldiers when they spent the night in her courtyard. She is now eighty-three and, in spite of her age and no teeth, is very pretty. It is clear she comes from a high-class family who must have had some money. The house is large with nice woodwork and fine artifacts. She is connected to Baoxian, an American-Chinese solar researcher who is a nephew of a famous Nashi historian, Fang Guoyu. The nephew was here earlier this year to pay his respects to his dead uncle.

That famous night, her son was a small baby and she carried him on her back while she prepared the dinner. Relatives and neighbors helped her, but she did the cooking. She used her own vegetables and rice. "They didn't want anything greasy," she told us. Her family were sugar merchants and had a restaurant, where her mother taught her to cook. She did cook for an office, but is retired now and only cooks for special occasions such as weddings and funerals.

We stopped in a tailor shop (there are many of them). The tailor and his son make exquisite aprons, all appliqué. The Bai aprons are blue with several rows of trimming, and a smaller white apron, also trimmed, is worn over it, and in back. We walked through a typical rural Chinese kitchen, about eight feet square. The stove is a square cement block with a fire box under it and a large hollowed-out place for the one wok, which is built in, that most families have. There is also a built-in water tank with a faucet, like an Aga stove, which always has hot water. A draft arrangement makes it possible to start a fire with just a little straw and have it heat up quickly. Straw, wood, and coal are kept nearby in a pile.

The kitchen is open to the courtyard and all the rooms have doors. On two sides of the garden are high walls. The lady of the house makes extra money from two persimmon trees, vegetables, and medicinal herbs she grows on a small piece of land. A large vat was at the end of the garden, for making wine, which they said they don't do anymore. We were told that this family is well off, but not as high up as the Nashi lady's family. So there are differences, and class, too, even in a communist society.

We walked through the old town of Dali, which is laid out in a square. The north and south gates still stand. In the middle of the town there is a rectangular space, the equivalent of a town square, as well as a spot in front of a pagoda, with two huge trees, that is a market place. Women were selling quantities of brightly colored knitting wool, sunflower seeds, pieces of meat, and odds and ends. So far this town is unspoiled and just the way it always has been. The streets are narrow and unevenly paved with stones, and there are no new buildings. We were led to believe that it is being preserved as a national monument, and I hope that's true. A new town is outside the old.

We stopped at an artist's house that is in the same style as the others we have seen today—substantial, with fine woodwork and courtyards for vegetables and flowers. An upstairs is being added to this house and it is filled with his lovely paintings of the favorite Chinese subjects—birds, flowers, and landscapes.

Houses in this area are big compared to many we have seen. All are entered through a gate and a courtyard with lots of flowers, vegetables, and fruit trees. People seem better off and better dressed. Bai women's clothes are pretty and always look clean. The Nashis' are blue with white straps across the chest and sometimes an odd-looking pad on their backs to protect them from heavy loads. It is shaped like a cross with extensions that look like wings on each side. Sometimes, under a basket, they wear a cape of animal skin. Most of the children look grubby—noses running and dirty clothes. However, most wear some kind of sandals. Only a few are barefoot.

After supper Harrison met with two old codgers, each also with a story of one or two days with the Red Army. One was a nice-looking, talkative man who came from a family of some substance. He said life under Chiang Kaishek's rule was terrible. People had no representation at all, no pride in themselves or what they did. His family owned property and the government wanted to take it. His father and brother resisted and were put in jail. He himself was away working on road construction at the time. When he returned, he demanded his father and brother be released. He was told he would have to pay 50 yuan ($25.00) and he didn't have it. He threw a scene, accused the police of being bloodsuckers, hurled a bench at them, and he was put in jail. He said it smelled terrible (I wonder how it could have been worse than some smells we encounter). He had only two meals a day of watery porridge and became so thin and weak he could hardly stand. He never saw the light of day. His family sold everything they had and got the father and brother out, but he stayed for six months, until November 1935, when the Red Army opened the doors of the prison.

He said that when the prisoners were released and their chains taken off, a Red Army man talked to them. He explained that the soldiers were sons of peasants and workers, that they were there to save ill-treated people, and to fight Chiang Kaishek and the Japanese. When the soldiers had money, which they often did after confiscating warlords' and evil gentry's supplies, they paid for what they got from peasants and town-folk. When the Red Army had no money, they paid in opium, which they also got from raiding rich people's supplies.

The next man worked with his uncle-in-law, who was a druggist and owned his own store. They had heard stories that the Red Army burned and destroyed and that the county had made efforts to fight them. Then they heard the magistrate make his speech about welcoming the soldiers. His uncle-in-law said, "We are doctors; we have nothing to fear." For six hours they worked steadily making up medicines and supplies for the soldiers.

THURSDAY, MAY 3
Xiaquan

Back with organdy bedspreads and pink basin. Today everyone was tired from yesterday at Dali and Lijiang, which I must admit I found exhausting. It is nine thousand feet above sea level here and we climbed and walked a lot. So we just had a sightseeing day on the way back here, where we are spending the night.

Dali is one of the 129 new places that have recently been opened to foreigners. There has just been a special Bai festival there that occurs for twelve days in the third lunar month, which is early April. The British Columbian people we met on the train last week were wondering how to get here. We described the man with a beard and shorts, and the guide said, "Yes, he's here." Over the door of a hotel in Dali, a sign in English reads, *Inside there are calm rooms specially prepared.* Maybe he is staying there.

We saw Butterfly Springs, so named because every spring big butterflies congregate here in a huge mass. A tree grows next to and bends over the pool and people throw in coins and make a wish (an unthinkable idle pastime when we first visited China). On the path to the springs several Bai girls were selling refreshments—bottled pop, sunflower seeds, little cakes, etc. One girl told Miss Li she could make twenty yuan a day, much more than Miss Li makes, but she has to pay a tax. As we were leaving we saw two men in blue uniforms approaching. We thought they were local police, but they were tax collectors. So free enterprise pays off for the government, too.

In a Bai restaurant we ate lunch together—we three, Miss Li, Zhang, the General, the driver, and the funny little local guide whom Harrison thinks looks right out of Chekhov. He is very small, thin, nervous, and wears glasses. Because Americans are supposed to love potatoes, we had potato chips made right there, and they were delicious. Also, something they said was fried milk. It must be very thin batter deep fried, crispy and good. And fresh fish from the lake.

We stopped at the Temple of the Three Pagodas, but there's no temple left. It was destroyed during the Qing Dynasty (1644–1911). At a gate in the middle of what is left of the west wall is a sign: *No admittance.* I looked inside and saw a sentry box but no sentry, barbed wire strung about, and barracks. We were told it is housing, but not for whom.

The pagodas, however, still exist. They date from the Tang Dynasty (618–907), according to the Chinese. The largest pagoda is in the middle and rises thirty feet high. The two smaller, and much prettier ones, are on either side. The largest was damaged in an earthquake several hundred years ago, resulting in a large crack. A fairly recent earthquake shook the pagoda and closed the crack. There used to be doorways on four sides of all the pagodas so people could go inside and climb up to the top. These have been closed off with cement. Maybe this protects the pagodas from excessive traffic, which is what we were told. Maybe it is to keep inquiring eyes from looking into what's beyond the wall.

We visited the showroom of the Dali marble factory. The Chinese are very proud of this marble; it's gray and white and famous for the pictures one can see in the natural markings, of trees, flowers, or some other suggestive shape. The only items I would have liked to buy were a mortar and pestle, but they're too heavy to carry. Along the streets people were selling pieces of marble and Miss Li bargained with a vendor for a paperweight and a small replica of one of the pagodas. I never imagined bargaining in this society.

Once more, we have clean, comfortable beds. Never again will I take my bedroom at home for granted.

FRIDAY, MAY 4
Kunming

Today's was a long drive, the reverse of Monday's over the same road. Silk must be made here, though no one has mentioned it. Jack said that a Nestorian priest smuggled silk worms out of China in a walking stick, and that's how the rest of the world got silk.

Tea grows where it is high and dry, north of Dali, and is famous for its delicious taste. I am surprised, because I thought it grew only where it is wet and there is plenty of rain.

We saw more mountains with a sprinkling of snow; the area is referred to as Switzerland.

There are shrines along the road, and good-luck papers and symbols on houses, put up for New Year's and weddings. The papers are red with white characters. When a person dies, strips of white paper with black characters are pasted around the door, wishing the spirit well. On most doors and gates are two big posters of fierce warriors, to guard the house. An especially paranoid emperor had real warriors guarding every door and gate in his palace. His prime minister figured that was a waste of manpower, and substituted pictures. Red Army soldiers are pictured on the newer door guards.

In the middle of an enormous wheatfield I saw a lone watering can. So much is done by hand. Carrying water long distances, weeding, harvesting wheat with a sickle or a curved knife or machete; bundling it up, carrying it on one's back to the threshing ground, often threshing it by hand flails, then winnowing the grain in baskets by hand.

After wheat, or first crops, are harvested, green manure is planted and let grow until one or two feet high. To prepare the land for the next crop, it is hacked by hand with a heavy hoe, left to dry out, flooded, plowed, harrowed, stamped down by one man riding a flat board pulled by a water buffalo or cow, then planted, all by hand. Not one inch of land is wasted; no mess at the edge of the field that a tractor can't get to.

Lots of pack animals, little burros and horses, are walking on this road.

We stopped to climb up to a temple and had a wonderful view of Kunming and the lake. Immediately below was a Normandy-style house with gardens and fruit trees and a swimming pool. It looked as if it belonged in France, or maybe Long Island. It was built by a warlord and now belongs to the government. A lot of the lake is being filled in and reclaimed. A big fish hatchery is down below too.

When the Services were living in Kunming in the thirties, the foreign residents liked to picnic here. They would take a boat across the lake, climb up to the temples, and eat their lunch feeling as if they were on top of the world. There wasn't any smog in those days.

SATURDAY, MAY 5
Kunming

Jack has had bronchitis for a few days. In Lijiang two doctors saw him, and today he went to the hospital to be seen by more. He has some new Japanese antibiotics, new cough medicine, and looks and seems better. No doctor has taken his temperature.

In the afternoon we had an interview with Xiao You, who says he is related to General Xiao Ke. As there are only about 136 family names in this country of nearly one billion people, everyone must have many cousins.

Mr. Xiao You is seventy-five now. He was involved in revolutionary work in 1928, secret underground activities. He helped set up a peasants' association, a children's corps, and a secret government. He organized a guerilla group. After joining the Red Army he was first political instructor, then went to the Security Bureau and became special security representative of the Fifth Army Group.

Harrison asked him if he had seen or met Mao, or other generals, and how they impressed him. He said he first saw Mao on horseback, a tall, thin man, courteous and polite; cordial when talking even to the ordinary soldier. Often soldiers had no idea who they'd been talking to. Mao gave the impression of a scholar, a learned man, an intellectual.

Zhu De seemed like a military commander, but he had no airs. He was plain-living, mingled with rank and file, played basketball and ate with them. Peng Dehuai, commander of the Third Army, was very serious, solemn-looking, heavily built, gave the impression of a solid commander, seldom talked.

He said he only saw Mao's wife being carried on a stretcher shortly after crossing Hunan Province, very close to Guizhou. He didn't see Zhu De's wife, Kang Keqing, until Yan'an. Bodyguards were called special security agents and received special training. When they got to Yan'an, security was referred to as the Department of Social Affairs.

Harrison asked what happened to Li De and Bo Gu after Zunyi, when they were put aside and their strategy abandoned. Mr. Xiao said that the

97

common soldiers were angry at them, felt they were responsible for losing the soviet base. But Mao insisted they be well treated, nevertheless.

Miss Li was busy with arrangements, so another girl from her office came with me to a department store to buy some "washing powder." This girl told me that her parents were cadres and that they were sent to different places in the country during the Cultural Revolution. They were "criticized," she said, but she didn't go into details. There are two girls and two boys in her family, she was only thirteen at the time, and they were the go-betweens—were allowed to visit their parents once in a while and would bring each one news of the other, as well as whatever news they could give of what was going on in the country. We know that this was the case for many people who were in jail at that time. If it hadn't been for the children, they would have had no outside contact at all. The children learned to fend for themselves; some lived in gangs on the streets.

When we passed the cosmetics counter, I asked who uses them. Everyone uses something, she said. She uses rouge on her cheeks in the summer because she feels she doesn't have enough color. She does not use lipstick, because her lips are red enough. She does not pluck her eyebrows but uses a depilatory to remove the underhairs. I was horrified and told her she'd blind herself, but she insisted it's safe. I need a nail file and she had never heard of such a thing, thought it sounded dangerous. She cuts her nails with scissors, then rubs them with the blade of the scissors to smooth them. She has no plans for marriage. We agreed a good man is hard to find. She is young, and she can wait. "Anyone can marry," she said.

I told her that in Beijing we were told by a Chinese woman that people in the countryside were destroying their girl babies, and we didn't believe it. She said, yes, it's true, but not in the cities. Jack saw a poster that admonished, *Don't abuse a woman because she has had a girl baby.*

SUNDAY, MAY 6
Dukou

We are in our fourth province—Jiangxi, Guizhou, Yunnan, and now Sichuan. Two more to go.

This morning, near Kunming, we went through Fumin, which was the town closest to Kunming taken by the First Front Army with Lin Biao commanding. The Second and Sixth also went through Fumin.

On April 29, 1935, Jack and Caroline Service were living in Kunming, then called Yunnanfu. It was an outpost city of 150,000 with a slightly French atmosphere. Britain, France, the United States, and Japan had consulates. A few French businessmen, American missionaries, Greek hotel proprietors, along with the government representatives, made up the foreign population. Jack was in the United States Consulate and Caroline was expecting her first baby.

There had been rumors that the "Red Bandits" were approaching, and plans had been made to evacuate the women and children. Caroline had started to pack a trunk of baby clothes she had bought from Montgomery Ward, her wedding silver, and Jack's gold watch. On this night—or rather, at 2:00 A.M.—a messenger pounded on the gate and delivered a warning from the American consul, Arthur Ringwalt, that three thousand Communists were at Debangqiao, about eight miles east of the city, and more were just behind them. The French had provided a train to take women and children from Kunming to Tonkin (North Vietnam), and it would leave at 7:44 A.M.

Caroline finished her packing, put two Siamese kittens in a basket, and got on the train. The kittens were for her mother-in-law in Shanghai, and somehow they got there. The watch was never seen again. The train was full; the families left, but the men remained.

The Red Army never went into Kunming, never made any effort to take it. They could have done so easily, because there were only five hundred local militia stationed there, no soldiers. It was a ploy to confuse the Kuomintang and make them send troops to defend Kunming while the Red Army went somewhere else. Caroline and the other wives returned after a while, and the Red Army continued north.

We had a long hot drive and the driver seemed pretty tired. We had one stop for a picnic lunch, and we found a quiet, secluded, fairly shady place, rare in China. It is rice-planting time in this area and every paddy was being planted with seedlings from the seed beds. Long lines of people, mostly women, were leaning over, up to their knees in water, planting rice all day. Their backs must be awfully strong or else hurt a lot.

There are lots of eucalyptus trees and very barren high mountains that have been planted with pines. In some places they are doing all right; in others, not. It is a huge undertaking, but poor as the soil is, if they can get those scrub pines growing, eventually the soil will build up and other trees and shrubs will come in naturally.

We had a wonderful sight of the Yangtze from a high road. I thought Sichuan Province would be drier and poorer than Yunnan, and we expected the worst. We have been pleasantly surprised. The land looks very fertile, with irrigation and wonderful vegetables. Here we found a nice guest house, which Harrison thinks they fixed up for us. Maybe, but Chinese engineers and government officials come here often as there are a huge steel mill and other industries. Formerly a tiny town, Dukou is a city of 800,000 people, 350,000 in the actual city, the rest in the suburbs. It is

4,030 feet high. It was established by experts, military, engineers, builders, scientists, before the Cultural Revolution. Part of the big steel mill was completed in 1971. There was no damage during those violent years. Scientists and anything to do with Lin Biao and the military were not affected. The reason all the generals we've talked to were imprisoned is because Lin Biao was in charge of the army then, and he wanted to get them out of the way so he could have supreme power. I believe there are many fairly new heavy-industrial cities tucked away where few realize.

We were greeted effusively by a contingent from this province, including several people who will accompany us. Miss Li goes back to Kunming early tomorrow morning with the driver. I hated to say good-bye to her. She is utterly adorable and has been lovely company for all of us. She is hoping someday to come to the United States to study. [We heard from her in the autumn. She is at a college in Georgia.]

MONDAY, MAY 7
Tong'an

This morning we drove up and down the same kind of mountains as yesterday, to the other side of the Yangtze, or Golden Sands, River. I asked about the reforestation of such a huge area that is so inaccessible, and was told it is done by scattering seeds from airplanes. Harrison doesn't believe this, because on the mountains are narrow terraces obviously dug out by hand, so that whatever is planted won't wash down with the first rain. However, if seeds are scattered from a plane, it would account for the irregular growth, dense in one place and bare in another. Eventually, in fifty years or more, there will be good forests on all these mountains.

We are in a wonderful old landlord's house that is now headquarters for the local government, police, etc. As it is dark we haven't been able to see much, but can tell there are many courtyards and rooms. The WC is quite far off, and when I first headed that way, five girls looked at each other and preceded me. So I waited outside until they came out. We have an old-fashioned black lacquer commode in our room, undoubtedly the landlord's, or modeled after his.

Tomorrow, weather permitting, we get up at 5:00 and walk about nine miles to the Golden Sands River at Jiaopingdu (*du* means "crossing" in Chinese.) This river crossing was one of the most important episodes of the Long March; there are no roads to it, only footpaths, and Harrison insists he should see it. It is about 150 miles away from the crossing near Dali, and Mao, Zhou Enlai, and many others crossed here. We will spend the night, in God knows what, and walk back the next day and spend that night in Huili. I hope it won't be too much for us.

Huili 10:00 A.M.

What I have always dreaded about this trip has happened. Harrison's heart is beating irregularly and he is so exhausted he says he can't finish this trip. I'll go back to Tuesday morning at Tong'an.

The weather was good. We were awakened at 5:00, had breakfast at 5:30, and were driven about a mile and a half to where we began this idiotic walk. There must have been thirty or forty local people joining us. We are the first foreigners to come to this area; everyone is excited about our project, and none of our companions had ever taken this walk before. They came from Chengdu, from the province, the county, the prefecture.

Before starting we were each given a big straw hat and a sturdy cane. First we climbed straight up one thousand feet. No wonder there are a lot of goats here; it is just right for them. Jack made it easily. He walks every day up and down the California hills and his legs and muscles are in A-1 condition. Harrison and I are in good shape for what we do normally, but not for anything like this. And neither were some of the others. Everyone went at his own pace, Jack and Zhang way out ahead and everyone else strung out with Harrison and me and the people assigned to be with us gradually falling to the rear.

When we reached that first peak, I should have said, "That's enough, we'll go back from here." But I didn't. For three miles or more, we walked on the side of Fire Mountain. At least the path was flat and fairly smooth, though it was terrifying to look down. Another mountain was just across the divide, dark and rocky. It reminded me of rides I have had in Montana when I wondered what would happen if the horse slipped. We climbed around Lion's Head—which from the other side does look just like a crouched lion, the head very clearly defined—and down to a flat place where a fierce battle was fought. The Red Army vanguard had crossed the river from Yunnan Province (we were going the opposite way; the next day we saw the terrain as they did) and, with very little rest, were sent ahead to clear out the enemy, the Sichuan unit that held the mountain. From their vantage point of three to four hundred feet above, the enemy could clearly see the advancing soldiers. The Red Army soldiers were tired; they were in full view of the enemy as they struggled up the cliffs; they had inferior weapons. But with all these disadvantages, they won out. The Sichuan unit ran away.

Nothing has made us feel the reality of what that army of young boys did as seeing that battlefield. How they must have hated the regime of warlords and landlords to fight the way they did.

The country we walked over, and the country we've been driving through, is nowhere near as populated as most of China. It is mostly mountains—barren, rocky, high, and terribly steep.

Walking on the flat was all right for both of us, but when we proceeded to go downhill for the three-thousand-foot descent on a stony and rocky trail, we began to give out. My left knee, which sometimes bothers me at home, began to hurt, and Harrison's knees turned to rubber. We finally got down to an old riverbed where I had anticipated a nice grassy path along the side. But not at all. We walked for two and a half more miles on rocks and stones. There was no grass or anything soft anywhere. Harrison was swaying from side to side in front of me, and he took one terrible fall, spread right out on the sharp gray stones. He said it was good for him—got some adrenaline stirring, but it was awful to see. I couldn't bend my knee, had to swing my leg to keep it straight, the way I remember my cousin Richard Tudor (who had had polio) swinging his paralyzed legs, encased in braces as he walked on crutches. Extraordinary to think of him. He died when he was sixteen, and I must have been twelve or thirteen. He didn't have any real life.

Everyone tried to help us, but there was nothing anyone could do. A young man kept saying, "You're cree-pled," and he was right. We continued our painful way and finally, after nearly seven hours of walking, dragged ourselves up to a nice airy building above the Golden Sands River, with a balcony on the top story and a wide terrace on the bottom. We could hear the river; there were ripe papayas on trees in front; I fell into bed and said I would have to be carried out—so would Harrison. No more walking like that for us.

I slept all afternoon, but Harrison went down to the river and met with some of the boatmen who, forty-nine years ago, had ferried the soldiers across. It seemed like yesterday to them, they said. They had helped locate thirty-six boats; the crossing took nine days and nights and not a man was lost. Horses and mules swam. Jiaopingdu was a turning point, a very important episode for the Red Army. They had been in the field, so to speak, for seven months; their losses had been heavy; they were down to about twenty-five thousand men. But Mao's way had paid off. They had crossed the Yangtze. They had shaken off the pursuing Kuomintang. Their spirits were high. They had unforeseen hardships and squabbling among themselves ahead, but they would never again be so threatened by Chiang Kaishek.

Back to Tuesday. It seems two hundred days ago, though it's just two. We had supper on the porch—Chinese spam, which is very good, and papaya right off the trees. We went to bed almost immediately and fell asleep listening to the lovely sound of the river. Next morning (only yesterday) we were awakened before daybreak. Candles were lit along the balcony; it looked beautiful. Harrison and I were pretty stiff, and as we had said we couldn't walk back, it was arranged for me to ride the little horse that had carried packs the day before, and Harrison was to be carried on a stretcher by two stalwart boys. I thought he wouldn't acquiesce to that, but he said all the Long Marchers were carried when they were wounded, so he would be too. The young man who owned my horse led him, so all I had to do was sit there. Strangely, my knee didn't hurt, bent for the stirrup.

Jack and Zhang had already left; a fairly big group came with me, and Harrison was sitting on the stretcher, ready to go, with the General and others staying with him. We went quite fast, and every time I looked back I could see no sight of Harrison and the General. When we got across the rocky riverbed, we waited and waited until finally they came into view. Harrison was walking, swaying the way he did the day before, with a man on each side. I was furious, and terribly upset, and couldn't imagine what had happened.

It turned out that the two boys were not strong enough to carry Harrison, and the handles on the stretcher were not long enough for the boy in back to see his feet.

On the walk to Jiaopingdu we had had three pack animals—my horse, a mule, and a little burro. The last was the only one needed to carry things on for the trip back; we had eaten and drunk all the supplies and there were only the few things we had brought to be carried. When it became apparent that the stretcher wouldn't work, a call went out to try and find a saddle for the mule that was walking ahead of me, led by his keeper, a girl with pigtails wearing a pink shirt. Heaven knows how word was sent, or how a saddle was found, but as we were waiting by the old riverbed, a man came down the mountain with one. It was made of wood and had very short stirrups, the same as Mongolian saddles.

Harrison was heaved up on the mule, and even though it was uncomfortable, at least he wasn't walking. A man with a first-aid kit was with us, and my stirrups were extended with gauze bandage. And when Harrison's saddle broke, it was tied up with the same. This mule had never had a saddle or person on his back before, and it is a miracle he carried Harrison without mishap.

Everyone stopped for a rest at the flat before Lion's Head—the scene of the battle. Several pack trains passed, and many herds of goats being taken to higher pastures. All the way back the burro carrying our bags walked ahead, with his keeper, a man of at least seventy, and a little boy following right behind. The man leaned a little forward and kept his hands clasped behind his back, the way diplomats do, and never altered the pace of his sinewy legs. He makes that trip every day.

The last one thousand feet downhill were awful, even on a horse. I never could have made it on foot.

People don't ordinarily ride animals here; they are used for carrying packs and pulling carts. But when we returned and had said good-bye, my boy jumped on his little horse and galloped away. I have seen two horses with saddles, but no one on them, and occasionally I have seen children sitting astride water buffalo when they're being taken out to graze.

Jack and Zhang were ahead of us by two hours, and the General, who went very slowly, was almost that much behind us. He is fifty-nine, I am seventy, Jack is seventy-four, Harrison seventy-five, and Zhang thirty-five. Jack made the trip more easily than the rest of us, even Zhang.

We had more spam for lunch in a room filled with flies, and left right after for here. We have been boiling hot and perspiring for two days, and this room is cold and damp. Harrison had a chill in the middle of the night, which is always a danger signal for him. He took aspirin and hot water, and I put every blanket in the room on him. He sweated it off, but is weak and exhausted and his pulse is irregular. We are waiting for a doctor.

SAME DAY: THURSDAY, MAY 10
Xichang, 5:30 P.M.

This morning at Huili, two doctors and a nurse examined poor Harrison, took an electrocardiogram, and said what we knew, that there is a little irregularity. It was decided to let him rest in the morning and after lunch come here, where there is an army hospital and more doctors. We were a caravan of three minibuses. Besides all the people from this province who accompany us, we had the two doctors. Harrison sat in the front seat so he wouldn't bounce around, and we had a drive of nearly four hours, going very slowly. This is a beautiful place with a big lake, Qiong Hai, and we are in a very pretty guest house. As soon as we got here, three more doctors came, took another EKG, and gave Harrison a more thorough going-over. They feel there may be some heart failure that the pacemaker is covering up. They will do blood tests to clarify some suspicions.

So here we are. Harrison is lying in bed with his sweater on, covered with a quilt and sleeping. I don't know how I feel. I can't allow myself to think he is really ill, but again, I can't help but think he is. I hope I don't break down. I feel stretched fairly tight. While I have recovered from most of my stiffness, my knee still hurts when I step down, and my emotional state is pretty shaky.

We never should have come on this trip. I have been against it for over ten years, ever since Harrison started talking about wanting to retrace the Long March. Maybe if we had just stuck to the bus and not undertaken that terrible walk, we could have done it. I had no idea it was going to be so difficult; I wasn't in on any of the talks and plans. I thought Harrison had more sense about himself, but I guess he didn't realize what the terrain is really like. No wonder there aren't any roads there. But I blame myself. When we got halfway up that first steep hill, I should have said, No, this is not for us. Well, I didn't. Thank God for Jack and Zhang and the doctors who seem to have appeared out of nowhere.

FRIDAY, MAY 11
Xichang, 4:00 P.M

Usually I write at night, but everything has been so mixed up the last few days, I write whenever I can.

Last night the doctors got some result from a blood test that makes them think Harrison has had a heart attack. The two doctors who came with us from Huili spent the night here; they took turns sitting outside our door all night. We had to keep the light on and one of them came in every half hour, or more often, if they heard Harrison cough or move. A glucose solution is dripping into him because he is so dehydrated. At noon four doctors, two from the army hospital and two from the civilian, took another EKG on a huge new Japanese machine, and we are waiting to hear the results.

Just as I wrote this, Zhang came to tell me we can go to Chengdu tonight on the train. The doctors say it's okay. They will just take Harrison's blood pressure once more.

I can't believe it after all this anxiety. I don't know what to think. My feeling all along has been that Harrison undoubtedly strained his heart, that he is completely exhausted and dehydrated, and needs at least a week of rest in bed. But with all the talk about the possibility of an attack and injury to his heart, I wish we could stay another day. Well, once we get on the train he can sleep all night, and from Chengdu we can call his doctor in New York, which has not been possible from here. When we get to Chengdu I will insist he stay in bed, and from now on I won't give in when my instincts against something are so strong.

SATURDAY, MAY 12
Still at Xichang, 9:15 A.M.

Nothing works out as expected on this trip. Last night we had supper in this room, which we are still in, went to the station with Dr. Du, the lady

M.D., and Dr. Chen, a whole bag of medical supplies and an oxygen bag, which we haven't seen since we were in Tibet. It was just after nine; we were sitting in a private waiting room and the train was due any minute. Suddenly a great burst of conversation started up among our Chinese companions. The train was just coming in. There had been a dreadful accident about two hundred kilometers away—a freight train had been caught in a landslide in a tunnel. The stationmaster hurried to tell the engineer. They did not tell the passengers—there would have been panic, with everyone wanting to get off the train, and no facilities in Xichang for taking care of so many people. No new passengers got on, no one got off, and the train chugged out of the station on time. Jack watched it and said there must have been at least one thousand people aboard. The accident occurred near a small town, and I suppose that by the time the train got there some arrangements had been made, at least food and water provided. Thank goodness we found out before we got on the train. What could have happened is a nightmare to contemplate.

We are scheduled to fly to Chengdu at 1:00. A group of local officials were planning to go to a meeting there by plane, but they were "requested" to give up their tickets to us. They will travel in the two buses we have had in this province and it will take two days and a night instead of an hour and a half. We have no say in arrangements like this and I have to admit it suits me fine.

So, here we are, waiting again. We have been unbelievably lucky in our misfortunes, if that is the way to put it. That terrible day, returning from the river, it didn't rain. We have had the best possible doctors—maybe the best anywhere. Their devotion and constant attention is reassuring and comforting. And it was fantastic luck to find out about that accident only minutes before getting on the train last night.

I am sorry not to have seen anything of Xichang. It is naturally beautiful, with a big lake and good climate. It is being turned into a tourist attraction and resort, and two chemical factories that were polluting the lake have been closed down. This is a Yi minority center, but the Yis are only one third of the population. However, we are told that 40 percent of the officials have to be Yi people. The others in our party have been doing some sightseeing and they report seeing many Yi women in their native dress. Many women wear pants instead of the traditional skirts.

This is the place Chiang Kaishek took off from when he fled to Taiwan. Another Kuomintang general left from here ten minutes before the Red Army took the airport.

There is an army base here (hence the doctors and good equipment). It must be air force. We have heard several supersonic explosions, or breaking-the-sound-barrier noises. Harrison says they are fighter planes and he didn't think the Chinese had this kind of plane. I think probably they have everything.

EVENING, SAME DAY
Chengdu

The same caravan that went to the train last night went to the airport. There we waited nearly an hour. It looked like rain, the plane had not arrived, and I was beginning to think the flight would be canceled. But nothing awful happened. The plane came in; our bags (and those of the other forty-eight passengers, including several Japanese, who always have more and bigger bags than we do) were pedaled out by one man on a bicycle with a cart attached. He had to make about eight trips. Our hand luggage was personally inspected quickly and politely, except for Harrison's typewriter, which completely baffled the inspectors. They had never seen such a strange machine as his old Remette.

The flight took fifty-five minutes, and we are now settled in a nice airy room in the Jin Jiang Hotel, named for the river here. Everything works in the bathroom and there is hot water all the time. Luxury.

The little we saw of the city is much more attractive than what I remember from four years ago. White oleanders, plane trees, and feathery fir trees line the streets, and the boulevard leading to the big statue of Mao (one of the few left) is really beautiful. Flowers and shrubs surround this hotel and we can see two tennis courts from our window.

As soon as we were in our room, the doctors took Harrison's blood pressure—it is still too high. But he came to the dining room and ate a little supper.

SUNDAY, MAY 13
Chengdu

No one came in during the night. Harrison slept all night and was hungry for breakfast. After breakfast his blood pressure was taken and at last it is normal. His heart is beating normally too, they said. But he still has a cough and is continuing antibiotics.

Until here, I had been afraid to have myself checked—afraid I might have something wrong that would compound our problems. But I am okay—everything beating and sounding as it should. Both doctors said they could tell I am strong because I recovered so quickly from that ghastly walk. I think I am strong too, but I remember my childhood years of always being sick, and it seems quite remarkable. Perhaps it's from necessity. The doctors didn't charge me anything for a pretty thorough checkup, and I couldn't help but think that a New York doctor would have sent me a bill for at least seventy-five dollars.

After lunch another Dr. Chen, a lady professor-cardiologist who speaks English and who has just been at the University of California at La Jolla, examined Harrison. Everything seems to be mending, slowly, but she wants him to go to her hospital for a few days to be observed. So we will go tomorrow at 8:00 to a high cadre part of the hospital where I can stay too. At first I was desperate about this, but now am thinking of it as a new adventure. I have no choice, actually. The hospital is not far, so perhaps I can walk back here every day for a breather.

At 4:00 we met for an hour with General Ding Ganru, who had made the Long March. He looks very young, but is sixty-seven and has had two heart attacks. During the Long March he was with the rearguard unit of the Fifth Army. He said the worst and most difficult times for him had been the Grasslands, the Snowy Mountains, and the minority people.

The Han, who constitute 96 percent of the Chinese population, have always felt superior to the minorities (The Tibetans, Mongols, Manchus, Yi, Miao, and other tribes). This is probably still the case in most places. For centuries they had driven these tribes out of their territories up into the mountains, where living was almost impossible, and under the Kuomintang, conditions became worse and worse. The poverty was frightful. Rumors about the Red Army being red devils made the minorities as suspicious of the Red Army as they were of the Kuomintang. They fired on the soldiers as they went through the valleys, and hid their food and supplies. He said the Miao people were naked except for an apron in front, and that they ripped the clothes off any straggling soldier, who then froze to death. This is a pat story and Jack is dubious about it.

He also talked about the Qinggangpo battle and said it was very usual for Zhu De to be on the battlefield. He added that Mao and the others were often at the front.

The worst hardship was never having enough to eat. In Tibetan areas they went against the nationalities policy of the Red Army and smashed old statues of Buddha that were stuffed with grain. It had no taste, had been there for years, but they suffered no ill consequences. They washed the feces of the army that preceded them, took the undigested grain and boiled it. They had no new uniforms after Zunyi, were always cold. Until the fourth crossing of the Chishui River, the Kuomintang was in hot pursuit. After that, they were not troubled very much by the enemy, though they had many problems among themselves.

When they finally got over the mountains and through the Grasslands and were in Gansu, life was better. They could communicate with the people; there was plenty of food. They were told to eat sparingly at first, but many soldiers couldn't restrain themselves, and ate until they died.

We are comforted by talking to Harrison's doctor in New York. He says the Chinese doctors are doing everything right; he thinks it is sensible to go to the hospital for observation and rest, and we will call him afterward.

MONDAY, MAY 14
At the Sichuan Medical College Hospital

We came here this morning, Harrison and I, Jack, Zhang, and the two doctors from Xichang, Dr. Du and Dr. Chen, who have been with us every instant. More doctors examined Harrison, took another EKG, and prescribed breathing oxygen three times a day. Tomorrow more heart doctors will come to consult. We have a bedroom, sitting room, and bathroom, and I will sleep on a cot next to Harrison's bed. An adorable nurse speaks a little English. She will come at midnight to take his pulse. He seems definitely on the mend to me. I hope we don't have to stay more than two or three days.

FRIDAY, MAY 18
Back at the Jin Jiang Hotel

We stayed at the hospital until this morning—four days and nights. On the second day seven heart specialists examined Harrison and all the EKG tapes and came to the conclusion that he did not have a heart attack, nor is his heart damaged in any way. Because of fatigue and dehydration he suffered loss of blood and oxygen to his heart, but breathing oxygen and drugs can fix that.

Visitors came every day bearing flowers and fruit, and we made a good friend down the hall. When Harrison first arrived, he found a welcoming note from "a fellow American patient" who told him not to worry about anything, he would have the best of care. She had no idea who the new patient might be; she was just being friendly and reassuring. She turned out to be Margaret Graham, a woman who lived in China as a child and had known Jack Service. Her father taught archaeology at the college here, and ran the museum. After that he spent twenty years doing research on the Miao people for the Smithsonian Institution. She is a widow whose home is in Tucson. She wanted to come back to China to teach, but was told she was too old. So, she told me, "I wrote to a fellow Sichuanese who is older than I and is high in the government, and told him my problem." The fellow Sichuanese was Deng Xiaoping. Soon after that, she received several offers, and chose this place. She teaches English in the medical college. It was cozy having her down the hall and I visited her regularly, as did Jack.

I went back to the hotel each day, took a bath, had lunch, and did some shopping. Once, after a visit to a department store, Jack and I took a pedicab. I am amazed they still exist. I rode in one in Cambodia in 1966, but never in China. It is a queer sensation, being pulled or pedaled by another human being, and except for being amused at the picture we must have made, I didn't really enjoy it. Ours had a plastic-covered seat and looked quite clean. As we got in Jack said, "All you might get is fleas."

Wednesday Dr. Du and Dr. Chen, the Huili doctors, came to say good-bye. We had a nice talk about our experiences together and Dr. Du gave me so many compliments I could hardly stand it. She said my devotion to my husband had impressed them, that I was a model wife, an example, and that they had all learned from me. The Chinese say the ideal relationship between husband and wife is when they treat each other as guests, and we seem that way to them. They think we are a "model couple." I didn't know how to reply to so much praise and said I would answer the way the Chinese do, that "it is my duty and my responsibility." Every time I have said how grateful we are for all the loving care and attention they have given us, that is what they reply. It has been a rare experience for us. Our American doctors are not like this. They go home and leave their patient to a resident or a corps of nurses and machines. Here an experienced doctor sleeps in the hospital so is always available, and, as I have written, in the beginning, either Dr. Du or Dr. Chen sat outside Harrison's door all night and checked him every half hour.

They got up to leave and we started to say good-bye. When I got to Dr. Du, I broke down completely, threw my arms around her, and burst into tears. She did the same. We have been through this without being able to really talk to each other, and yet our hearts and feelings are alike. My defenses came crashing down and the bottled-up feelings of the last week came pouring out. I recovered enough to say good-bye, and then they were gone.

They saved Harrison. I have no doubt of it. If they had not been at Huili, God knows what would have happened.

It is interesting that all the doctors, except for Dr. Du, were called Dr. Chen or Dr. Wang. One Dr. Wang had just come back from Paris, where he had given a paper on heart problems and treatment. I remember that in 1972, when we asked if Chinese doctors had any contact with doctors in other countries, to compare notes, the answer was that they read medical journals. Now both doctors and professors go abroad and exchange knowledge with their foreign colleagues.

We had lunch with Jack. He must be delighted not to have lunch with just me anymore, though he is, and was, very polite about it. After a rest we met with a Sichuan Tibetan, Mr. Tian Bao, or Sand Ji Yaoxi in Tibetan. He isn't a real Tibetan, but one of those born in the Tibetan area of China. Tibetans came down from Tibet four to five hundred years ago and settled on land much easier to live on than their native country—not so high, not so cold, wonderful wide plains for grazing animals.

Tian Bao had no name until he was six years old, when he was taken to a lama and his name was drawn out of a jar. He lived in the monastery until the spring of 1935, when the Red Army came. Of three brothers, he and the youngest were to be lamas. He said the rule was that no matter how many sons, only one stayed home. The rest went to the monastery. The system was primarily Tibetan; there were no Han people except for occasional traders and peddlers. There was no government, but there were chieftans in the minority tribes, rich men who owned land and rented it to the poor, just like Han landlords. Most families had guns and horses for protection.

Tian Bao first heard of the Red Army in 1933, heard that a revolutionary base had been set up in North Sichuan. One report was that the poor people were happy; the landlords' and chieftains' properties had been confiscated; the Red Army was a good force led by a fierce man named Zhu Mao. He didn't know until later that there were two men, Zhu De and Mao. Another rumor, supposedly spread by the Kuomintang, said that the Red Army came to kill Tibetans and eat their children. When the Red Army was approaching in 1935, the chieftain became panicky and ordered every man to defend the area against them. Noncombatants were sent to the mountains. Tian Bao and others left the monastery and joined the Communists. They were welcomed, he said, given clothes and food, and they helped in confiscating the chieftain's goods. Here, the Red Army didn't follow their rules of not touching minority landlords' property. The reason given was that the First Front Army was just passing through, they needed the supplies, had to slaughter cattle and take what they found. The Fourth Army was in the area for several months and had time to make propaganda and teach people their aims.

He told us that when the people in the mountains decided to come down and see if all the good things they were told about the Red Army were true, they sent the grandmothers first. When it was certain that they were treated well, the rest of the Tibetans returned. Being a grandmother myself, I don't appreciate that obviously they were expendable.

It is sheer heaven to have Harrison out of the hospital. He is very thin, but his color is good. The doctors say he must be careful not to catch cold or get tired.

SATURDAY, MAY 19
Jin Jiang Hotel, Chengdu

It was nice to wake up here rather than in the hospital, in spite of all the tender loving care we received.

This morning we visited the Long March section in the Provincial Museum, which was neither new nor inspiring. Evidently, there used to be a much larger and more comprehensive exhibit, which, for some reason we can't fathom, has been reduced. Looking at what there is took only fifteen minutes, and then we had a good interview with three historians.

Harrison is trying to find out the reasons for the conflict between Mao and Zhang Guotao. Zhang was Mao's biggest rival, had his own Fourth Front Army, had been in the field independently for five years, and was called "Chairman" by his men. When Mao and he met in the village of Fubian in Sichuan in June 1935, Zhang Guotao had a much larger force—he claimed it was one hundred thousand men, but it was actually eighty thousand. They were in good shape, had plenty of food and proper clothes, and their animals were healthy. Zhang, according to people who saw him, was white, soft, and fat. Mao's First Army was down to a few thousand men, exhausted, thin, and poorly dressed. Because of his superior strength, Zhang Guotao figured he should be commander-in-chief, and he said the decision at Zunyi was invalid. He was a member of the politburo, but he had no support in his claim. Mao, in spite of losses and bedraggled forces, had the backing of the party and the devotion of cadres and soldiers.

A meeting between the two commanders was arranged, and on a cold rainy day, Mao, with Zhou Enlai and Zhu De, waited in a flimsy tent for Zhang to arrive. Mounted on a white horse and surrounded by body-guards, he came galloping up, splashing everyone in his way. Mao emerged from his tent, Zhang dismounted, they embraced, and, arms around each other (according to Zhang's memoirs), walked into town to a celebration banquet. They had not seen each other for twelve years, but they had never been close. They had very different ideas, disagreed about where the armies should go, and never came to terms.

Zhang Guotao had the reputation of arresting and executing officers he didn't trust. After subsequent meetings, Zhu De went with the Fourth Army, supposedly as commander, and Zhang as political officer. But Zhang would not relinquish his control and, according to some reports, held Zhu De a virtual prisoner. Mao and Zhou Enlai continued together and reached Yan'an nearly one year before the Fourth Front Army.

In 1938 Zhang Guotao left the Communists and joined Chiang Kaishek. Later he escaped to Hong Kong, where his family was allowed to join him.

We are heading southwest tomorrow, then north, to see some of the places where these events occurred.

I am sorry I haven't been able to do any sightseeing, or go back to some of the places we visited on our last trip to Chengdu. I especially would have liked to see that fantastic irrigation system—the Guanxian Dam, according to Nagel's guide; the Dujiang Dam system, according to the

Foreign Language Press in Beijing—and the Two Kings Temple on the side of the hill nearby. The dam has been functioning since 250 B.C., over two thousand years, and brings water to over one million acres. It has made the Chengdu plain the richest agricultural area in China. Three harvests a year of rice, sugar cane, tobacco, and other crops are normal.

Margaret Graham told me that an American engineer who has been here twice, advising the Chinese on some project, was taken to see the irrigation works. His reaction was "Of course, the Chinese didn't do this. They must have had help from Europeans." He didn't seem to realize that this was developed before Christ. Most of Europe was populated by warring tribes, except for the Romans. And even if one of them had thought of this great scheme, how could he have gotten to Chengdu?

SUNDAY, MAY 20
Ya'an, on the Qingyi River

Ya'an used to be the capital of a province called Sikang. But Sikang was split up, some given to Sichuan, some to Tibet, so now it is just a town in Sichuan Province. It still has the feeling of a capital. Large trees line the streets, vigorously pruned as in European cities, and the river is big and important. Logs cut from the mountains were floated down, but there are no signs of that now.

We left Chengdu right after lunch and the drive was pleasant and easy. Gradually, the flat rice lands gave way to more hilly country. The altitude here is three thousand feet. We drove through Baizhang, a town where Zhang Guotao fought the Kuomintang in November 1935 and suffered a terrible defeat, upward of ten thousand casualties. He was hoping to capture Chengdu "to eat rice," he told his men, the direct opposite of Mao's strategy of leaving cities alone and concentrating on villages and countryside. Zhang retreated, came back up north, and never tried to go south again.

Jack saw a poster that read *It is a glorious thing for a couple to have only one child.*

MONDAY, MAY 21
Shimian (Means "Asbestos")

In 1951 an asbestos mine was discovered here, hence the name. We left Ya'an around 8:30 this morning in three vehicles. A jeep carried the local people and a doctor ahead, while Harrison, me, our lady doctor, and Mr. Zhang rode in a Toyota Landcruiser. Everyone else followed behind in another—Jack; Mr. Guo, the very nice man who has been with us since Dukou, where we said good-bye to Miss Li and met the Sichuan contingent; Mr. Wang, the young man who told me I was "creepled" on that big walk; and several others. We drove through country I never expected to see in this province, wet, misty, mountainous, with a few azaleas still in bloom, like Jiangxi or Guizhou. I had thought Sichuan was dry and dusty all the time, but this is the beginning of the rainy season. We went up as high as six thousand feet but are now back by the Dadu River, which we have heard and read and talked about so much.

I have seen a lot of flowers that are just like ours—buttercups, self-heal, wild roses, and some like multiflora roses. Azaleas and rhododendron in the highest places, and the pale purple lilies we saw in Guizhou.

We got here around three. After a short rest, we went, in three buses and a jeep (I can't figure out who all the other people are), to see a memorial to Prince Shi Dakai, the last of the Taipings.

The religious-political movement known as the Taiping Rebellion was started by a schoolteacher from a small village near Guangzhou, after he had four times failed the civil-service examinations. Influenced by some gospel writings given him by Issachar Roberts, an American missionary, he had visions of a Heavenly Mother, believed he was Christ's younger brother, that he had visited heaven and been ordered by God to free the world from evil. He enlisted a cousin to help him spread the word, and soon acquired more apostles, who went through the countryside preaching salvation from gambling, opium, and the rule of the Manchu demons.

From 1850 to 1864 the Taipings gained millions of supporters all over China, controlled sixteen out of eighteen provinces, and established their capital in Nanking. They had a well-disciplined army, taking orders from heaven, and initiated a land-reform program which, though the land belonged to God, gave individual peasants fields to use.

But it couldn't last. The leader was too unstable to rule; his followers began to quarrel and turned on each other's armies. The emperor's forces grew stronger, and in a Gotterdammerung of burning and killing, it came to an end.

In 1862 a terrible battle took place at Zidadi (a town that was washed away in a landslide in 1902) between the rebelling Taipings and Ching Dynasty troops. Shi Dakai's wife had had a baby and his army took time to celebrate. They were surrounded by the enemy, all ways out were blocked, and the prince surrendered. His people killed themselves or were executed and thrown into the Dadu River. He was taken to Chengdu and sliced to death, as I wrote earlier.

Chiang Kaishek likened the Red Army to the Taipings and said he would annihilate them at this same place, but it didn't work.

We are on the second floor of this guest house; the rooms open onto a long balcony. The Chinese have rooms here too, but they eat somewhere by themselves. We three eat in one of the bedrooms, emptied of beds and basins. A man and a young woman, both in starched white coats, are at our beck and call, but there's not much to call for.

TUESDAY, MAY 22
Luding

This morning we drove to Anshunchang, situated near the site of the old town of Zidadi. A memorial to the Red Army, a young soldier's head carved out of big stone blocks, is near the river. Modern and strong, it is very simple, inside a small square enclosed by a fence, with pretty flowers at the base. The sculptor was killed at age thirty-two by a rock falling on him on the same road we took today. It wasn't a landslide; he was out of the car and a rock rolled down and hit him on the head. He never saw his monument. The General knew him.

In 1935 the Red Army had to get across the Dadu River, and there were no bridges then except the one at Luding, about ninety miles from Anshunchang. (Today we counted fifteen suspension bridges between Anshunchang and Luding, two for cars and trucks.) The Luding Bridge was built in 1701 and swings over the river for 370 feet. Nine chains fastened into the rocks at each end make the floor, with planks laid on top, and two chains are on each side for railing. The "Imperial Route," the main road from Beijing to Lhasa, was from Beijing to Xi'an, Chengdu, Luding Bridge, Kangting, Lhasa; and when Nepal paid tribute to Beijing, they came this way.

In 1908, when Jack Service's parents were on a walking and camping trip in this still-remote area, his mother wrote: . . . *but when one notes the open spaces, the irregularly laid planking of the flooring, the infrequent palings connecting the side chains, and the general airiness of the whole construction hanging so jauntily over wild and swirling water, one cannot help but feel that the bridge is sketchily built. However, the location is important and if one lets the imagination play on the scene, one can visualize a thousand interesting caravans which have for scores of years passed over this old trade route. Travelers from India, Tibet, Nepal, and other parts of High Asia, have safely crossed the raging Tung (former name of Dadu) by this tenuous web of man's ingenuity. It holds the charm and glamour of mystery hidden away in this obscure Chinese valley.* They walked over; a companion was carried in a sedan chair whose poles broke halfway across, so she walked the rest of the way. Animals had to be led, one man at the head, one behind to steady them.

It was clear that it would take days for the Red Army to cross the river

115

in the three boats available, so the decision was made to march. With practically no food or rest, fighting an occasional skirmish with random enemy troops, they covered the ninety miles. Soldiers tied themselves together to keep from falling off the cliffs in case they went to sleep while walking. At one point they spotted Kuomintang troops across the river, marching toward the bridge, reinforcements for the troops already there. The Red Army knew the enemy's codes; a bugler sent a message that they were friendly Kuomintang troops and had just wiped out a band of Red Bandits. The enemy soldiers camped for the night. The Red Army marched on. At daybreak they arrived, spent the day reconnoitering, and at 4:00 P.M. they stormed the bridge. Twenty-two volunteers made the assault and only three were lost.

I don't see how they managed. It is a peculiar sensation to walk on a suspension bridge. It can get rolling and swaying back and forth, and the Luding Bridge is high over the violent rushing river. Though they were covered to a certain extent by their own soldiers firing over them to the bridgehead, they were facing enemy guns, while hitching themselves across, hand over hand, on the big chains. Planks had been removed from the bridge and the bridgehead set on fire. Harrison thinks that perhaps this screened the attacking soldiers, hid them a bit.

Somehow or other they made it across and took the bridgehead. The Kuomintang troops who didn't give up fled. The whole operation took two hours. One more display of the determination of those young soldiers to get rid of the system that had bled them for so many centuries and make their country a land where people could live and work and have opportunities, and not just be stuck forever as peasants and workers with absolutely no say, no voice, no right to object, no rights at all, used and abused by landlords and a feudal system. Every day here, when I meet men and women who represent their country, their province; the doctors who are so well trained and dedicated; the historians, museum directors, army people, government workers, who mostly come from peasant families and are doing their work so conscientiously, I am impressed all over again with what has been achieved in thirty-five years. We drive through villages where, granted, everyone is poor compared to a lot of the world, and people work hard and don't have lives anything like mine, but they look healthy and happy. There are no more epidemic diseases; children are well taken care of, inoculated, and vaccinated; old people are not abandoned or segregated; the children are well dressed and most girls, even in the simplest villages, wear the same clothes girls in cities do—nice-fitting pants and a shirt or jacket, often shoes with heels. At least half the women I've seen have curled their hair. That may not seem important, but it is symbolic of the state of mind of the average Chinese woman. She wants to look her best and does what she thinks will make her look that way. Personally, I like their own natural thick straight hair, but obviously, some of them don't.

At dinner Zhang and the General joined us and we had an awfully good time. Much too much food and lots of beer and jokes and affectionate talk. Harrison has had the daily EKG and blood-pressure tests, etc. (They now do that to Jack as well and he is very annoyed.) One doctor leaves us tomorrow and another joins us. We are back in the bus together and life seems to be returning to normal. I felt well and happy today for no specific reason, and always worry that if I feel this happy, something terrible will happen.

WEDNESDAY, MAY 23
Danba, Also on the Dadu River

Today we were a cavalcade of seven cars. We are curiosities and everyone wants to come along with us for the novelty.

We left Luding early and took a very roundabout way because the roads were poor or nonexistent. We drove through mountains that come straight down on each side of the river, high and green, looking like the movie about Mao that we saw in Beijing. At times in the distance we saw snow-capped peaks, like the Snowy Mountains the Red Army went over, beautiful in the clear blue sky. On all the high places there are lovely flowers, especially a low shrub that has tiny thick leaves like a jade plant, and pretty purple blossoms. In some places it covers big areas and, from a distance, looks like heather. The stems are stiff and woody and we were told it is used to burn but isn't very good. A yellow flower, a "herald of spring," looks just like a poppy but the leaves are a combination of a lily and our wild, thick mullen. No one with us knows the name of anything. Many flowers are the same as ours—dandelions, buttercups, wild iris, and even tiny strawberry plants that grow on all the sandy, dusty roadsides. I took a picture of the yellow poppy flower and said I didn't want to pick it, would leave it growing, but just wanted to remember it. Immediately, the two blossoms were picked by other people. I noticed many truck drivers had these flowers hanging in their trucks. The Chinese haven't been educated enough (any more than most Americans have) about protecting flowers and shrubs. There are signs warning *Protect forests* and *Playing with fire by children is strictly forbidden,* and others like that. They are trying to teach people to protect trees. Flowers and shrubs come next.

Most of the country we went through is populated by Tibetans and reminded me of Sikkim, except the people look dirtier and shabbier. Some of the women and girls are beautiful, but there are lots of footloose-looking boys and very odd older men with no teeth and layer upon layer of clothes, generally wearing a huge felt hat. Their houses are made of stone, as we remember them in Tibet, but these are two-story with pretty windows and trim. In fact, these houses look like the former rich people's houses in Lhasa. The ones we remember from the country were like flat-roofed rabbit warrens, each enclosed by a wall—a microcosm of a village, a labyrinth.

We had lunch at a bus and truck stop, a big kitchen that turns out quantities of meals to travelers, a fast-food joint of a type. The best dish was soup with big bean sprouts and shreds of meat.

At the highest point, Zheduoshan (over 14,000 feet in altitude), the front police jeep and our car stopped as we had lost sight of the rest of our cavalcade. They drove up after a while, everyone got out and asked, "Didn't you hear the signal?" The engine of the blue and white car had caught on fire. One of the jeeps went back to help and somehow the disabled car was turned around and coasted down all those mountains until it got to a place where it could be fixed.

Several of our companions felt the altitude, were faint or sick or unnaturally sleepy. Harrison and I don't seem to mind it much because we move slowly and don't try to do anything.

We stopped at a monastery, or lamasery, that was damaged in the Cultural Revolution. It is one of the places the Tang Dynasty princess stopped on her way to Lhasa to marry King Songtsen Gampo in the eighth century. He also married a Nepalese princess at the same time and, according to the stories, lived with them both in a palace he built where the Potala is today.

As we came into more Tibetan country, the small bridges changed. Instead of the rounded stone bridges we have seen almost everywhere, now they are cantilevered and flat, made of wood. They are nowhere near as pretty as the Chinese bridges.

There are prayer flags everywhere. The Chinese say they are just on graves, but we see them entwined in bridges, around houses, on tents in vegetable fields.

There used to be many bandits, and as late as the 1920s a Dr. Shelton, a missionary whom Jack's parents knew, was killed by them.

It was a long drive, 266 kilometers, really too long for one day on these roads. Yet the last part, going through the narrow, high mountain valley with a violent stream and the most eerie rock formations with rhododendrons and other gorgeous flowers growing out of them, was more than ample compensation.

This guest house is quite pretty and we can see a little of the river from one window. Two men from Chengdu made a vanguard trip to all the places we have seen, and will go to, in this province, and prepared our hosts along the way. In every place there has been pink toilet paper; in many, new furniture; and always one or two girls or a bossy woman to take care of us. Every meal has been a feast, whether we like the food or not. People have done their best for us and we certainly appreciate it.

THURSDAY, MAY 24
Maerkang (Chinese) or Barkam (Tibetan)

Something I will never get used to is the lack of privacy in rural China. Jack is always saying, "Didn't you go to boarding school?" But my school recognized the desire for being alone at times, and even in a washroom for a whole floor of girls, toilets were separated by partitions and doors, and showers by curtains. Early this morning Harrison and I went out together to the toilets. Outside the guest-house door are several steps and a wall at the top. On and behind the wall were at least seventy-five people, men, women, and children, waiting to catch a glimpse of the queer pale visitors. That was embarrassing enough, but when I got inside the women's section, which had twelve holes—six back to back with a partition between them, but none between the six on either side—two ladies were squatting next to each other in a most friendly fashion. I went to the back. No one was there, but in an instant I was joined. When I told Jack I had been in there with two Chinese women, two Tibetan women, and a hen that walked all around, he shook my hand and congratulated me. I have arrived at a certain stage in this culture.

Last night we heard what we thought were several loud cracks of thunder, but this morning we learned it was blasting in a mine nearby. It caused a landslide just across the bridge from the center of town, which had to be cleared away.

Today we had only six vehicles in our caravan. The police in the front jeep wave red flags from both sides at all approaching trucks, jeeps, and wagons, which then pull over to the side of the road and wait for our group to pass. We drove on a very narrow road on the other side of the Dadu River, which is called Dajinchuan up here. There are logs in the river, some floating with the current, many more hung up and stuck on rocks. I can't believe this is a sensible way of getting wood out. By the time the spring rains and melting snow raise the water level so they can float again, most logs are banged up and waterlogged (I never realized that is where the expression came from).

All through the first long valley there are big beacon towers on the highest ground at strategic points, some still in good condition. For hundreds of years, until not too long ago, men watched from them for enemies, then, by lighting fires, sent signals to the next tower, telling that tribe to prepare to defend their territory.

We are still in a Tibetan autonomous prefecture. The houses look more substantial than yesterday, often three or four stories high. The stories above have brightly colored and decorated windows and an open place under the roof for drying and storing meat, vegetables, and wood. All houses are made of stone; some are plastered over and have fancy curves on the roof. The country is primarily grazing land, but areas that can be used for vegetables and grain seem to be planted. Occasionally, walls are made of mud or dung.

At 11:30 we stopped at Dajinchuan, a town with the same name as the river, and had light refreshments—tea or an orange drink; hard-boiled eggs, a sort of Cracker Jack popcorn square. The head of the county and his deputy answered Harrison's questions, though they said they had not been planning on an interview.

The county has 70,000 inhabitants, the town 20,000. There are 39,000 Hans, close to 29,000 Tibetans, and 200 Qiang. Bais and Miaos have married into the community as well. Pears account for one-third of their income. The rest is forestry, apples, peaches, pomegranates, and oranges. They also have good crops of wheat, corn, beans, winter wheat, and barley. It's too high for rice. They plant corn after wheat, which is planted in the fall. In the lower areas they get two crops a year. The peasants are making money with this new "responsibility" system. People in the rural areas now make as much as 290 yuan a year, where they formerly made around 40 to 50. Ninety-five percent of the villages have electricity. Infant mortality is higher among Tibetans than among Hans. According to the latest census, there are 4.5 people in each household.

As we are scheduled to be here for three nights and two days, I decided it would be wise to expect the worst. But it turned out differently. There are two suites in this guest house with real bathrooms, and we and Jack have them. The only flaw is that a pathetic-looking sheep is tied to a post right under our window. She has been given a few greens, which she hasn't eaten. It is clear she will be slaughtered—probably for us—and I can't bear it. She has been baaing ever since we got here, obviously is lonely and frightened. If she is to be killed, why can't she be left where she's comfortable until the last minute? I would love to be able to do something for her, but what? The Chinese must think animals have no feelings. The other night I was watching TV and there was a program about getting rid of dogs with rabies. One dog was clubbed to death and thrown into a pit. The other had a rope around his neck and a man swung him around until he died. I didn't watch anymore. Why don't they shoot them? I don't believe they have so much rabies. I think it's an excuse to get rid of dogs.

After supper, when Harrison went directly to his typewriter, I took a short stroll with Jack, and a security man was right behind us the whole time. Jack tries to get out for a walk before breakfast every morning, and almost always someone spots him and either joins him or follows a little behind. Some mornings he can't get out of the guest-house gates, which are locked up tight. One morning in the hotel in Chengdu, it was raining, so he walked around the hotel and came upon some Buddhist monks chanting their prayers. We surmise they were guests in the hotel.

FRIDAY, MAY 25
Maerkang

Right after breakfast Jack took off for Xiaojin in the other Toyota bus with Mr. Wang (one of the two vanguards who made arrangements for our trip in this province), a doctor, and two other people; and another bus went along, with five men, police, security people, and officials from the county. They will visit the place Mao and Zhang Guotao met, and other places where they had meetings and discussions in June 1935.

After saying good-bye to Jack we went to the local museum and looked at still another exhibit of the Long March. There are pictures here we haven't seen before, of mountains and the countryside, that give us a better feeling of what it was like in 1935. In the museum office where we met with local experts, a huge round electric burner, usually used for boiling big kettles of water, was burning, for heat in the cold damp room. Harrison is still trying to find out more about Zhang Guotao and his Fourth Front Army. Before he and Mao met, not far from here, he had been in control of a large area for about nine months, calling it the Northwest Confederation. There his eighty-thousand men were well fed, but when they came here it was different. The population of this place is now eighteen thousand; in 1958 it was fifteen hundred, in 1935, less than that. There were only a few houses and monasteries, so we don't understand what the Fourth Army ate. The local people had scarcely enough for themselves, and the Red Army quickly ran out of food.

After the initial meeting at Fubian, there were more discussions and changes. Zhang Guotao was made political commissar instead of Zhou Enlai; Zhu De was commander-in-chief, and Mao the leader of all. It is not clear to me why Zhang Guotao got Zhou Enlai's job, or what position Zhou Enlai then had (chief of staff?). The politics—the in-fighting, the disagreements, the intrigue, the headmen being displaced or promoted or passed over—is so complicated I don't know if I will ever get it straightened out. Harrison says not to worry: "No one has it all straight." And I must say we hear varying versions of the same events everywhere we go.

Harrison asked how the army treated the lamaseries. The answer was what we have been told before, that the troops were instructed *not* to interfere with the religious practices of the people. The lamas ran away at the approach of the Red Army, and the soldiers stayed in the lamaseries but were not allowed to touch anything. However, after a while, when food became scarce, discipline was relaxed and they did help themselves to what they could. So the fine intentions didn't always last.

This was an opium-producing area, and right where we were sitting there was a market for exchanging opium with traders and caravans in return for grain, clothes, fabric, money. Opium was harvested in September, so the trading market took place in the fall.

The Red Army also used opium as money for trade. They confiscated it from landlords. In some instances they could only recruit addicts, so they took them on and gradually cured them of the habit. The soldiers were forbidden to use it, and I have never heard any tale of even one soldier taking opium. An elderly Chinese doctor who was brought in by the Fourth Front Army had the habit, but he was such a good doctor they supplied his needs.

I asked if the lamas used it, and this caused about a five-minute talk among the Chinese. They said it was a difficult question. It was forbidden by the lamas' religion, but who knows? Their life was prayer, but they were landowners; they grew opium. Maybe they took some in their back chambers.

Old people around here remember Zhang Guotao as a tall, white, fat man with a big scar on his face. He cursed a lot and was very violent. Sometimes, right in the midst of meetings, people were dragged out and executed. Perhaps they were "offenders in the Fourth Army," the museum experts suggested.

Before Liberation, as in 1935, there were just a few houses and lamaseries in this area. In 1953 the Tibetan self-autonomous region was established.

A lot of things are going on here, including an enormous amount of building—new apartments every inch. There is a printing plant that prints books, textbooks, notebooks; a prefectural newspaper put out by another press three times a week, in Tibetan and Chinese. A food-processing plant, a drug factory, a match factory, an agricultural-machine factory, and, some distance away, a factory where wooden shoe trees are made. Timber is big business and there are two truck transport companies, one belonging to the county, the other independent. The factories are small, probably employing one thousand industrial workers in all (Harrison, for some reason, thinks it's nearer five hundred). Government workers number three thousand, including hospital personnel. Others are service people, salesmen, clerks, etc. There are army barracks nearby, which we know because yesterday when we were driving by the gate, a young soldier driving a jeep came rushing out, never looking to see if anyone was coming, and we nearly had a big smash-up. Our driver kept his head and swerved to the right and we missed by about an inch. I thought Italians made a lot of angry noise at accidents, or near-accidents, but I have never heard such a commotion as our companions made. Zhang and the driver jumped out of our car; the security people ahead backed up and got out; the General got out, and the sight of him shut the soldier-driver up immediately. In the end, even mild Mr. Wang was yelling. The army guy will get a good dressing-down (he's already had one) and may lose his license for three months.

Maerkang is one of the off-limits-to-foreigners places we have seen that seem very much on the go.

When we got back to the guest house, Harrison said, "You were right; the sheep has gone, and there are signs of slaughtering." Blood was all over the ground and on the wood-slat bench that people sit on—which folds down flat to make a platform for killing. I have seen pigs being butchered on them. Poor little thing. She cried all night, and then this. I know I eat meat, and I like it, but I can't eat an animal I have felt for or identified with. We have been told we are to have a Tibetan meal of mutton tonight. Not for me.

Looking across at a balcony on the nearby apartment house, I saw clothespins holding clothes on the line, the first I have ever seen in China. Clothes and other laundry are simply hung over the line or stretched on poles through the sleeves. A huge bird that looks like an eagle is hanging outside a window, obviously aging. But it is right in the sun and must be getting awfully smelly.

In the afternoon we drove six kilometers to Zhuokeji. Where two small rivers meet is the most magnificent house we have seen, though it is crumbling fast. It was one of several residences, or yamen, of a chieftain who used it when he was traveling. It is a five-story structure with a beacon tower standing high on a rocky mount—stone on the outside, wood within. Balconies run around the upper floors. (After we got home, Harrison found some reminiscences of Red Army soldiers that described this house at the time the Red Army arrived: *Columns lacquered in red, green, and black; wood carving and enamel with precious stones. Tapestries and scrolls hung on the walls, and rooms were furnished with silken couches, teak beds, and tables inlaid with mother-of-pearl. There was a library of Tibetan and Chinese classics and the only glass windows for hundreds of miles in all directions.*)

On the ground floor were the kitchens and stoves. Security people and traders stayed there. On the second lived servants, troops, guards, and others who worked for the family. The family lived in comfort and luxury on the third, and visiting lamas on the fourth. Just above the balconies were two odd-shaped rooms under the peaked roof, where prayers were held. Animals lived under it all, with a door opening from the outer walls, not into the courtyard. An enclosed small room, more like a balcony, is stuck on the outside of the house on the family's floor. A chute runs from it down to a walled-in space on the ground level. This was a toilet. We see these protuberances on all the more substantial old houses in this area.

Some of the lovely woodwork on the balconies and doors remains, but most has been taken, probably to burn. All the paint and decoration have gone. One family lives on the bottom floor but is moving out soon, and then what is still left will be vandalized if nothing is done. Chickens and pigs wander around the splendid courtyard at will, and birds are nesting in the upper stories.

The General feels the way we do, that such an extraordinary building should be preserved and restored. When the Red Army came, the chieftain fled, and, since it was the most luxurious house around, Mao stayed in it for a few days. So perhaps that would be an incentive to save it. Clearly, the people here don't have any appreciation of what a gem they have, and they have no money for this type of project. It would have to be funded by some group in Beijing. We are going to write to everyone we can think of who could help.

We visited a Tibetan peasant family who live close by. Their house is large and well built and they have an income of 4,000 yuan a year, unheard of until recently, and probably several times as much as most government workers earn. This disparity is bound to cause trouble. Someone told us that the peasants are making so much money they don't know what to do with it after buying bicycles, TVs, radios, clocks, tractors (which don't always work everywhere). He said a favorite story is of two peasants who came to Beijing with their pockets full of money and went to Maxim's for lunch. They spent 180 yuan. That used to be three months' salary for Foreign Ministry workers. There are many stories of peasants buying airplanes, buying expensive cars and going into the taxi business, making the most of the responsibility system.

At supper a big covered (thank goodness) dish of meat and bones was on our table. We didn't eat it. I think chicken will be the extent of my meat eating from now on.

SATURDAY, MAY 26
Maerkang

Today was very relaxing. Went shopping and bought a few Tibetan items—two money belts, sashes, and a headdress. One man in our group bought a pressure cooker just like one I have at home. The sun was hot and it was lovely out, so we headed toward the river for a little walk.

Immediately a lady was sent to accompany us, and a security man walked behind. The lady led us to another store, where downstairs were tools, light bulbs, nails, and radios; and upstairs nothing but shoes, men's and women's, and a few toilet articles. A small special room had wool for knitting, some shirts and jackets.

Jack came back earlier than we had expected—just after lunch. He brought me a big bunch of rhododendron and no one had a "flower bottle" (as they refer to a vase) big enough, so I put them in a cuspidor, which was just right. I showed it to the women in the office on our floor to point out that I was doing what Chairman Mao had taught—"to make do" with what you have, to "innovate." They laughed.

At 5:30 we had dinner with two Tibetan officials from this prefecture. They wear real Tibetan clothes—a medium-length coat, like a Mongolian *dal* or Chinese coat, over shirt and trousers, with boots and a big felt hat. One kept his hat on during dinner. The other, our host, is thirty-five, and so handsome I could hardly believe it. They have nothing to do with Lhasa and Tibet, they said, but think the Dalai Lama should come back. They aren't believers, but their parents once were. They said the policy is that when a boy reaches the age of eighteen, he can decide for himself if he wants to be a monk. Parents can't send them, or the lamasery take them, without their choosing to go. But the other day, at the lamasery near Danba where the Chinese princess stopped on her way to Tibet to marry the king, we saw thirty or more lamas chanting and praying in the adjoining temple, and among them were several boys who looked no more than ten or twelve.

Dinner was genial—just the two Tibetans, Jack, us, Zhang, the General, Mr. Guo, and two local officials. One of the latter is happy that he is going back to Chengdu after twenty years here. The rest of our group was celebrating noisily in the other room, and the General kept going out to make toasts with them. They made a lot to me and I was very touched. The General said he was going to tell his wife she should "learn from me," as Mao used to say, "Learn from the West."

At dinner our host spat his fish, and other bones, into the hot towel that is almost always passed to each person as we sit down at the table. Generally, they are taken away after everyone has wiped his face and hands, but tonight they were left on the table. When our host wanted to wipe his hands again, he just shook the bones out on the floor behind his chair. More delicate than spitting them all out on the tablecloth, which is quite acceptable.

The menu was translated literally from the Chinese. There were eighteen dishes, plus two beautiful platters of hors d'eouvres. On the first platter a big bird was carved out of a huge white turnip, with greens surrounding it and little birds and flowers in the green leaves. The menu read:

125

1. Double Phoenixes Play with Peony
2. Golden Hooks [shrimps] Hung on Jade Plate lettuce
3. Oxtail bamboo shoot cooked in soy sauce
4. Roast fresh Pork sweetened
5. Cold sliced chicken in pepper oil
6. Buddha's Hand like vegetable rolls
7. Shreds twining kidney beans
8. Spare ribs stuffed with scallion stalks
9. Soup of Gorge Pearl Meatballs
10. Hundreds of birds court Phoenix
11. Fish fragrant Pork Fillet
12. Duck squares with crisp walnut
13. Phoenix-tailed Lettuce Soup
14. Five Willow Fish
15. Steamed Fritillary chicken
16. Boiled beef
17. Three colored silver tree-ear
18. Pepper spiced sauté meat flowers
19. Sichuan Noodle with Pepper Sauce
20. Egg white snow maches potato

Some of these names make sense, some don't. Tree ears are mush-rooms and there are several kinds in varying colors. We still can't figure out what "fritillary chicken" is. Beans wrapped up in onion or chive strips, and the noodles, were delicious. Tiny asparagus was cut in pieces for one of the cold dishes, but we can't guess which one it was from the menu.

After dinner we watched a too-long movie: about northern Sichuan. Tomorrow we are off again and will probably be uncomfortable for the next ten days.

SUNDAY, MAY 27
Hongyuan, Altitude 11,550 Feet

This morning we said good-bye to some of our Sichuan friends and left in only three vehicles. Mr. Guo, Mr. Wang, the two drivers, and the doctor who joined us at Chengdu are still with us. A lady doctor from Shanghai has been added to our entourage, plus a girl who is her assistant. It is comforting to have them, but it is clear to me Harrison is all right now. He looks well and seems absolutely normal, and is being sensible. We are high up here, 11,500 feet, so we just do everything slowly.

Leaving Maerkang we followed the upper Dadu River and its tributaries. Part of the First Army took this route; the rest traveled a bit to the east. There were no boundaries in those days; it was just territory occupied mostly by Tibetans. This county was created in 1962 and encompasses eight thousand square kilometers. Today it has 27,000 people and 500,000 animals. Seventy percent of the population is Tibetan; there are 200 Hui, 150 Qiang, and the rest is Han. In 1935 there were no roads, no people, no food. The weather can change from warm sun to a blizzard in minutes, and the Chinese are nervous about high altitudes. No wonder the soldiers were terrified, miserable, and sick all the time.

Potatoes are blooming in the vegetable fields and people were weeding with short-handled hoes. We are told that in summer the Grasslands are a magic carpet of flowers. Now it is too early, but on the mountainsides are cascades of rhododendron, and blue and yellow flowers grow on the stony hills. Elderberry bushes remind us of home more than anything. They smell just as delicious here but are smaller than ours.

Yak and sheep graze in the huge plains and the peaks of the Snowy Mountains are visible. They seem to reach halfway around the sky. Occasionally we saw a yak with a saddle. Walls around pastures are made of dung, and prayer flags wave on shrines at intervals along the road.

We stopped at a Tibetan village to have a picnic lunch that had been brought with us. The sun was hot, the way it is in Colorado Springs in the middle of the day, and we were shown into a dark, cold room with a stove that didn't give out much heat. Tables and chairs were being brought in, and I said to Jack that I was going to sit outdoors. He told our hosts, whereupon the furniture that had just been carried in was carried out, plus four wicker settees, and everyone had a lovely lunch in the glorious air. We had meat slices in a huge bun, eggs, all kinds of drinks including beer, Laoshan water, pop, fruit juice, and the canned oranges Harrison likes so much. But the best part of lunch was the yogurt that the Tibetans make out of yak milk. It has more body than ours, and they pour their wonderful coarse-grained sugar on it and eat it by the quart.

I am relieved that in this Tibetan country we haven't been offered a whole lamb, or the head, or the eyes. The food has been good, with lots of vegetables. After supper we watched two endless movies showing everything from dancing girls to yak and sheep breeding to medical experiments on rabbits—all the great achievements of Sichuan Province.

MONDAY, MAY 28
Nuoergai

We left Hongyuan and drove through country that is so much like Mongolia I felt as if I were there. The same wide plateaux surrounded by rounded green high hills. But, unlike Mongolia, almost everywhere we looked, there were snow-capped mountains in the background, sometimes covered with clouds.

We have been in Tibetan country for six days. About seven hundred years ago, when the Tibetans began moving in here, it belonged to China. During the centuries, first China was strong, then Tibet. At this time China was weak. In the Qing Dynasty, when China was the stronger, about half of the Tibetan area was incorporated into China. But except for levying a few taxes, the Chinese let Tibetan chiefs continue to run things, and after Liberation they were still left alone. The way of life continued to be primarily Tibetan until the Cultural Revolution, when all hell broke out. Animals were slaughtered; agriculture was changed with no thought of the climate; lamaseries destroyed, lamas killed. Since the end of that terrible period there has been a gradual return to a way of life that recognizes what the Tibetans have always known—that yak and sheep and horses can live in this altitude, that it is more suited to animal husbandry than farming, that rice will not grow, that barley will, and so on. Also, there seems to be some freedom of religious belief. That has always been in the Chinese Communist constitution, but not always honored.

There are prayer flags everywhere, around the herdsmen's tents, at small shrines near rivers, and all over the hills.

To make a courtesy call, we stopped at a lamasery that is close to where the White River, which flows through the Grasslands, meets the Yellow River. We were greeted with dusty cheesecloth scarves by about forty-five lamas. Most of them looked old and bent-over and filthy. Inside we sat on the floor and drank, or pretended to drink, hot butter tea. The smell from unwashed bodies and clothes and butter lamps was worse than any of the other ghastly smells in this country. I don't remember any monastery in Sikkim smelling like this. As was the case in the lamasery we visited the other day, boys who look younger than eighteen were among the lamas. Someone did say that if, by chance, a family has more than two or three children, extra boys can go to the lamasery at an early age.

We walked to where the rivers meet. It is not very impressive. Both rivers were still, almost like ponds. When we started out this morning it was clear and bright and the sun felt hot. But suddenly it changed; the sky grew dark, rain began to fall, the wind blew wildly, the rain turned to sleet. As quickly, it changed again—first sun, then storms; and while we stood on the easy sloping bank looking at the rivers meeting, it began to snow. So we have had a taste of the weather the Red Army encountered. This is the end of May; there are only five frost-free days in the year, in July, so it can snow every month at any time.

The two Tibetan prefects who met us at the border of this county were waiting for us when we stopped for lunch. One is handsome, as many

128

Tibetan men are, and wore a wonderful sheepskin-lined coat. We talked and drank tea before being led by a beautiful, tall Tibetan girl who wore red leather shoes with three-inch heels, to a square stone-and-mortar room that usually serves as a stall for animals. Here we had our meal. We had that wonderful yogurt again. Harrison has always hated yogurt, but he loves this.

Nuoergai is pretty much an outpost town. Most Tibetans live on the range in tents and tend their herds. They come into town on horses, leading yaks, to get supplies and food. We thought our accommodations would be terrible, but once again we are pleasantly surprised. We have two rooms and two big beds; two electric heaters to take the chill off; two washstands, five basins, three spittoons, one sofa, four armchairs, four folding chairs with mat seats, rugs in both rooms, and an enormous amount of drinks. Several kinds of wine, Laoshan water, beer, two thermos bottles, cups, glasses, and a kettle so we can boil water ourselves.

We had a feast of a supper in the most awful place. We crossed the courtyard to another building and walked through a long, dark, dank corridor with rooms on each side. People who work in this guest house, and nearby, live here. All the doors are locked up tight with big padlocks. I have never seen so many locks and bolts on every door, car, window, gate. At the end of the corridor a room was made into a dining room, with a curtain down the middle, we three on one side, our Chinese companions on the other. An electric heater burned here, too. We were told the other day that electricity here costs one-tenth of what it does in Beijing.

TUESDAY, MAY 29
Nuoergai

We have had a very pleasant stay here, and very comfortable. This morning we went to Baxi, where Mao had his last argument with the Fourth Army and then went on his way. The local historian accompanied us and told us that Nuoergai has a factory for making sausage casings, another for leather and fur garments, and a small power plant. He showed us a small group of buildings out on the plain and said that was the old village. It was moved to its present site because it is closer to the lamasery. They use the buildings for shelter now. They have peat, coal, wood, and dried dung for fuel. I couldn't understand how there can be any wood, thought it must come from far away, when all of a sudden we left the grassy plateau, drove up a not-very-high hill, and there on the other side were big evergreens and an extensive forest. This is the watershed of the Yellow and Yangtze Rivers, and it is hilly and green. In the Cultural Revolution trees were cut haphazardly and people just took what they wanted. Now the government has a scientific program, but it will take a long time to make up for the damage. There are still a few big old trees ready to be cut, and there are huge logs in the courtyard here.

A local historian says that Tibetans in this county have been here for twelve hundred to two thousand years. They have lived a nomadic life, which the Chinese don't understand at all. They bury their dead by putting the body in the river and letting the fish and birds take care of it. We went by a flat place with prayer flags all around it, next to the river, where they have this special ceremony. They also do what the Tibetans in Tibet do—chop up the corpse and let animals and birds eat it. And they use coffins and regular burial in the ground when there is enough wood. Mothers carry their babies inside all their strange wrapped garments. Sometimes the baby is upside down, the head hanging out, and usually they are naked.

Harrison and I didn't walk up to the remains of the temple from which Mao made his speech to some detachments of the Fourth Army about going north. It was too steep and there is nothing to see. The Red Guards wrecked the temple, not realizing Mao had been there. He told the soldiers they could do whatever they chose—come north with him, or go south with Zhu De and Zhang Guotao and the rest of the Fourth Army. They chose to go back, but as we know, the Fourth Army suffered defeats and losses and ended up in Shaanxi one year after Mao.

Mr. Wang was told to stay with us, and he suggested we look under the little bridge in the valley below the temple, where we waited for the others. A yak's head was hanging there, about two feet above the water. The Tibetans believe that a water-ox god lives in this river (they are not in all rivers) and that if enough attention is not paid to him, he will make trouble for the bridge. It could be washed away in spring floods, for instance. So a yak is sacrificed and his head hung under the bridge.

The flowers are lovely and it is hard to imagine how they could be more profuse or beautiful. There is a tiny, very dark purple ground cover; a light blue one that resembles a small orchid; a heavenly thorny bush with pink flowers; a yellow shrub just about to burst into bloom; and everlasting, just like ours.

On the way back we stopped at Banyou, where the Red Army set up their headquarters and Mao stayed nearby. Most troops went over to Baxi because it was a village with houses where they could stay. We saw the yellow willow trees (the only kind that can grow in this altitude) at the site of the headquarters. Here and there were huge piles of yak dung that has been dried in flat sheets. It is used for fuel and for building houses and walls. Lots of dogs, big ferocious animals who must be watchdogs. People came out of their flimsy houses or tents to see the strange pale visitors, and children surrounded us.

The smell was terrible; they must never take their clothes off or wash.

But I don't blame them. It's too cold most of the time to undress. The county magistrate describes the climate as "an extended winter."

But the children are appealing, curious and friendly. There is a school for the first and second grades, which all children have to attend. After that, they have to go into the town if they want to continue school, and hardly any do. They would have to ride the distance, and besides, even the smallest children help with all the work and take care of the babies, of whom there seem to be many, certainly more than the two supposedly allowed minority families.

There are hundreds of prayer flags and obviously the lama religion is thriving. Most people here are believers; 80 to 90 percent turn out for religious holidays. Jack got a letter stamped at the Baxi post office. In the days of the Long March there was no mail service here.

In the afternoon we visited the local museum. No matter that the exhibits are limited and just like what we have seen in other museums; it is quite wonderful to have a museum in an out-of-the-way place like this. At the library they claim to subscribe to several hundred newspapers and periodicals, and there are two rooms with tables and chairs where people can come and read. We wondered about that—the magazines looked as if they had never been touched.

At dinner we said farewell to Mr. Guo, Mr. Wang, and the drivers from Chengdu, and hello to the people from Gansu, the new province we will be in tomorrow. They had driven over the provincial border to meet us, which is an unusual gesture. Miss Zhou, who was with us in Langzhou four years ago, is head of the Gansu group. At first we didn't recognize her because now she has curly hair. But she is still the same serious young woman. Though the Chengdu people will remain with us until Thursday, this is the official, and social, good-bye.

There were millions of courses and toasts, and I made some tonight. To the doctors; to Mr. Guo, who has taken such wonderful care of us "in sickness and in health"; to Mr. Wang, who was responsible for the comforts along the way; to the driver, Mr. Ho, who drove me back and forth to the hospital in Chengdu; to our other driver, Mr. Li. Jack made one to Mr. Wang and said Mao had crossed the Grasslands once, General Qin twice; the Fourth Army three times; but Mr. Wang will have crossed them four times after he leaves us.

WEDNESDAY, MAY 30
Diebu

It was raining and cold when we left Nuoergai at 8:15, but not frosty, as it was yesterday. We have six buses and jeeps now that the Gansu group has joined us. We drove through the biggest pasture in the county—about

131

sixteen hundred acres. Even in the mist, perhaps because of it, it seems to go on forever. Ditches are being dug in the wettest of the Grasslands to drain them and make smooth pastures. When the Red Army crossed here, a lot of the Grasslands were like the worst today—clumps of grass in water. They had to jump from clump to clump, and trying to find a place big and dry enough to camp was just about impossible. There are, and always were, some big plains that are not this wet, but if you aren't familiar with the country, you don't know which way to go. It does seem that Mao didn't take time to find out which was the best route. Harrison thinks he was in a hurry to get away from Zhang Guotao. He did have Tibetan guides, but evidently they looked ahead across the plains and simply went in a straight line. No wonder it was the worst time for many of the soldiers—no villages, no people, no animals, nothing to eat, wet and cold. The only person who seemed to make the best of a bad scene was He Long, who caught fish in the marshy ponds.

Between November and May animals are in the winter pastures. Today many were being driven in the same direction we were traveling, northeast, to the summer grazing lands. Two herdsmen were riding behind hundreds of yak, each holding a big umbrella in one hand and the reins in the other. The number of animals is not increasing here, but pastures are being improved by seeding. Some fodder is grown, primarily for young stock. Barley is the mainstay of the Tibetan diet, along with yak meat and milk products. A lot of meat is sold—two million pounds a year. Slaughtering is done in the fall; there is a cold-storage warehouse.

I saw a man getting up on a yak's back and I noticed that he had the yak's head pulled all the way around to the side. A rope is put through the nose, same as a ring in a bull's nose, and a halter is attached to it. So the yak couldn't really move until the man got on and released his head.

Fences surround areas where fodder is planted, where winter food is stored, and where young animals are kept. They are about three feet high and often made of dung. Later we saw some made of stones. We wondered why dung walls don't get damaged by high winds. Possibly it is because they are not high. They look quite nice when, after a while, grass and flowers grow on them.

Just before 10:00 we came upon forty or more riders with our handsome county magistrate-host at the head of them. He led a guard of honor to welcome us and escort us to the great spectacle we were to see. It was pouring rain so we didn't get out, but stopped to say hello and recognize the honor guard. When our bus started up, with shrill cries and whoops, the horsemen galloped along beside us. As we slowly made our way, more groups of riders met us with the same cries, and rode on either side of the road until we had nearly one hundred riding escorts.

We turned into a big flat field and were greeted by a crowd of men, women, and children, dressed in heavy felt and fur or sheepskin-lined clothes and boots, lined up on each side of a tent, clapping a welcome. We were presented with white scarves (clean this time, not like the lamas') and went inside the tent. The top was made of flowered material; it looked like what we see on fancy umbrellas and awnings on patios and terraces at home. Rugs were spread on the ground; Jack, Harrison, and I sat at the end opposite the entrance, and everyone else along both sides. On a table in the middle were samples of Tibetan food: four big bowls of barley, barley flour, and two other kinds of flour, hunks of cheese and butter made from one hundred pounds of milk. We were given tea and yogurt. We have not been offered that rancid butter tea, thank goodness, nor traditional fatty mutton dishes. Harrison thinks that someone passed along the word that we don't like them. Whatever the reason, it is a relief.

In the freezing rain we stood and watched some horse races. First three men raced against each other, then two girls, followed by two young boys. They raced down to a mark, turned around, and raced back. We gave our scarves to the winners, tied them around their necks. It is nice to see handsome horses. These are bigger than Mongolian horses and have beautiful silver-studded bridles, good leather saddles, and gorgeous saddle blankets.

We didn't stay for more refreshments but started off again on our way. Almost immediately we came into very different country. We began climbing up between two mountains, got to the top, and all of a sudden the hills were made of stone. There were only a few scrubby trees. The pass is 11,550 feet high. We have been so high up for so long that I am used to it and don't need a pill to sleep anymore.

We went down into a small valley and soon came upon cultivated fields, lots of pigs and a few cows. I saw only one yak. Women were working in the fields of wheat or barley. They are farming Tibetans as opposed to herding Tibetans. They don't have grazing animals which have to be moved from pasture to pasture; they live in their villages all year round. Their houses look flimsy and cold, are made of wood with strange wood fences and big pole structures for drying meat and skins and anything else that needs to be dried. We saw several lamaseries that seem to be active, and a brick factory, though most walls were made of mud.

We said good-bye to our handsome prefect, who somehow had gotten to the county line before we did, and to the blue-hatted policemen who had led us through so many bad spots on the road.

We have a feeling these Tibetans have some direct contact and relationship with Tibet, while those in Maerkang don't.

The others in the bus have made a rule that Jack can stop only a few times a day to take pictures, not every five minutes, as he would prefer. So he has to work the rest of his picture-taking into stops for other reasons. Often someone in the caravan needs a comfort stop, Harrison wants to take a picture, or I want to look at a flower. At one point today I needed a comfort stop, but there was no place, nothing but the road, steep, bare sides, and rocks. At last we came to a shrubby area and I said I had to stop. The driver slammed on the brakes, all the doors of the four cars behind us flew open, and everyone jumped out for the same reason. When we got back in our bus, Zhang said, "Everyone is grateful to you; no one else dared to say he would like to stop." One advantage of living this long; I dare to say when I have to go to the toilet.

Along the White Dragon River, which we followed, were several little mills for grinding grain and a power station. The flowers and shrubs continued to look familiar.

We arrived here at Diebu around 2:00 and Jack and Harrison and I had hard-boiled eggs and noodles sitting at a tiny low table in tiny chairs in our living room. They were like doll's furniture. At 3:00 we met with two Red Army veterans. The first is sixty-eight, has no teeth, and was fairly credible. He had never heard of the Red Army until it came through his village in Yunnan Province. It stayed only two days; he joined and went with them. He was in a scout group in the First Army, so they had provisions. He is the first person who has said he had no trouble going over the Snowy Mountains. He fought in many battles, day and night. His hands were injured going over the Luding Bridge. After crossing the Grasslands he was shot in the thigh and was left with a Tibetan peasant family. They took care of him. The Kuomintang did not come; a Tibetan chieftain ruled the area. He stayed here for two years, now lives in Maya.

The other man wasn't as easy to believe. He came from a poor peasant family in Yilong County, where Zhu De was born. He said he wanted to join the Red Army when he was twelve but was told he couldn't because he wasn't even as tall as a rifle. He obviously went along with some troops, was wounded in 1936, first put on a stretcher, then into a group that took care of sick, wounded, and stragglers. He was carried across the Grasslands. He said orders came to leave all sick and wounded behind, and with about one hundred other soldiers, he stayed. He had no answers to questions about whether they had money or anyone to help them, and we all felt he must have been a deserter, of which there were quite a few. In 1934 the Red Army was disciplined; there were no stragglers or deserters. One year later some soldiers were weak, sick, undisciplined, and there were many stragglers.

They told us what we have heard before—that villagers ran away when they heard the Red Army was coming, and hid or buried their woks and other belongings. When they returned, they found everything cleaned and shined and the courtyards swept. The soldiers used what they found, and left things in better condition than when they found them.

We had dinner cooked by a Chinese cook who had worked in the Chinese embassy in Pakistan. Mr. Zhang kept getting up from our table to help with toasts at the other table. Every time he sat down again he hit the leg of the table and the maotai and other glasses tipped over. Someone said the god of liquor would be angry with him, and I said I thought the liquor salesman would be pleased. The General liked that crack.

THURSDAY, MAY 31
Minxian, Gansu Province

Left Diebu around 8:00 after an affectionate good-bye to Mr. Guo, Mr. Wang, and our driver, Mr. Li. We again drove along the White Dragon River, which in Chinese is Bailong.

There is a lot of reforestation in this valley and many signs saying *Protect the trees*. The area is under the jurisdiction of the government. The purple-pink shrub I thought was a rose is definitely a rose and Miss Zhou says it grows only in this valley. A purple flower like our fireweed, only smaller, is everywhere, as is a bush that resembles bridal wreath. Important crops are apples and pears; vegetables are grown under plastic, and seedling trees are protected by straw matting held up by posts, something like Tibetan tents.

On the river is a plywood factory and a big power station with a long spillway. Under a wooden bridge we saw three heads hung to mollify the water-ox god; one was a goat. Lots of live goats, pigs, and dogs.

The Bala River, which we saw yesterday at Baxi, flows from the Grasslands and joins the Bailong at Nine Dragon Gorge, a long, narrow cut in the mountains. Some of the Red Army followed the river, and again we wonder why Mao took such a difficult route. The reason usually given is that he was trying to escape the Kuomintang. Most of this land was controlled by a Tibetan chieftain named Yang and he let the Red Army go through, even gave them food. We were told there were only two instances of trouble in his land; one soldier's rifle was snatched, and a sniper shot at them.

The Yang family has been around for twenty generations. During the Ming Dynasty the chief of this area went to kowtow to the emperor and take him gifts. The emperor gave him the name Yang, which was considered a big honor. The present Yang's father was the chieftain who let the Red Army go through his territory. He was assassinated by the Kuomintang. The Kuomintang wanted to keep his son on their side, so they made him a general even though he was only seventeen years old. But he went over to the Communists and is now vice chairman of the People's Provincial Congress. He lives in Lanzhou.

135

On the sides of the gorges there are narrow paths cut out of the rocks—scarcely room for a man—and on some, what are called "cliff bridges" were added. Wooden poles were driven into the cliffs and a few logs laid across to extend the path. There was room for a man and a horse, no more. Men were supposed to blow a bugle as they were walking on these cliff bridges, and if they didn't, a man coming the other way had the right to throw the man and his horse into the river.

At the end of the first great valley we began to see lifesize (or bigger) menacing figures made of straw or wood, placed at the entrances or gates of villages. They had real swords at their sides. Formerly these were to keep out demons and dragons; now they mean, "Don't come into our village if you have a contagious disease."

Before noon we got to the Lazikou (*kou* means "pass"), where there was a fierce battle between the Red Army and the Kuomintang. On a flat place about a quarter of a mile from the pass, Mao had his headquarters, and from there he directed the attack to take the pass so they could continue north. On the very spot where he plotted the strategy stood a big tent. It was flowery inside, just like the one yesterday. We walked down the road to the pass, so narrow one could almost jump across, and both sides too steep and rocky to climb. The Kuomintang held both slopes. At first the Red Army tried to scale one side. But it was impossible. With some Miao soldiers, a detachment went back and circled up behind the enemy and took the first top. When the Kuomintang soldiers on the other side saw what had happened, they fled. From then on the Red Army had primarily nature (and themselves) to struggle with until they reached the remarkable valley we arrived at this afternoon, where they could talk to the people in their own Chinese language and found plenty of food. As one man said, "Gansu Province was like a gas station for the Red Army. They were recharged."

After we had inspected the pass and wondered how it had ever been taken against such odds, we went back to the tent and had eggs, meat, cheese, fruit, beer, and tea. During lunch Tibetan women danced for us—the clumsy shuffling step we first saw in Sikkim. They simply stand in a circle and move to one side slowly. Every once in a while everyone jumps straight up, then they resume shuffling to one side.

After lunch we continued our drive and at first drove over a mountain pass at eleven thousand feet. The country soon became very different from what we've been in—dry, treeless mountains where reforestation efforts scarcely show, with remarkable lush valleys below. The rivers in the valleys were muddy from soil runoff.

The road was filled with carts piled high with small pieces of wood, saplings, and shrubs. The mountains are so bare it seems terrible to cut anything off them. But there is no real wood, no coal, nothing else to burn for cooking and heat. I don't know where they find even the poor stuff we saw. It must grow in the eroded canyons between the mountains.

Some of the carts were big straw baskets on wheels. They are open at the back end, look something like covered wagons. It's the first time we've seen them. Most are pulled by donkeys, some by yak, horse, or mule, and a fair number by men. Going up to the high pass, we saw a man sleeping on a blanket beside the road and another sitting, with his head on his knees, sound alseep in the middle. There are always children and animals in the road and I don't understand why nothing or no one is run into and killed. Perhaps they are and we just haven't seen any. A pretty tree with red feathery flowers grows in the valleys.

We noticed that as soon as we crossed into Gansu Province there were few, if any, prayer flags, though for quite a distance the population is primarily farming Tibetans. We asked if there is a different provincial policy and the answer was no. But there must be. The villages here are the same higgledy-piggledy collection of houses, fences, and general confusion as other Tibetan villages, and the absence of flags waving on everything is sudden and striking.

We stopped at Hadapu, a town with a population of six thousand, and six thousand must have been out to greet us. Every street was lined with people, ten to twenty deep; men, women, children, babies, standing in doorways, on steps and roofs. Of course it had been planned and there were policemen here and there to control the crowds, but at the same time there was something spontaneous about it. Every face looked curious, but they also looked pleased. We were told we are the first foreigners ever to be in Hadapu. How odd we must seem. Three tall, fair people, two with blue eyes, in strange clothes and stranger shoes. (Harrison's and Jack's boots are always noticed and commented on.) In the middle of black-haired, brown-eyed Chinese I feel like one of those colorless bugs that live under rocks—one of my mother's favorite ways of describing us when we looked pale and sick. She liked people to be suntanned, and every summer of our childhood we spent on the beach or in boats.

After Lazikou the Red Army came through the mountains the way we did and stayed in Hadapu for more than a week. At that time the population was about two thousand and there seems to have been plenty of food.

We walked through the clapping crowd to where Zhou Enlai stayed. One room is in its original state, with old wood and a ceiling made of long sapling sticks (like the ones we saw in carts this morning) holding up straw filling, freshly painted black. The varnish on the walls was sticky and the covers on the beds brand-new. Harrison thinks our visit is doing a lot toward preserving the houses where the leaders stayed. Many have been spruced up and painted, or at least cleaned.

We walked farther on to a merchant's house where Mao stayed. This is a substantial house set back from the street in a nicely planted garden.

I noticed several little girls with pierced ears and gold earrings. I thought this wasn't done anymore. I have never seen jewelry on women or children anywhere except in the Uighur communities in northwest China. But the last time we saw a *China Daily*, Harrison read me an article about people in Shanghai taking their gold jewelry to be redesigned, and another about how many people go to church these days. He said, "In China we put on our gold jewelry and go to church."

We still see bound feet on older women, and I saw an albino Chinese child—a curious sight. How hard it must be for her, but someone said there are quite a few.

While we were visiting Hadapu, we heard several loud blasts, louder than when planes break the sound barrier. At first we thought it might be a salute to us. But it was rockets being fired into the clouds to disperse the gathering storm. Hail is a serious problem; it damages crops when they are ripening. However, as we left, hail came down in sheets, so the rockets don't always work.

The guest house here at Minxian is pretty depressing. Our room opens off the main meeting room; the floors are cement; there is a pile of coal and sticks in the corner, a small stove in the center. We had supper in the big room sitting on tiny chairs at a low table, as in Diebu. I asked why they are so low and was told they're for when many people watch TV; those in front use the small chairs and those behind can see.

I don't really mean to complain. I know that lots of thought, care, and effort has been expended for us. Many of the rooms we've stayed in during the last few weeks are offices and have been converted to guest rooms especially for this trip. Furniture has had to be moved, brought in, sometimes bought or newly made. At Diebu, for instance, the cupboards in both Jack's and our rooms were new, still had shavings in the corners. The mosquito netting on every bed in Sichuan was new and had an embroidered valance. We have had hot water and soap, and what more do we need? Also, what more could we expect?

FRIDAY, JUNE 1
Dingxi

Today is Children's Day all over China. Schools are shut; children wear their best clothes, join in parades, games, and dances. In Minxian girls were heavily made up and wore big red bows in their hair. The holiday must also be an excuse to have market day. Every town we went through was thronged with buyers and sellers; people and animals, and all kinds of food and goods for sale. There were peanuts in profusion, huge potatoes, radishes, turnips, onions. Not so many greens as we have seen in other areas—perhaps it's too high. Red peppers, big doughnuts that made Harrison's mouth water, and eighteen-inch-long candy sticks of red and white. The red candy cannot be sold in Beijing because the red coloring is unhealthy. I guess people out here haven't been told.

In a Hui minority village, men wear white caps and women wear long black headdresses that hang down their backs. Many horses, pigs, and sheep.

We have a new guide jeep with two policemen in spanking-clean white jackets. They don't wave flags, don't really clear the way for us or the bus behind. They lean out the window and tell trucks to pull over and stop. Sometimes the trucks do, sometimes they don't. In fact, often the policemen just drive on and other vehicles get between us. Our driver is extremely good, competent and careful, as all of them have been except for the man who kept slamming on the brakes going to Tong'an that rainy night.

A leaking tire on our bus had to be changed. The police jeep stopped ahead of us, the police got out and just stood there, never thought of coming back to help. The other drivers pitched in, and so did most of the men; the tire was changed, and then had to be blown up with a hand pump. I asked how they could tell without a gauge if the tire had enough air. The answer was "Oh, they can tell." Obviously, they could.

Most of the day we drove up and down the strange, deserty mountains with terrible erosion that the Chinese are trying to cover with trees. There are caves high on the mountains; they are used for shelter and/or storage, not to live in. Old forts and walls sit on top of many mountains. When bandits were in this area, people moved into the forts with as many belongings as they could manage, to protect themselves from robbery and kidnapping. Kidnapping for ransom was an important means of income for bandits.

These roads that wind up, around, over, and through huge mountains, whether made of rock, sand, mud, or paving, are skillfully built and constantly kept up by road crews who are generally Chinese, even in the minority areas.

We have driven a long time without seeing much industrial development, but at noon we saw a factory, though no one could make out what it manufactures. We also saw a grain elevator in the afternoon. There were stone fences as well as mud walls. The soil is loess—fine powdered earth, wind deposits blown over from Mongolia for centuries. Here it is reddish or yellow-brown. It is still amazing to be in hot, dry country after the rain and cold we have been in recently.

Had lunch at Longxi, a small town with part of the old city wall from the Three Kingdoms period. Honeydew melons grow here, we were told. The history of this area starts with the sixth or seventh century B.C. but the Chinese were around here in 1760 B.C. The altitude is nearly eight thousand feet. Gansu Province is about twenty thousand square miles and has a population of 2.2 million. It is considered one of the poorest and most backward provinces.

Flax has been harvested and is on the roads to be threshed by jeeps and trucks driving over it. The seed is valuable for linseed oil, which is used in paint, and fabric is made from the fiber.

After lunch we entered a new county and the useless policemen in the jeep left us. We now follow a pale blue "limo" with curtains, in which the new county magistrate rides. The reforestation looks more successful here. Trees are really beginning to take hold. Poplars, which grow fast, are planted everywhere, but I don't see where the water comes from. The river is completely dry now. Over the summer they expect some rain, but not much. We notice that on mountains and hills trees are planted from the top down. It helps control erosion.

The houses are made of adobe mud and are the same color as most of the landscape except for the bright green terraces and struggling trees. Purple iris is growing in courtyards.

We saw our first camel (and it turned out to be the only one on the entire trip) this afternoon. It was being led along a street and was reaching high into the trees, eating leaves and branches. I have been wondering why we haven't seen any before. We're in camel country, it seems to me.

Here, in Dingxi, we are in a hotel and the luxury is unbelievable. We have a comfortable bed; the washroom, which consists of six sinks on each side of a big square room, is near; hot water is brought in kettles. The WCs are down the hall and the women's is Chinese, clean and private. We were driven in the blue limousine to the bath house, to which we could easily have walked, where Harrison and Jack had showers and I had a wonderful hot bath in a huge tub. A barber and hairdresser have their shop in the same building. There have been bath houses at several of the places we've been, but, like this one, they have been in a separate building, and they were not always open.

SATURDAY, JUNE 2
Dingxi

Today we drove to Huining, where the Fourth Front Army met with some of the First Front Army when the Fourth was on its way to join Mao in Shaanxi in 1936. The First Front Army sent a fairly large detachment to accompany them to Shaanxi, as this was still enemy territory.

On the way to Huining the reforestation on the mountains is spectacular. I prophesy that in one hundred years, maybe less, they will have forests of evergreens and real forest floors instead of poplars growing out of the desert. Trees looked more established and healthier than what we saw yesterday. Possibly there is more water. "Maybe groundwater" is always the answer I get.

We passed through a small town where there was a donkey in every yard and many on the road. It wasn't a real market day, but private-enterprise vendors were on both sides of the street selling vegetables, eggs, animal skins; blouses, trousers, shirts, jackets, and lots of children's clothes. Girls were wearing bright-colored jackets.

It took only two hours to get to Huining—we arrived at 10:30 at a guest house with separate one-story buildings of five or six rooms each, like barracks, but with gardens of trees and flowers. We were shown to a room with beds, sofa, two big chairs, a desk with drawers on one side and in the knee hole a five-inch-high platform to keep your feet off the cold brick floor. I can't imagine it being cold here, but it does cool off at night even in summer, and they say it is cold in winter. The floor was swept and the furniture was spotless. The desk was newly varnished.

After the usual rest and tea we visited the west gate of the old city wall. We were told it was built in the Ming period and is authentically restored. Perhaps, but it has windows now, and no gates that were used for defense had regular windows. We saw a photograph of the wall and gate as they were at the end of 1935, falling down brick-and-plaster with a big crack. As a memorial to the Long March, it would seem more fitting tc restore it to that state instead of the elaborately painted and decorated gate that it was in the fourteenth or fifteenth century. However, the windows let in light, so we could see the relics of the Red Army—bowls, a kettle, a lantern given by a soldier to a peasant who gave him a meal, and so on. The two armies actually met at the north gate, but that has long since been destroyed.

We had lunch and another longer rest. When I woke up, I related to Harrison all the moves I had made in World War II with three children and two dogs—from Connecticut to North Carolina, to New York City, to Colorado, to Oklahoma, back to Colorado, and finally to California. It seems so long ago, and was—forty years.

In the afternoon we had several interviews with local historians, a magistrate, and six veterans of the Long March. Harrison ascertained that it was frosty in the morning when the two armies met in September and October of 1936. Millet was stacked up waiting to be threshed. Corn, potatoes, buckwheat, and squash had been harvested. The peasants were in the fields, plowing, spreading fertilizer, getting them ready for winter.

Residents at that time numbered about two thousand, the First Army detachment one thousand, and the Fourth Front Army forty thousand. So how did they get enough to eat? The answer was what we always hear—they confiscated the supplies of landlords and evil gentry and bought food from peasants. Prices were five (Chinese) dollars for a hundred-pound hog; two dollars for a fat sheep; one dollar for five chickens; fifty cents for a hundred pounds of vegetables, and ten cents for more than a dozen eggs. There was a celebration feast when everyone met—chicken, mutton, pork, and a home brew, minmin jiu.

The first veteran was a Mr. Yang, who is now seventy. He was articulate and interesting with a good memory. He came from Wanzai County in Jiangxi Province. In 1929, when his town was liberated, his parents were dead and two older brothers were active in the underground. Though he was only fourteen, he joined the Red Army as a regular soldier and was given a spear because they had no more weapons. He was transferred to the telephone and communications operation but also took part in battles. In 1931 he was with the Fourth Army. In 1933 he was sent away to study communications, and when he returned to Jiangxi, he was technician and repair man as well as chief telephone operator.

He only felt terror when going over the Grasslands; he couldn't talk to minorities, there wasn't much food. "This was a bad time," he said. Of 150 operators who started at Jiangxi, 110 made it to the Grasslands. Others had a bad time on the Snowy Mountains because they could not breathe.

When the armies split into groups and detachments, he and forty of the telephone operators went with Zhu De. They crossed the Grasslands twice in 1936; only eight survived. Of those, seven went with the First Front Army and he stayed in Huining.

He met many of the big leaders. Thought Mao was a good leader, always worrying about his men. Zhu De was heavily built, "opened his eyes wide" when he talked. He often saw Kang Keqing, Zhu De's wife. She had a horse and a mule and carried two pistols. She was kind to soldiers and telephone operators, spoke to them of the importance of their work. She had her own quarters and position. Generally she and Zhu De lived separately, he said. Amazing, in China, where families usually all sleep together.

Zhou Enlai was sometimes there, sometimes not. Mr. Yang felt he was off on important missions.

The next man was sixty-three, he said, but he looked older than all the others. He joined the Red Army in July 1933, when he was only a boy, because of the propaganda: "Defend your homeland—go north and fight the Japanese." He worked at division headquarters, ran errands, carried water. He was in many battles, was injured by enemy planes and put in the hospital. He ended up being an orderly to a commander. He, too, said it was difficult in the minority areas. No communication, cold and very

142

heavy snow. He remembered that Zhang Guotao lost control of himself in a battle, got into a panic, and lost his straw sandals.

Next was Mrs. Chen, who came from Sichuan Province, as they all did except for Mr. Yang. She is sixty-eight. She was in a platoon of women, working in a hospital unit, of the Red Army. They were in Wangping for one year, in Lushan County for another, then went on the Long March.

She remembers there was nothing to eat except grass, wild wheat, and berries. When she got to Huining, she became a straggler—not exactly a deserter, she explained, but someone who left the army because life was so hard and hopeless. An old woman who was gathering firewood up in the hills found her and took her in. She is, or was, married, and has two sons and daughters.

She must have been an outstanding beauty, for she is quite handsome now, even with a very wrinkly face.

Another man, Mr. Fu Juyu, is seventy-three and has a wispy little beard, like Ho Chi Minh. In 1924 he joined a peasant uprising that was not successful. All these veterans, except Mr. Yang, the telephone operator, were with Zhang Guotao and the Fourth Front Army.

The next man said he joined the revolution at age eight. That means his family, eleven in all, just went along with the army, followed on behind, as many people did. They were terrified of the Kuomintang, who took dreadful reprisals, especially if they knew or suspected a member of a family worked in the underground or was in the Red Army. These followers were asked to bring their own food.

At the start his father and sister became separated from the family and were never seen again. An uncle was killed by Tibetans; his younger brother died of an illness—there was no medicine or care. In the end there were only his older brother, his aunt-in-law, and himself. He was given to another family to bring up as an adopted son.

These are stories from people who came from the most humble backgrounds. How I wish Madame Soong were alive. I want to talk to an intellectual, to a rich-born person who joined the revolution. There were many of them, yet we seem to talk only to people who emphasize their peasant origins. Not that there's anything wrong with it—I just wish I could talk to someone who grew up differently.

We had a pleasant dinner with the magistrate and returned to this comfortable hotel.

SUNDAY, JUNE 3
Lanzhou

We left Dingxi after breakfast. Here in the northern country, breakfasts are different. No more xifan, the rice gruel we have become so used to, but ludou, a gruel made with whole wheat and little beans that look like lentils. Neither Harrison nor I like the taste. Yesterday morning we had soybean milk that was very good; this morning, cow's milk. Both were served warm in a bowl. The Chinese especially like youtiao, a long doughnut-type fried twist that they dunk in soy milk. There are always two or three dishes of pickled vegetables, and here, peanuts, which pleases Harrison.

All day we drove through more mountains and dry desert land in various stages of reforestation. The responsibility program applies to forestry as well as to crops and other enterprises. A family may be allotted as much as eighty acres on a hillside. The state supplies the seed trees and the family does the work. They can keep the land and pass it down to their heirs as long as they live up to their end of the bargain and care for the trees. Every bit of the work is done by hand—digging out the terraces, dragging trees up to the top, and planting. Trees are set about three feet apart.

Some people think these hills were once forests; others think not. I believe that most of China, except for real deserts like the Gobi, was once covered with trees. The ever-increasing population, not knowing any-thing about replanting and replenishing (and needing wood for houses, fuel, and fodder), simply denuded the country. In wars, and especially in the civil war between the Communists and the Kuomintang, there was a lot of burning and scorching of the land. When you think how, for centuries, the Chinese have scrupulously cared for their arable land— have produced food and still do, on the same plots—it's strange to see how severely they abuse their forests.

Rape is flowering, and we passed many fields of wonderful bright yellow. Bee-keeping families were camped by the road with their boxes of bees. We were not aware that the Chinese use honey, but on this trip we have seen trucks laden with beehive boxes, on the road or parked beside fields of flowers in bloom. Honey is used to flavor eight-jewel pudding, and is given to children. A lot is exported to Poland.

Corn is about six inches high, and we saw cauliflower growing, and piled up by the road.

About an hour from the city of Lanzhou we could see smog ahead. This is a highly industrial city, developed after Liberation from an old city of the Sui Dynasty. Large groups of people from coastal cities, especially Shanghai, were sent out here to work. At that time the Chinese wanted nuclear plants and industry as far away from the United States as possible. Now we are more friendly and the Russians are not, and all these installations are here, in good range of any Russian missiles. How insane we all are—working hard to make arms that we can never use without destroying the world, and changing sides so often.

In spite of the smog, the valley is very fertile and vegetables grow in abundance. The Yellow River flows north of Lanzhou, and the Wang River, which we saw on the way here, is about an hour away. We saw a big pumping station and pipelines for irrigation.

In the city some girls wear dresses, or blouses and skirts, and high heels, which change the wonderful natural Chinese posture and walk. I saw a girl pushing a bicycle who had several silver chains around her neck, just like girls in New York.

We are staying at the Sound Sleep Guest House, which is very attractive. We have real sheets and hot water. It turns out we will be here only tonight and one day. The train to Xi'an, our next destination, is booked up except for tomorrow night. Jack will stay here until the fifth or sixth and take the two-day train he wanted, to Beijing. Caroline is coming before our trip will be over, but we will be back the twelfth, I believe.

It will be strange without Jack. He is such a fixture in the front seat of the bus with all his camera equipment beside him, dashing out to take pictures, crawling down ravines, up steep hills, making everyone nervous. And his knowledge of this country has been invaluable.

MONDAY, JUNE 4
Lanzhou, After Supper

This morning we met with three veterans of the Long March. The first two, Mr. Wu Seng and Mr. Zhang Renshi, were with the Second Front Army. He Long was their commander. They must see each other often and reminisce because they remember the same things. Mr. Wu looked serious and wore heavy-rimmed glasses. But at times he was quite funny. He is seventy-three and came from a poor family in Hubei Province. He and his father worked as hired hands, which means they worked for a landlord on a permanent basis. He joined the Red Army in 1931 to emancipate himself, and others like him. He said many young men joined. He remembers fighting five or six engagements every day. In 1932 they were being squeezed by the Kuomintang in the third encirclement campaign, so they pulled out to set up new soviet areas in the border regions of Hunan, Hubei, and Sichuan Provinces. He remembers crossing the Golden Sands River (where we saw it near Dali) as the most frightening time for him. The water rose swiftly; they had only one real boat, in which they put women and animals loaded with silver dollars. He said they had rafts and boats made of hide. (Harrison seems to question this.)

Mr. Wu suffered five wounds. He was fortunate that his wounds healed quickly without infection. After one wound he was carried on a litter for a few days. Another time a bullet went through his lung and out his stomach. He was taken to a peasant's house; a long bandage was put through the wound and pulled back and forth to clean it. The pain was excruciating, but in three days he was able to get on a horse and go along with his outfit. That treatment reminded me of the radical mastoid operation I had in 1938. The dressing was three feet long and had to be pulled out of my ear and a clean one put back in, every day for more than a week. I had a regular anesthetic the first time, but nothing after that.

Mr. Wu also lost a finger in the War of Liberation.

In the Grasslands they ate boiled weeds. He read a pamphlet that explained what was edible, but many soldiers didn't know the difference, ate poisonous weeds and died. They boiled their hats of yak skin and any other leather they had. If they found a yak, they killed it and ate every part, even intestines and bones. (An English friend told me that during World War II in England, her family always ate the bones when they could get a chicken.)

He saw lamaseries, but they were not allowed to enter them. The Grasslands was a big empty area—no animals, no birds, no people. The land was rubbery. They fished, but he didn't say what they caught. Having seen much of the Grasslands the Red Army crossed, I imagine there would be small fish. But we are surprised he said there were no birds. According to other reports, there were large flocks.

Mr. Wu got to Yan'an and stayed in the army until 1952, when he became deputy director of construction in northwest China and lived ten years in Xi'an. He was both director and political commissar when the bureau moved to Lanzhou. During the Cultural Revolution he was "in trouble" for four years, in prison for one. ("In trouble" usually means under house arrest; "struggled with" means being harassed, criticized in front of mobs, beaten—anything the Red Guards felt like doing.) After his troubles, in 1970, he was renamed director of the Material Bureau of Gansu Province. He has six children and six grandchildren.

Mr. Zhang Renshi was the only child of a peasant family. His mother died when he was four. He lived with his father and an uncle, who were hired hands, and joined the Red Army when he was fifteen. He is sixty-seven now. At the time of the Long March he weighed 132 pounds, but now he is huge—weighs over 200. He is living at the hospital while he is being treated for diabetes.

He told us that by the time his army group got to the Grasslands they had lost 80 percent of their men from sickness, cold, lack of oxygen, starvation. It was like a sieve, he said; a few survived, the rest went through. He had some fried bean flour that no one had wanted. He ate it on the Grasslands when there was nothing else. On the threshing floors near villages, soldiers found old grains of wheat left over from the previous season.

Mr. Zhang was wounded five times: twice fighting the Kuomintang, twice by the Japanese, and once in the War of Liberation.

He and Mr. Wu talked about He Long and Xiao Ke. The two generals had joined their forces to make the Second Front Army, but each commanded his own men. Xiao Ke was thirty-one; most of the troops were teenagers. The generals were good friends and the soldiers were happy about it. When He Long was with the Kuomintang, he was married. But after the Nanchang Uprising he joined the Communists, and that wife did not go with him. Later he married Jin Xianren, sister of Xiao Ke's wife, Jin Xianfo. We said we understood they were both beautiful, but Mr. Wu and Mr. Zhang didn't agree. Said they were "just average."

They told us that He Long used to play checkers with the political commissar, Guan Xiangying, and the stakes were their mustaches. He Long had an especially thick one. He lost occasionally and soldiers would ask, "Where is your mustache?" But it grew back very fast.

We asked if He Long went on the battlefield, and they said he always showed up at the front, just didn't get wounded. But in the Japanese war he was affected by poisonous gas.

He was loyal to the Central Committee and Mao's ideas, and even though at one time he was three years without radio communication, he followed Mao's line as well as he could. His troops were especially successful in rainy weather, when enemy planes couldn't fly.

Xiao Ke was thin and bald, due to some illness. When the troops saw his bald head, they thought it very funny. At first he didn't mind being laughed at, but after a while he did. His troops were known to be very tough. The Kuomintang knew this and told their soldiers, "Whenever you hear he's coming, you better run."

The third veteran was Zhang Shengji, sixty-eight years old. He comes from Jiangxi Province. His father was a Red Army guard and was killed in an effort to capture a landlord's village. After that, in 1931, Mr. Zhang joined the Communists. He was in the rear guard of the First Front Army and never knew what was going on; he just followed the soldiers. In September 1934, when the First Army started to move, he didn't know about the encirclements, was told they were going to Hunan to set up a new soviet base. The troops were in high spirits. They marched by night and hid by day. He remembers it was still hot in Jiangxi, and recalls abandoning heavy equipment in a river. He was with the last group of the First Front Army that crossed the Snowy Mountains. They were told to whisper, to save their breath because of the altitude. They were the last to go over the Grasslands.

In the afternoon we went for a drive around the city, and to the Yellow River on the north boundary. The handsome iron bridge was built in 1907 and is a series of steel arches. Probably the steel came from Wuhan; it was being produced then. But there was no railroad until the 1950s. All steel was hauled in carts. To get the parts here and put them together must have been quite a job.

We visited a lovely old courtyard house that used to be the Eighth Route Army Liaison Headquarters. The headquarters was first set up in 1937 and existed until about 1943. It was a recognized communications link with the Soviet Union and a base for underground activities.

We bought airmail stamps and stickers for the forty-four postcards we have written and had dinner with the deputy director of the Foreign Office. The governor of the province had planned to be our host, but he was in Chengdu at a meeting.

The deputy director was very pleasant and we had another farewell dinner—to Jack this time, though we will see him again in about a week. We toasted each other and became quite sentimental. The General toasted me and said I kept everyone in a good humor. I don't believe Harrison thinks that. I have never been any good at cheering him up or getting him out of a grouch. Harrison toasted Jack; Jack toasted him. I toasted everyone, especially Miss Zhou, who has been so helpful and done so much for us.

We are all ready to go to the train at 11:00. Jack insists on coming to wave good-bye, as does everyone else who has been with us in this province—the doctor, Miss Zhou, the party historian, and the professor. So in a few minutes we will be off on the last lap of this long, tiring, interesting, and unique trip.

TUESDAY, JUNE 5
Remnin Hotel, Xi'an

We arrived in the late afternoon and were met by three people in two cars—a lady doctor, a manager, and a local interpreter, all named Wang. On the train we were told it was 100 degrees here yesterday, but thank goodness it rained and has cooled off. We are in the same huge hotel we have stayed in twice before, but this time we are in a part that has been done over. It is like a hotel anywhere, with a few Chinese touches. Our room has two comfortable single beds and we have real sheets again. We have a desk, two armchairs, a table, and a big closet. There is a light above each bed for reading and one on the desk. Everywhere else Harrison has had to ask for a lamp. The Chinese who run the guest houses we've been in had never heard of such odd behavior—a peculiar foreigner who stayed up half the night typing.

The bathroom is more than adequate, even has a bidet. The floor is made of nice tiles that are quite well installed. The toilet works and doesn't drip.

It doesn't seem as if the Shaanxi Province people know anything about the point of our visit. Nothing has been arranged for Harrison, and they keep suggesting entertainments and sightseeing. These are fine, but not what we are in China for this time.

WEDNESDAY, JUNE 6
Xi'an

As nothing had been planned for us, we spent the morning reading and writing. I started to read my diaries from the beginning to see how they sound. On all our trips I have kept a journal and have never thought I could make a book from what I wrote. Yet I have—six times. So maybe I can this time. But I have written so much—six big notebooks already. I don't see how I can ever edit it properly.

We walk over to the big building for our meals. It is nice to be able to order for ourselves. Last night we had just two dishes and rice; this morning we breakfasted on fruit, toast and jam, and coffee with hot milk.

There are lots of tourists and we are appalled at the Americans. They are so fat, so sloppy. The men look worse than the women, with sport shirts half tucked in, shorts revealing hairy legs, and many shaggy beards and mustaches. I don't notice them so much at home, but here in this land of clean-shaven men, the Americans look awful. It's hard to be neat when traveling—no one knows that better than I. But it is possible to wear simple clothes and not call attention to oneself.

In the afternoon we drove out to see the famous clay figures that were discovered in 1974. The General and the lady doctor went in one car; Harrison and I and a new young man went in the other. We drove out the familiar way, but there have been many changes since we were last here. It is greener; in four years trees have grown, and the surrounding mountains are brilliant with trees and vegetation. There is a tremendous amount of new building, especially apartment houses. I wonder about putting housing in agricultural land when the Chinese say they will not be able to feed their people in 2000 if the birth rate keeps up. Besides all the housing, we passed several cement factories. But even with all the building, there are many pomegranate orchards, the trees laden with heavenly red blossoms. We've seen a few trees here and there, but nothing like this. The river is the Bahe (which means "river") and it flows into the Wei, which flows into the Yellow River.

This is a very fertile plain. When irrigated, it can produce in great

149

abundance. We understand that the responsibility system here has created benefits for the energetic peasant, who now can own his land and pass it on to his children. If he works hard and takes care of the soil, it will produce heavily and he will reap the profits. Under this system the quality of produce is much better than formerly. A peasant can make as much as 200 yuan a month and can buy a tractor, motorbike, even a car. A man who has been to the university and works for the government makes 48 yuan a month. There is a small increase of 5 yuan every few years, so by the time a government worker gets to be sixty he may be making 150 yuan a month or thereabouts. Our companion told us about a friend of his who works for the government. He makes 48 yuan a month. He is engaged to be married; his fiancée is a teacher and is paid a salary the same as his. When they get married, they will live in the young man's room in his parents' apartment—a room about ten feet square. The parents will buy furniture for them. He doesn't think this is a fair system. Neither do I.

Of course, in our country the blue-collar worker generally makes more than teachers, and politicians are always complaining they don't have enough, saying they have to be rich to go into government.

This young man saw President Reagan in April, when the president flew to Xi'an to see the clay figures. He was impressed with his "lovely cowboy smile" and general good nature. Said he was pleasant to everyone, even reporters.

We talked a little about the Cultural Revolution. He was very young, but his parents were afraid he would get mixed up with, or become, a Red Guard, so he was sent away to live with his grandmother. His father and mother are engineers and had to go wherever they were sent. Fighting in the streets of Xi'an was terrible.

The museum looked the same as it did four years ago, but inside the big dome that covers the vault, there were more figures standing guard and more excavation. In 221 B.C. Qin Shi Huang, a statesman of the rising landlord class, ended the struggle of the Warring States and founded the first multinational feudal state in China's history. He instituted unified local administrations, legalized private ownership by landlords and farmers, and standardized laws. When emperors or kings died, it had been the custom to put in the tomb everything they might need in the next world, from food to cooking utensils, clothes, and jewels, even animals and soldiers, who were buried alive. Qin Shi Huang, being an enlightened ruler, instead had life-size figures made of clay, and it is estimated that as many as six thousand were buried in groups to defend his tomb. Originally they were painted and held real weapons. The story is that a rival king, who hated Qin, broke into this vault after Qin died, stole all the weapons, smashed many of the figures, and set the place on fire. This explains why some of the statues in the display cases are black.

This remarkable find was "stumbled upon" in 1974 by workers digging for an irrigation project.

Work goes on all year, but during the tourist season the fragments of the figures most recently excavated are removed to adjacent buildings and put together there. The figures not yet completely uncovered are every which way in the earth—a head here, hands there, a torso sticking up.

In December 1980, two bronze carriages, each with a driver and four horses, were found near the actual tomb, which is some distance away. This is a large mound, now covered with vegetation, and not open. There are records describing the interior, which had palaces, a ceiling with stars made of pearls, and a physical map of China that covered the floor and had mercury flowing in the rivers. I am afraid that is probably all gone, plundered over the years. [In 1985 the Chinese announced that there is reason to believe the tomb is intact, has not been plundered, and that when it is possible, it will be opened.]

One carriage, with horses and a seated driver, has been restored and is in a glass case. It is smaller than life-size and utterly beautiful and adorable. The original workmanship has been duplicated carefully and lovingly. It is a joy to look at and be near. I hated to leave. The other carriage is being put together in the workrooms.

We had dinner with a provincial official whom I didn't like. I rarely have such a reaction, but this man was self-centered, arrogant, and rude. I was sitting next to him and he turned his back to talk to Harrison and never addressed one word to me. He seemed annoyed that we had been on our Long March, and insinuated that no foreigner could write about it, especially if he were not a Marxist.

THURSDAY, JUNE 7
Yan'an

We had a long drive—370 kilometers—and we are all tired. I have always found sitting in a car wearing, and while we were blessed with good weather, some of the road is being repaired and it was very bumpy. We have the biggest, roomiest, and fanciest minibus so far, and it certainly makes a difference to be together. We now have four Wangs—the doctor, the manager, the young interpreter, and the driver. All the Wangs, the General, Zhang, and the Salisburys make up our party now. I miss Jack. He contributed so much with his knowledge of China, the language, and his special humor.

On the main street in Xi'an large pots of roses are placed on the center line that divides the traffic. They look lovely and no one seems to run into them.

151

Yesterday rain knocked down a lot of wheat. Today it was being harvested with a sort of cutting scoop, like a scythe with a basket on the end. It looks more practical than cutting wheat with a sickle. When it's cut this way, in one swoop, it falls into the basket and is easily turned over and out in rows. I noticed several women walking between the rows that had been cut and around the edges of the field, picking up the few stalks that had not been gathered.

I noticed long strings of garlic being sold in villages; buses being washed in a riverbed; brick houses and walls painted a pretty red; forts on hills, as in Gansu, and a few beacon towers. There were many bandits here—the valleys are narrow with high cliffs over the roads. Perfect settings for attacks and escapes.

The smoke and smog from cement factories were appalling, especially in Yaoxian County and Tongchuan City. The smoke coming out of the chimneys is thick, yellow, and repulsive. They must be making enough cement to supply the world. We met a great many trucks loaded with coal, and some pulling trailers full of it. But we never saw a mine or where there might be one. A railroad was started here, but work on it has been postponed, or possibly abandoned.

We stopped for lunch at Huang Ling—named for the Yellow Emperor, a mythical character rather like King Arthur. This emperor supposedly is the ancestor of all Chinese and lived more than five thousand years ago. He was benevolent and good and his people loved him. When it was time for him to die, a dragon came to take him to heaven. The people tried to prevent his being taken away; they held onto him for as long as they could. A few pieces of his clothes came off in their hands and are buried at Huang Ling in his big tomb, we were told.

We had a picnic near some cedar trees that the emperor himself is said to have planted. We stopped at a temple where the trees are enormous and peonies and roses are in bloom. I keep thinking about ours at home—they must be either in bud or out already, depending on the weather.

I have heard many cuckoos and today saw one. There are two or three species in the United States, but I have never seen one and have only heard them in Italy.

On a special day Chinese people come to the temple to pay their respects to their original ancestor and leave wreaths.

We can't get over what has happened to Yan'an. Twelve years ago it was a small town devoted almost entirely to Mao and the Red Army history. Today it is a bustling, messy, unattractive industrial city of one hundred thousand people. It is too bad. I would have thought they could put all that industry somewhere else and make this a real Red Army museum city. We can't find the hot, dusty brick hotel where we stayed in

152

1972—no one knows if it has been torn down or drastically altered. The people from this province who are accompanying us don't seem to know about anything that dates back more than a year or two.

Wuqi (Pronounced "Wooshee")

The Long March ended here when Mao arrived on October 19, 1935. Mao ended up in northern Shaanxi purely by accident. After breaking with Zhang Guotao, he had to go someplace. He headed north. At Hadapu he read in the newspaper that there was a Communist force headed by Liu Zhidan in a soviet base in northern Shaanxi. So they went there, making Bao'an their base. It was so far away that they had relative freedom.

In 1936 Chiang Kaishek was kidnapped by the Young Marshal (son of the Old Marshal, the dictator of Manchuria, which had been taken over by the Japanese). This crisis resulted in an international outcry and the joining of the Nationalists and Communists into a united front against Japan. There was to be no more fighting between them while the Japanese remained a threat.

Mao then moved his base to Yan'an and did not leave. Troops were sent east to fight the Japanese. After World War II ended with the defeat of Japan, the civil war resumed; the rest is history.

Our retracing of the route is done, but we have a lot more ground to cover before our Long March is completed. We hope for more interviews in Beijing. Then we have the long trip home. And for the better part of a year we will both be writing our books.

We left Yan'an around 8:00 and drove first to Bao'an, which is now called Zhidan, after Liu Zhidan, a general who was killed in the Eastern Expedition. The drive took a little more than two hours, through mountains and valleys that became browner and drier by the minute. There has been some reforestation; in fact, some mountains and hills have about a twelve-year growth. Where there are no trees, wheat has been planted, even on the tops of mountains. It is thin and sparse, and it is tragic to realize people work so hard for such a meager result. It is too high for irrigation. One Chinese man said, "They have to depend on the Almighty for rain." (That is certainly a switch from 1972, when any mention by us of God, religion, legends, or fairy tales was met with "There is no room for such superstitions in our socialist society.") Maybe eventually these mountains can be watered from planes.

Looking at the sad plots on the hills, one of the provincial men said, "You can see the hunger for land." The central government wants to reforest all those hills and has told the people they will provide them with grain if they will give up their old ways. Maybe the government will be able to convince them, but maybe such changes will have to be enforced.

Millet, buckwheat, and some potatoes are also planted way up high. I saw a man sitting in the middle of his vegetable patch smoking a long Chinese pipe. I have seen a few of these pipes on this trip. They are about eighteen inches long and have a small bowl. Tobacco is grown in many provinces; the Chinese used to smoke a lot. In our group, only the General smokes, and occasionally the local and provincial people we pick up do, but it doesn't seem to be anywhere near as prevalent as formerly. Young men working on the roads often have a cigarette in their mouths, like a permanent fixture, and people enjoy a smoke when sitting under a tree by the road or playing chess or checkers. I have seen only one older country woman smoking. Someone told me it is still frowned upon for women to smoke.

At Zhidan we had interviews with two more old veterans. The first man came from Jiangxi and joined the Red Army in 1930. He said he participated in all five encirclement campaigns. Harrison asked him if he had had any experience with the Yi people. He said a group of them descended, with yells and whoops, on him and about five other soldiers, grabbing their weapons and pulling off their clothes. He was a machine-gunner, so they couldn't get his gun—it was too heavy. He said they wore a kind of robe. Others have told us they were naked, but that seems to have been proved wrong.

On the Grasslands they didn't see a human being other than themselves for eight days. After they got to Maerkang, they killed one thousand yak, he said.

He got through the Long March without injury but lost an eye in the Japanese war and was retired from the army in 1941. He married and settled here. I asked him if he didn't miss Jiangxi, it's so different, and he said, "Yes, it's beautiful there." In 1941 conditions wouldn't have permitted anyone except a soldier on a special mission to travel anywhere, so he stayed.

The second man is sixty-five, bald, and has no front teeth. He joined the Red Army when he was fifteen. Soon he became an orderly, then a messenger, and ended up as bodyguard for a division commander. He had been much affected by what he heard about the Red Army. Everyone was equal; soldiers and generals ate the same food, wore the same clothes. The day he joined, more than thirty were conscripted. He was with the Fourth Army and crossed the Grasslands three times. This was because Zhang Guotao wanted to go south to Chengdu, and take the city so they would have enough food. As we have learned, that idea proved disastrous. Harrison asked him what the soldiers thought of Zhang. He said

Zhang appeared kind to the soldiers, but everyone knew that he had a terrible temper and often killed people. He said Zhu De was in trouble once, had been humiliated and made to carry water for troops for three days. (We have been told this was not true; he was just deprived of power.) He was present at the meeting of the First Front Army and the Fourth, saw Zhang Guotao and a man he was told was Mao. When he saw them, they were walking; horses were being led.

After a sumptuous lunch of fourteen dishes—not counting soup, rice, and steamed bread—for the two of us, and a ten-minute rest, we went to the tomb of Liu Zhidan.

A central pagoda with two smaller ones at each side stands at the top of a steep path. Several men were chipping away at huge blocks of stone, chipping them into the right size and shape for steps. It will take months but will be an improvement.

Tablets with inscriptions extolling the virtues of Liu Zhidan, by Mao, Zhou Enlai, Zhu De, and many other generals, are in the central pagoda, and more inscriptions are on the walls. Up a flight of stairs, his coffin, covered with a red flag, lies in an otherwise empty room. The shrine is set in simple gardens and walkways lined with roses and peonies.

It was put up in 1942, was defaced by the Kuomintang, then restored. The Red Guards had their turn during the Cultural Revolution, smashing many of the tablets and inscriptions. But this desecration, also, has been repaired and tablets replaced or restored.

Liu Zhidan came from a landowner's family but was a revolutionary from the start. He joined the Communist Party in 1925 and enlisted in the Whampoa military academy the same year. He openly disagreed with his family's policies and sided with the peasants. He organized uprisings and established a soviet base in this area. He was a popular hero and beloved by his soldiers. He was head of the Twenty-Sixth Army but in 1932 was framed by Du Heng (a follower of Wang Ming and Moscow), and temporarily "set aside," as they say.

From the shrine we drove here, to Wuqi. We passed many nurseries of young poplars. In one place the road by the river, built up about six feet high, had washed away, so we drove down in the riverbed for a mile or so. Riverbeds are generally wide, with sand, dirt, or stones on the sides and just a tiny, shallow stream in the middle. On the side of a mountain road men were cutting rocks out of the cliffs, then lifting them onto another man's back. He held the bottom of the stone, the way one holds a child, and, leaning almost to the ground, carried the rock across the road to a truck where another man helped him put it in the trailer.

In one small town an animal fair, or sale, was in progress. Horses, mules, cows, sheep, and goats were tethered in the riverbed. People were walking from every direction, and a traveling troupe was performing

Peking Opera on a makeshift stage. We didn't stop, because it would have stopped the show.

We stopped for a while at the house where Mao stayed when the Long March was over. It stands high on a hill and is kept in nice condition. In the courtyard, I took a picture of Harrison and the General crossing swords, to celebrate the end of the Long March. [It turned out very well and is on the jacket of his book.] We then drove to the west and looked through binoculars at a flat place on a mountaintop from which Mao directed the last battle against the Kuomintang at that time, the day after the Long March ended. A single tree grows there—a replacement of the original.

Then we drove to this guest house. We have a bossy woman looking after us, and she keeps coming into our room and pointing to the toothbrushes and toothpaste, urging us to brush our teeth. I have the feeling whatever I do will be wrong in her eyes. When we were having tea with our group, when a cup needed filling and there was a little left, she just emptied it out on the brick floor, tea leaves and all. The air is terribly dry here, so the liquid vanished in seconds.

There was time before supper to talk to one more old veteran, Yuan Yaoxiu, who is seventy-seven years old and a native of Wuqi. Harrison asked him mostly about Liu Zhidan. He had red cheeks, Mr. Yuan said, always talked a lot, and his voice could easily be heard by one thousand people. He could talk for hours without notes. He walked steadily and was very thin. Was loved by his soldiers and the people. Everyone knew he was rich—his father was a landlord—and that he did not live as his family wished him to. In 1929 there was a terrible drought, which led to the famine of the next few years (Edgar Snow wrote a graphic description of this in the chapter "Death and Taxes" in *Red Star Over China*). During this awful time Liu Zhidan returned from school and his family asked him to write notices about the rent and taxes due. He refused to do this, went to the hired hands and said, "How long do you want to go on like this? Join the revolution."

He was a Robin Hood, according to Snow—took money from the rich, even expropriated his family's property, and gave it to the poor. Robin Hood was my favorite hero when I was growing up, and Liu Zhidan appeals to me more than anyone we have heard about so far. I wish I could have met him. I am a little weary of the same old refrain—"coming from a poor peasant family." I wish I could meet more people from landlord families, people who had something to lose and yet joined the revolution. We have known some—Zhou Enlai, Madame Soong, and some of the generals in Beijing. But I would like to talk to more. The peasants had everything to gain. To be well off and realize the system was rotten and cruel, to be willing to give up everything to change it—that is a different story.

156

The provincial magistrate is a tall, handsome man. He has a high-bridged nose, like a lot of men in northern China, and looks a little like an American Indian. One man has a black armband with white characters. It means a parent or parent-in-law has died.

SATURDAY, JUNE 9
Back at Yan'an

We left Wuqi at 8:00. Everyone had awakened early, and the weather was clear, cool, and dry.

Along the drive, we noticed that sheep have just been sheared. They look a little embarrassed the way our dogs used to when they were shaved before we took them to Cape Cod every summer. Many gray-white pigeons or doves, usually in pairs. I am surprised to see anything wild in this country, from flowers to birds to animals, but I believe the bird population is increasing.

We stopped at the town where we had seen the animal sale. It was still going on. Hundreds of people were walking to town from every direction, as they were yesterday. They had nothing to sell, were just coming to have a good time and maybe buy an animal or go to the opera. Many babies and small children with young mothers, all dressed in red. The Peking Opera players were lounging behind the stage, so we didn't interrupt anything, but we had only been out of the bus a few minutes before we had a large, curious crowd accompanying us.

At one place in the road poplar trees have been planted in three levels, or tiers, and the ground is so hard and dry they look as if they were growing out of cement. Something we wonder about is why so many trees are planted either in or just along the riverbed. I would think that bottom land would be rich farmland, but maybe it gets washed away in floods and trees hold the soil.

We stopped at the Date Garden, an attractive series of cave houses and courtyards that used to belong to a landlord. Naturally, Mao took it over. He, Zhou Enlai, Zhu De, and many others lived here for well over a year. It is on a hill at the edge of the city. Dates, pears, and lilacs grow in the courtyard, and a natural-wood pagoda is in the center. At the bottom of the hill is a small canal, more like a fast-running brook, which was built when the generals lived here, "to bring water to the peasants beyond," who had never had any before.

We arrived here in Yan'an in time for a late lunch, after which we visited the enormous museum. I thought we'd never get out. We drove around the city, and saw the Dixie Mission's headquarters, which is abandoned and falling to pieces. Woodwork is broken, paper and glass torn out of windows. The area in front is a parking place for bicycles.

157

We then drove around trying to find our old hotel, and we are more shocked and saddened than we were the other day. Yan'an, the home of the Red Army, the place where its heart was, has become just one more fast-growing industrial town. Buildings are too close together, streets are crowded, and the smog is so thick we can't see the famous pagoda unless the wind is blowing hard. But the worst is that no one knows anything about their recent history, which took place right here. Many well-known revolutionaries lived here for several years, but now there is no trace of them. No one knows where their caves were. Only the Date Garden is kept up, yet in front of Zhou Enlai's house, bricks and stones were being laid, as if a wall were planned.

Someone said that the official thinking had been "Yan'an is an important place in our history; it must have factories and industries"—all the elements that at that time were considered the most important. It is a tragedy. In the United States we destroy our past every day, but what's happened in Yan'an is like tearing down Independence Hall or Benjamin Franklin's Library in Philadelphia or building a factory on the Gettysburg battlefield.

SUNDAY, JUNE 10
Back in Xi'an

We left Yan'an this morning in smog so thick you could cut it with a knife. Even though it's Sunday most factories seemed to be open. An added curiosity is that we were told that the factories are not very big and that the output of goods is of poor quality. A factory for assembling watch parts that were made in Xi'an is closed. Too many watches were made; there is no market for them. The industry that is ruining Yan'an doesn't seem to be worth the price.

In Yan'an we saw, for the first time on this trip, wagons pulled by four animals, three ahead and one in the middle behind. Usually the three front animals are small, either mules or horses, and a larger one behind. It upset me to see a man hit a mule good and hard with a shovel.

The back of a big truck was crammed with boys and girls going on an outing. They were dressed in their "Sunday best," as we might say. The girls wore hats to ward off the sun. The boys were near the cab, in front, the girls segregated in the back half. We saw blindfolded donkeys pulling grindstones round and round in a small circle. I should think they would get terribly dizzy even with a blindfold. We saw unfinished parts of the railroad that was started to carry coal (which is now carried in trucks). We passed a trailer that had been attached to a truck. It had lost its wheels, lay on its side, and coal was all over the road. One old man, who may have been the driver, was waiting for the police to come. A team of five bicyclists in athletic uniform was followed by a motorcycle with a sidecar. The provincial cycling team practicing.

The wild flowers amaze me because they are all in bloom at once—buttercups, dandelions, forget-me-nots, thistles, ugly dock, and morning glories, not quite blooming but already twining dainty murderous stems around everything. Locust trees are laden with flowers.

A boy and girl sitting under a tree were called to our attention by one of our companions. "Look," he said. "Very romantic." We talked about men and women and their behavior and customs. He told us that in some places people are so conservative that a husband and wife could not talk to each other in public. He also told us that in his family's village of over one thousand households there had been no landlord, only two or three rich peasants, the rest middle-income farmers, no poor. They paid rent and taxes, but it was not clear to whom.

We drove through high flat plains that looked very fertile and had healthy vegetation. There must be water somewhere, but we didn't see any pipelines or reservoirs.

The roadsides were filled with traveling beekeepers. They start in Hunan Province in early spring, end up in Inner Mongolia, and go back in the fall. It must be a strange life, living in a tent, spending two or three days in one place, generally right beside the road, with fifty or more boxes of bees. They collect the honey; then everything is packed up and they move on. Occasionally we see bees—those who didn't get back to the hive in time—following a truck. Wild flowers are profuse now, and when they return from Mongolia, buckwheat will be in bloom, we are told. We wondered about the children of these families (because we saw quite a few, certainly more than one per family)—whether they go to school, or if the bee season is more or less summer vacation.

On the last huge plains before Xi'an everyone was harvesting wheat as fast as possible while it was still dry, and putting it in the road to have cars and trucks do the threshing. There are signs all along the road saying that this practice is prohibited, but no one pays any attention. It is dangerous. But it is a free way to get the kernels separated from the straw, and less work than running over it with rollers attached to a one-man tractor, or putting it into a hand-turned separating machine, or whacking it over the back of a chair. *All* the work on these vast fields is done by hand or with an animal—cow or mule, sometimes horse. Every inch of land is utilized—not wasted around the edges as it is if a tractor is used.

We are in the same part of the hotel as before, but a different room. Harrison is angry and upset at the poor treatment he has had in this province. We think it stems from our host of the first night here, the man who said no one who wasn't a Marxist could write about the Long March.

The people who have accompanied us are pleasant and friendly but don't know much themselves, and treat us as tourists.

MONDAY, JUNE 11
Xi'an

Today was a complete flop for Harrison, a big waste of time. But it is nice for me not to have to go outdoors to the toilet; it is nice not to have to wash in a basin; it is nice to anticipate getting back to Beijing and staying in one place for a week; and it is especially nice to think about going home.

We interviewed two veterans and Harrison didn't get much new information from them. The first, Mr. Zhong, was born in Jiangxi Province in 1919. His family were "poor folks," he said. For four months a year they didn't have enough to eat. Twice Zhu De and his army came to his area and made a good impression. Soldiers didn't rob the people; officers and men were decent to each other. He joined the Revolution when he was only twelve, and the Red Army a year later. He was too young to have a rifle, so he worked in propaganda, putting up slogans and posters. After that he worked in the hospital.

Harrison asked where he was in October 1934 when the Long March began. He was in the hospital at Ruijin. He went from there to Yudu. He said he recalled that it was raining when they set out, that the road was slippery and they had to light torches. We have been told by most of the veterans we've talked to that the weather was dry and the moon was bright.

Mr. Zhong said that the young people in the Red Army found the hardships much less difficult than the older soldiers did, so they recovered quicker. Being so young, they didn't think about much, only food and the great adventure they were undertaking. It's the first time anyone has said that. He did not have trouble on the Snowy Mountains, was not short of breath. Crossing the rivers in the Grasslands was the most dangerous part of the march for him, because he was so small. He could easily have drowned. Officers took horses back and forth across the river, and young boys held onto the horses' tails so they wouldn't be swept away.

The next man, Mr. Ye Yingli, was born in 1916 in Hubei Province. He, too, was poor, and herded cows for a landlord from an early age. He was a member of the Communist Youth League, the young people's underground movement. In 1930 his county was not yet liberated, was full of Kuomintang soldiers. But in 1931 the Red Army had wiped out the landlords and their system, so Ye joined the army at age fifteen, probably the average age of the Red Army soldiers.

160

He worked in communications in the Fourth Front Army with Zhang Guotao as chief. He said Zhang did have a bad temper, flew into a rage if crossed. But Mr. Ye doubts that he executed people. Harrison asked if he ever heard Zhang get angry with Mao, and he replied, "No." But he did hear a struggle session between Zhang and Zhu De—very harsh words. This was when Zhang wanted to go south to Chengdu and Zhu De wanted to follow Mao's way, north. The soldiers were all aware of this split, he said.

We spent the rest of the day writing postcards, cashing checks, going to the post office, buying more silk scarves for presents. The temperature was around 100 degrees. After supper we learned we are to have one more interview tomorrow with "someone good," and will fly to Beijing at 3:30, depending on CAAC, the most unreliable, unpredictable airline I've ever encountered. Our departure time has changed three times already.

TUESDAY, JUNE 12

On the 3:30 P.M. Plane From Xi'an to Beijing

This morning in Xi'an I wrote in my notebook, *Up with the birds, except I don't hear any.* It's true there aren't many, but there are more than there were in 1972, when all of China was reaping the results of the "Getting Rid of the Four Pests" campaign—rats, mice, flies, and birds, I think they were. At any rate, right after breakfast we paid a visit to Dr. Wang's hospital. The Army Medical University and Hospitals is a huge medical complex with three other establishments besides this one, which dates back to World War II, when it was in Shaanxi under the Eighth Route Army. It was transferred to Xi'an after 1949.

Professor Chen Yua, the vice president, is eighty-two years old but looks much younger. He greeted us and sat with us while a spokesman gave us the facts.

Three types of doctors are trained here: general practitioners, doctors trained in medicine and treatment relating particularly to the army and air base, and gastrointestinal specialists. There are fifty-four departments, thirty-six of which can give postgraduate and doctorate courses. Three hospitals are attached to the medical college. There are 150 professors and assistant professors, over 400 lecturers, and 2,800 students. They study for five to six years and take thirty-four to forty courses. More than one million patients are treated yearly.

Students come from two backgrounds: Some are good high-school students who join the army when they enroll in the medical college, and the rest are soldiers. The percentage of male students is 80 percent or higher. This surprises me, because we have met so many women doctors in China since 1972. But maybe it's because it is an army hospital. In the nursing school, which is a three-year course, 95 percent are women.

They have exchanges with medical colleges and hospitals in other countries. Professor Chen (another Dr. Chen) went to Columbia University Medical School, for instance. Many doctors go to the United States for conferences. The head of the orthopedic hospital has been in Iowa and Wisconsin and speaks English.

Before we started on a tour of the buildings, I said we felt we were very fortunate to have had such a good, sensible doctor as Dr. Wang with us, and guess what the answer was? "She was just doing her duty."

At the orthopedic hospital we saw pictures of limbs that had been cut off or crushed, and the miraculous repair jobs that doctors had done. Several patients were brought in to show us fingers and hands that had been severed and sewn back on. One girl's arm had been cut off at the shoulder, and although it rested in a sling, she could move it, and the doctors said she would eventually have use of it. Most of these accidents were caused by machinery in factories. Workers must not be sufficiently trained to be careful, or perhaps their safety devices are inadequate. In 1972 we saw examples of this kind of surgery in Shanghai; their knowledge and expertise seems to have increased enormously.

We saw one extraordinary case of plastic surgery. A girl had been born with her face still in two sections, the way we start in the womb. Her head was much too big; her eyes were too far apart; her nose was in halves on each side above her mouth—a big space in between. At age twelve, in a series of I don't know how many operations, her face has been remade. She has a cut down the middle of her face, but her nose is in one piece and in the right place and her eyes are normally separated. Several pieces were taken out of the middle of her skull and the two sides pushed together. The shape of her head and her face are now normal. They said her brain has not been affected.

I never imagined anything like this. Our doctors probably do such operations, but I haven't heard of or seen any, and I doubt if many American doctors would spend so much time for no monetary remuneration.

The medical complex is bigger than the Forbidden City, which has an area of 250 acres. The buildings are not high and there are pretty gardens everywhere and lots of trees. It is a beautiful campus and hospital, very inspiring.

After our hospital visit we met with two party historians and a professor. The historians dodged all of Harrison's questions, the professor hemmed and hawed, and it seemed pretty pointless when the "someone good" walked in, accompanied by her husband. She was Liu Lizhen, daughter of Liu Zhidan. She is a tiny shy woman, fifty-three years old, with an endearing smile. She wore a blue-and-white-checked shirt, tan

162

trousers, and carried a small bag. At first she seemed nervous and kept fiddling with the zipper, but in a short time she relaxed and talked easily and naturally. She is a doctor.

Her husband is Zhang Quan, editor of a newspaper in Xi'an. He is big, friendly, talkative, and, it turned out, very frank. After they came, the historians and the professor never said a word, and acted relieved. It's so odd; there is the shrine at Zhidan, the place has been renamed for Liu, and he was a beloved hero, yet people seem reluctant to talk about him. It may have something to do with the people who are running this province. They seem just like the officials we met in 1972. [When we got back to Beijing, we heard several reports that backed up this idea. For instance, we were told that in some areas the people who were prominent in the Cultural Revolution are still in control, and maintain the values of that era just under the surface.]

From the daughter and her husband, we heard more about this fascinating Liu Zhidan. As I have written, he played a prominent role in establishing a revolutionary base in his native northern Shaanxi. His band of about five thousand men controlled twenty counties in Shaanxi and northern Gansu and directed guerillas in more than thirty counties. This small group was able to keep occupied two hundred thousand Kuomintang troops who otherwise would have been a big danger to the Long Marchers.

Du Heng, the man who framed Liu Zhidan, was the provincial secretary of the party. He removed Liu and took over the Twenty-sixth Army himself. Only a few kilometers from Xi'an they suffered a terrible defeat. Liu Zhidan escaped, went north, and created a new force.

His troubles came from the followers of the Moscow line, whose ideas ran afoul of Mao's. Though Liu Zhidan was not in communication with Mao, he had the same theories. In September 1935, the Twenty-fifth Army came north into Shaanxi. Cheng Zihua, one of the generals we met in Beijing in March (the man with the badly damaged hands and arms) was political commissar of this army. When we met him, I wrote, "He has a nice face." But knowing what we do now, I wonder. Cheng and his Twenty-fifth Army joined in a plot against Liu Zhidan. After the successful battle at Laoshan, led by Liu Zhidan, Liu's enemies turned against him. Almost all those above the rank of regimental commander were arrested, many executed. The high-ranking officers were held for interrogation. Liu Lizhen was just a little girl at that time, but she remembers that a big pit was dug and the officers, her father included, were to be buried alive.

Fortunately, Mao arrived at Wuqi in the nick of time, heard of the plan for the killing, and said, "Let no one be executed." He dispatched two representatives and a company of soldiers to stop it.

Harrison asked if there was any punishment for those responsible for the arrests and executions. Only removal from their posts, they said. No one was imprisoned, no one killed.

Liu had been handcuffed and his legs put in chains, so after he was released, it was painful for him to walk for some time. Liu Lizhen said she was shy with her father when he came home; it took her quite a while to feel comfortable with him. She said her father and mother got along very well, but they did not have much time together. He was fatally wounded in 1936, fighting the Japanese.

Her mother was in the hospital with typhoid fever when Liu Zhidan died and so did not attend the burial. In 1943 the coffin was moved to its present place. Liu Lizhen was thirteen at the time, and she remembers peasants kneeling by the road and burning incense. Her mother had the coffin opened and saw that Liu's body was dressed in the army coat she had made for him. His only other belongings were his pistol and his horse. She had them given to someone who needed them.

His daughter said his only heritage was his spirit. Though only eight when he died, she cherishes his memory. Even now, when her mother meets old friends, they weep. They will never forget what he did and gave for the revolution.

Liu Zhidan smoked a great deal and his widow, to this day, burns a cigarette in front of his picture.

During the Cultural Revolution, Liu Lizhen, her mother, and all the family were made to go to the countryside to work. Her husband worked in a production team in a commune, she in a county hospital. Her mother said, "The Cultural Revolution is like the purge of 1935; it is nothing new. We are just being persecuted again, this time from the left." After the death of Lin Biao, the family moved back to Xi'an.

After lunch we were getting everything together to leave at 3:30, and Liu Zhidan's widow stopped by. She had been at the hospital in the morning for a checkup. Her name is Tong Guirong. She is seventy-nine, is "in the same class," as they say, with Deng Xiaoping, meaning they have birthdays the same year. She is tiny, smaller than her daughter, feisty and funny. She walks with a cane. Harrison asked her where she met her husband, and she replied, "It was an arranged marriage. I didn't want to admit this, was afraid you'd laugh at me." But, she went on, most marriages were arranged then. Liu came from a "wealthy" family, and so did she, though her daughter said that didn't mean they were rich but that they could make ends meet. She repeated, "It was, and is, a very poor county."

Tong Guirong said she was being nursed at her mother's breast when the marriage was arranged. They were married when she was seventeen, Liu eighteen. But clearly it was a romantic relationship that happened in a romantic, exciting, and dangerous time.

164

So the "someone good" turned out to be one of the best meetings we have had and Harrison is pleased.

Beijing

We are in the central, and oldest, part of the Beijing Hotel, the section I remember as charming, with small rooms, high ceilings, and nice old woodwork. Now it has been completely redone and is like a stylish hotel anywhere in the world, not especially Chinese. The bedroom is huge and the enormous bathroom clean and fancy. We have seen the Services, are unpacked and settled and have a good four-day schedule. We will be seeing three great ladies, President Li Xiannian, and Party Secretary Hu Yaobang.

At four o'clock we went to the Great Hall of the People to meet with Chen Pixian, vice chairman of the Standing Committee of the National People's Congress (the Chinese equivalent of a parliament). The main purpose was to talk about Chen Yi, the man who was left behind in Jiangxi in 1934 when the Long March began. At one of our first interviews I wrote that Chen Yi was in the hospital, looked out the window and saw troops moving. So "he called in Zhou Enlai and asked him what was going on," I wrote. Chen Pixian said that Chen Yi had been wounded and so would not have been able to travel; he knew the area better than anyone; it was felt his staying would raise the morale and give confidence to those who were left in the base area. So he was appointed to remain and organize resistance. He was not consulted about this decision; Zhou Enlai went to see him in the hospital and told him the plan. Harrison suggested that maybe Bo Gu and Li De did not want him with them. They were running things then, before the Zunyi conference. Chen Pixian said he was very young at the time and didn't know what went on in high circles; however, "I would be inclined to agree with you," he said. Harrison also suggested that perhaps Chen Yi had not been happy about being left, and not being consulted; that he'd agreed because there was no choice.

Chen Yi was in the hospital because of a wound in his hip that would not heal. Chen Pixian said that what we have heard is true; he had himself tied to a tree, and a bodyguard squeezed out the infection and rubbed tiger balm into the open wound. After that treatment it healed.

Chen Pixian was with Chen Yi for most of the three years of guerilla activity and obviously admired him enormously. He told us that the Kuomintang was so afraid of him they had sixty thousand dollars on his head. After the Communists went up into the mountains, they lived like hunted animals, eating what they could find in the woods, and living in holes and tents made of branches and leaves. As we have heard from other survivors, they hid by day and at night would go down to the villages, often disguised, to get food from the peasants and to have meetings and underground activities. Anyone suspected of having anything to do with the Communists was eliminated, and thousands died. He told us that one night some soldiers crawled into a cave and went to sleep. In the morning, as they were waking up, a tiger walked out from behind them, paid no attention to them and went on out the entrance, minding his own business. They never knew if he had been in the cave when they crawled in, or if he had come in after.

When Jack met Chen Yi in the forties, Chen Yi said, "All these others will tell you how they are proletarians or come from poor peasant backgrounds. But I won't give you any of that nonsense. My people were well-to-do. I come from a bourgeois background." One of the men I wish I had met.

Lin Biao hated Chen Yi and realized that as long as he was around, he, Lin Biao, would not be able to take over the military. He was responsible for the attacks on Chen Yi, and for his bad treatment during the Cultural Revolution. He did not go to prison, but was struggled with and harassed and was under restraint, as was his wife. His wife died later, both deaths brought about by the psychological effects of their treatment.

In spite of this sad story about a wonderful man, the evening was rewarding and pleasant. His children, whom we met, are charming and friendly, and Chen Pixian was a warm and hospitable host.

THURSDAY, JUNE 14

At 8:30 this morning we met with Madame Liu Ying, widow of Zhang Wentian, also known as Luo Fu, the only member of the Long March group who had any firsthand knowledge of the United States. He had been in California for a year, worked in the university library at Berkeley, and for a newspaper in San Francisco's Chinatown.

Madame Liu was born in 1908. She wore a neat gray suit, has short, very black hair and glasses. She was friendly and easy with us. She is the tiniest person we have seen so far, hardly bigger than a minute. When Helen Snow saw her in Yan'an, she said she didn't know why the wind hadn't blown her away. Harrison said he wouldn't think *anything* could blow her away, tiny as she is. She studied in Moscow for three years, returning to China in 1933, to the soviet area in Jiangxi. She worked in the Young Communist Central Committee, was director of propaganda in Ruijin at the time of the fifth encirclement, which began in early 1934 and ended just before the start of the Long March. She went to rural areas to recruit soldiers because the Red Army had lost so many men. She remembers that when the Long March began, it was a fine day, and there was moonlight as they crossed the river at Yudu. There were thirty specially chosen women cadres, she one of them. Fifteen are alive today. Her job was to do political work and protect equipment. In especially difficult mountain areas, the porters could only walk about 2.5 kilometers a night. All their property from guns to woks to supplies was carried on shoulders; a press required six people to carry it. The bearers suffered sores on their shoulders and feet. The Red Army got bearers in relays from villages, but it was often hard to convince them to come. They were afraid the Kuomintang would kill them if it was discovered they had helped the Communists.

Because of all the equipment they were carrying, and the roads being narrow and slippery, many soldiers fell over the cliffs and died. Madame Liu doesn't remember when heavy machinery was abandoned, but she said most of the equipment that was left was buried after the Zunyi meeting. The places were marked so it could be picked up later.

She said that Mao did not have malaria at the beginning of the Long March; he had recovered, thanks to Dr. Nelson Fu. But he was weak and was carried on a litter. He slept on his litter all through the Long March, and often was carried because he worked all night and needed some rest.

Harrison asked her when she was married to Luo Fu. She said that she did not live with him until they got to North Shaanxi, but she worked in the Central Team and saw a lot of him on the Long March. He taught her how to take minutes of meetings and helped her in her work. She said she hadn't wanted to be married on the march. She didn't want to be tied up with children. She could not be like He Zizhen, for instance, who was pregnant at the start and just had to leave her baby. She said women who had babies either left them with peasants or just "got rid of them"; it was like throwing away excess equipment. There wasn't any choice; the revolution came first.

She talked about He Zizhen. Said she was quiet and seemed easygoing, but she had a quick temper. She was not always understanding of Mao's ideas, and at the end of the Long March she was ill and went to the Soviet Union for treatment. Mao let her go because he felt she had had no chance for an education, she had had so many children, and this might be a chance to study and also to raise her political ideological level. She was five months pregnant and had that baby in Moscow. That was the boy who died after getting sick in a nursery school. This was a terrible blow to He Zizhen, and she was ill, probably had a nervous breakdown, and was never her old self again.

Harrison asked Madame Liu if He Zizhen's going to Moscow had anything to do with Jiang Qing. The answer was no; Jiang Qing came to

Yan'an late in 1937. He Zizhen had gone to Moscow in 1936. Jiang Qing did what the writer Ding Ling told us many women did; she took advantage of the "vacancy," filled the empty bed.

Mao wasn't very good luck for his women, at least for those we know about. His original marriage was arranged, never consummated, and disregarded in the records. The marriage known as his first was to Yang Kaihui, by whom he had three children. She was left behind in Changsha at the time of the Autumn Harvest Uprising. In 1930 she, with her six-year-old boy, was arrested by the Kuomintang. She was tortured and shot, and the child was returned to his nurse and ended up begging in the streets of Shanghai. Eventually he was reunited with his father and was killed in the Korean War.

Mao was living with He Zizhen at the time, and married her at Jinggangshan. Later, when He Zizhen was in Moscow and Jiang Qing moved in, Mao had to get permission from the Party Central Committee to obtain a divorce and marry her. Some members were against it, and rumor has it that permission was given with the proviso that Jiang Qing *not* interfere in politics. The whole world knows her story.

There are tales of other women, too gossipy to repeat. Mao reminds me of that song from *Finian's Rainbow:* "When I'm not near the girl I love, I love the girl that's near."

Because of World War II, He Zizhen was caught in Moscow and did not come back to China until 1948. Mao's marriage to Jiang Qing was yet another blow to her. She was not allowed to go to Beijing and spent much of her time in Shanghai. When Mao died, she asked to come to Beijing to pay her respects. In a wheelchair, she went to the mausoleum and was moved to tears. A group of women from the Long March visited her; "Her memory was weak, but she recognized us as fellow Long Marchers." Toward the end of her life she was partially paralyzed, and she died of a stroke.

Most of the stories we have heard are tragic, but this woman's life is the worst to me—the saddest, most difficult, most pointless, most unrewarding.

Madame Luo Fu said that trouble for her husband started at the Lushan meeting in 1959, where he was accused of being part of an antiparty clique. He was removed from his position in the Foreign Ministry and sent to the Research Institution in Economics. He wrote reports and papers on the Chinese economy. In the Cultural Revolution he was called a revisionist, a capitalist roader, was attacked for his role in the "anti-party clique" and struggled against. In May 1968 he went to prison on charges of illegal connections with foreign countries. After a year of investigations, no proof of these charges was found and he was sent to Guangdong Province in the custody of the military. There he spent six years. He did have some freedom; he could read and write, and he continued his interest in economic affairs. But his health deteriorated—he had heart disease and hypertension. He asked to go to Beijing for treatment but was refused. Jiang Qing didn't like him because he had opposed her marriage to Mao. He asked to go to his home county near Shanghai, but this request, too, was refused. He was finally sent to a small place where the medical care was not adequate, and he died on July 1, 1976.

The poor lady was wiping her eyes as she was telling us this, and added that there was no memorial service, and she was not allowed to go to the cemetery. Later his image was rehabilitated and a memorial service was held.

Harrison asked what had happened to her. She said that when her husband got into trouble in 1959 she was asked to tell about his illicit connections with foreign countries. She said she could not, so she was accused of not being able to draw a clear line between her husband and her job, and she was transferred from the Foreign Office to the Institute of Cultural Affairs. In the Cultural Revolution, when Luo Fu was imprisoned, she was persecuted, asked to write about his foreign connections. "You must do it," they said. "It will be a service to the party."

But she insisted she could not concoct a story just to please them, said that Mao believed in "seeking the truth through facts." She went with Luo Fu to Guangdong, helped him with his paperwork, and took care of him when he was sick. They were given only a meager allowance to live on and no real medical care.

She got permission to return to Beijing after Mao died, in September 1976, and her record has been cleared; she has been rehabilitated and is now a member of the disciplinary committee.

At 4:00 we went to Zhongnanhai, the compound next to the Forbidden City where the leaders live and work, to have a talk with Party Secretary Hu Yaobang, the man who is supposed to succeed Deng Xiaoping. Outsiders are not invited there, not our ambassador or even President Reagan. It is a big compliment to Harrison and Jack.

As we approached the high red gate, two soldiers snapped to attention. Inside were two more soldiers, one directing us with elegant gestures worthy of a ballet dancer. This particular area was a park on the most southern of the lakes in the city. Many of the buildings are contemporary, but are only one story high and made of gray brick, unobtrusive and fitting into the landscape.

When our host greeted us, I instantly felt the intense energy and excitement generated by this extraordinary man. He is small compared to most Americans, but full of so much dynamite he sets the atmosphere on fire.

169

We sat in a big, light, airy reception room in the usual semicircle of chairs. A gorgeous picture done in glass relief of flowers and birds was on one wall. Two girls in smart, spotless, well-tailored tan pants and jackets served us tea. They wore tan leather shoes with heels and their hair was curled. Most girls curl their hair a little now, and they wear it any way they want to—long, short, medium, tied behind, or done up. In 1972 we saw only two hairstyles: pigtails (on girls and younger women) and the bowl cut.

We began by talking about the Long March. Hu Yaobang was eighteen at the start of the Long March and was appointed secretary general of the Young Communists Central Committee. He said there were thirty-two on the Central Committee and fourteen or fifteen made it to Yan'an. Today only five or six survive.

After being in Hadapu, the total force of the Red Army was ten thousand, down from the eighty thousand who started from Ruijin and Yudu. Hu Yaobang was asked to head a force to collect stragglers, because the army had scheduled a fast march into northern Shaanxi. He said the army moved so quickly that every day there were one thousand stragglers; they became an army in themselves. Because of their numbers, they were no longer afraid of punishment and many refused to go along.

Harrison said that explained something that had been puzzling him: We have been told that the First Front Army had only six thousand when it reached northern Shaanxi, and he has been wondering what happened to all the soldiers.

Hu Yaobang said that the Red Army's policy was to try to win skilled people from the Kuomintang—doctors, telephone operators, people who could operate heavy machine guns. Telephone operators who went over to the Red Army taught them the Kuomintang codes. Wang Bin was a surgeon in the Kuomintang, was captured, and joined the Communists. He took care of Zhou Enlai when he was so ill with hepatitis.

He said the Kuomintang was not in touch with the people, and in the beginning was poorly equipped. Otherwise the Long March would not have been successful. No one has said that just this way before. I have wondered all along why the Kuomintang was so terrible to the people, so cruel. If they wanted to be successful, why didn't they court the peasants, try to win them over to their side?

Red Army communications people were trained as early as 1930 in Shanghai and the Soviet Union. Zhou Enlai was in charge of this.

Hu Yaobang said the Long March is an inspiration to the people in China, and the world. It gives them tremendous spiritual encouragement, moves and inspires them when they hear of the courage, strength, confidence, and wisdom of that event.

He asked each of us to give our impressions of our trip. Harrison had been giving his all along; I said I had found the trip a moving experience, felt I understood the Chinese people and the revolution much better than I had. He asked me if I hadn't found conditions very primitive—wondered if they were more so than in other countries. He giggled when he asked this. I replied I hadn't traveled enough in remote areas of other countries to answer that, but I thought that wherever we went, no matter what the conditions, our hosts had given us their best and done everything they could to make us comfortable.

I mentioned the chieftains's house in Zhuokeji, near Maerkang, the fantastic structure we think must be saved before it falls down. He turned to the man on his left, who made a note of my suggestion, so maybe something will be done.

I said that family planning didn't seem to be working in the countryside. He said that women are so determined to have babies, sometimes they go away, to another village or province, and have a child. But even with the obvious success of birth control in the cities, there is a population increase in China of eleven million every year. The educated people, government workers, cadres, have only one child. They are too conspicuous to have more, even if they wanted to. But this policy is hard to enforce in remote areas. It is the same all over the world. The less educated are populating the earth.

Jack said that unless one had known the old China, it was impossible to appreciate the miracles of the new. I guess that's true, but without that advantage, we appreciate a great deal. He mentioned the great strides in roads, railroads, communication. He said that improvement in the relations of Han and minorities is obvious, but he is sorry to see such a revival of Lamaism—in his view, a backward social system, which opposes progress and modernization.

We walked out to the garden, where peonies and roses were blooming, and sat on stools around a little table for picture-taking. Dinner was in an adjoining room, an oblong table set for eight, four on a side: Miss Shi (the lady we met when the Chinese first came to the United Nations), Harrison, Hu Yaobang, and me on one side; Mr. Zhang, Caroline, Jack, and Mr. Qi (head of the Information Department) on the other. Mr. Zhou Nan, assistant foreign minister, couldn't stay for dinner; he had to go to the British embassy because it was the queen's birthday. A man stood in the doorway to the pantry; a woman in strictly Chinese clothes, trousers, and shirt stood in the entrance; and another man was positioned at the door to the garden.

The table had no flowers, but two beautiful enameled candelabra, with six or more candles each, and a big lobster shell stuffed with lobster salad, were in the middle. The lobster remained there until the table was cleared for dessert.

We had been told the dinner would be Western, and it was, but more

French than American. And there were almost as many courses as in a Chinese meal, but all served in Western fashion with knives and forks, no chopsticks. (Later, Hu Yaobang suggested that the Chinese people give up chopsticks and start using forks, said it was more sanitary. The whole manner of serving and eating meals would have to be changed, and I can't see the Chinese accepting that for a long time, if ever.)

There was bread and butter and two kinds of wine. Girls in dark red, tight-fitting dresses slit to the knee waited on us. The menu began with the lobster salad. Next was truffles and goose liver, very finely sliced in clear broth, served in individual baking tureens with a puff-pastry top, flaky and delicious—really out of this world. This was followed by escargots in garlic-butter sauce. The waitresses tactfully showed each guest how to use the special tongs and forks, as if we had never seen such a contraption, and passed baskets of sliced bread—French, rye, dark—and rolls. Then came a fish course, a big white fillet with mango sauce and tiny carrots and pieces of broccoli, just the way the vegetables at Maxim's are served.

After that each of us had a sizzling steak surrounded with sliced mushrooms, served on a metal dish in a wood platter. Paris salad, of lettuce, apples, and walnuts, came next. By this time I was pretty full, even though I had only nibbled at each course, but three kinds of cheese (brie, Roquefort, and a more simple yellow cheese) and crackers were passed. We ended with vanilla ice cream and fresh strawberries, and Zhang said, "This is what we talked about so often on our trip."

White and red wine, the product of Dynasty, the joint venture of France and China, were excellent. Harrison feels they put on such a splendid meal to show they can equal anyone, even in the foreign gastronomical field.

The conversation continued throughout dinner, with our host bouncing around on his chair and gesticulating to illustrate what he was saying. One of the waitresses stood behind him almost all the time, on guard in case he should fall off his chair or not land on it when he jumped up and down. She pushed it here and there to be sure it was under him.

Hu Yaobang is a remarkable man. A Chinese said to us, "Everything depends on him—he is wonderful, our hope." He is very aware of the rest of the world (something I can't always attribute to our politicians) and reads a lot, including American and European books in translation. He has read Nixon's books and is fond of Kafka.

FRIDAY, JUNE 15

At 9:30 this morning we went to the Great Hall of the People, to which we easily could have walked, and had a long meeting with Li Xiannian, the

President of China. We have seen him twice before and thought he was ill and old. He is old, must be in his eighties, but he looked better than either time before. He does seem a little wobbly to me, and when I mentioned this to a Chinese, he said, "That's one of the big differences between the United States and China; we respect and revere old people." But that wasn't what I meant. I meant that perhaps he is too old to hold an important decision-making position. However, his job seems to be mostly ceremonial. He went on a long trip abroad last winter, and he sees many visitors* But I doubt if he has much to do with policy. At any rate, today he had his facts about the Long March well documented and rehearsed.

He greeted us and, turning to Harrison, said, "You and I are on the way out." Cheerful thought.

We sat in a semicircle of chairs and they proceeded to have a very technical discussion of the Long March, of armies, mistakes, erroneous lines, divisions being wiped out, battles being won, skirmishes lost, commanders arguing, and a lot about Zhang Guotao and his disagreements with Mao. Li Xiannian was political commissar of the Thirtieth Army, which was part of the Fourth Army, and was with Zhang Guotao most of the time. He talked about being sent on the Western Expedition late in 1936, which was a total disaster. Zhang Guotao gave the order, but it really came from Mao, with the approval of Moscow. They were attacked by Kuomintang Muslim cavalry led by the brothers Ma—fierce, hard-riding horsemen wearing white hats. A women's regiment was tortured, raped, then killed or sold as slaves. Thousands of soldiers were killed and the survivors ended up in the Gobi Desert. Li Xiannian was rescued by a friendly plane and flown back to Yan'an. Soldiers who survived took a year to get back.

At 3:00 we met Madame Li Bozhao, wife of General Yang Shangkun, at the International Club. She is small, plump, has short, carefully combed gray hair and nice teeth, the way many Chinese have. She wore a tan pants suit, a ruffly white blouse, and tan leather shoes. She greeted us with "It is indeed a happy thing to see friends coming from afar to see China and to study the Long March, especially a renowned writer. I would like to share my experiences with you. I would like to go into details. The Long March is an important landmark in history. I would like to talk about my three crossings of the Grasslands."

She was born in 1910 and comes from a revolutionary family. Her father was a county magistrate and scholar. Her mother was interested in painting, reading, and writing. Her father died when she was six or seven, her mother soon after. Li Bozhao studied at Normal School, was influenced by her teacher, and began to be interested in the Communist Youth

*He came to the United States in July 1985, and we dined with him at the White House. He looked very well.

173

League. The party organization sent her to Shanghai, where she had intended to go to a university. Instead she was given the task of teaching women factory workers to read and write. Many were illiterate. At the time of the white terror, when Chiang Kaishek turned on the Communists and slaughtered thousands, she was arrested and imprisoned. The chairman of the Youth League bribed the guards in the jail, who let her out, and she went to Moscow.

There she belonged to an art group at Sun Yatsen University, wrote plays, and learned Russian songs and dances. She and General Yang Shangkun were married there in 1929.

She came back to China in 1930, when it was dangerous for anyone not sympathetic to Chiang Kaishek. She disguised herself as "an innocent girl," wore long pigtails and peasant clothes. When she got to Shanghai, the party decided it was risky for her to be there and sent her to the Communist soviet area in Jiangxi. She worked on the teaching staff of the Red Army school. In 1931 the Soviet Republic of China was proclaimed and she was assigned to the Ruijin paper, *Red China,* as an editor and proofreader.

There she had more contact with Mao and "learned a lot," she said. Collaborating with two men who had been on Zhou Enlai's staff in the underground, Zhu Di and Qian Zhongfei, she wrote a play, *To Die or to Fight—for Whom?* They put on plays in a regular theater; she wrote two by herself, one titled *We Must Win Victory.* She was president of the Gorky Art Theater, where excerpts from *The Lower Depths* were presented. It was difficult to train illiterate peasants to present this play, she said, but she persevered, and when they had learned some skills, the plays were presented to the soldiers.

At the beginning of the Long March, she was working in propaganda in the general political department of the First Army, and with them crossed the Grasslands for the first time. When the First and Fourth Armies met, she was sent to the Fourth Army to train cultural workers. When the controversy between Mao and Zhang Guotao became more heated, she got word from her husband that Mao and the First Army were going north and that she was to join him. But she couldn't get away, and didn't see her husband again for a year. Her second crossing of the Grasslands was with the Fourth Army going south. Later she was transferred to the Second Army and crossed the Grasslands for the third time. She said she was the only person who taught culture to three Red Armies.

She talked about some of "the thirty women comrades" on the Long March. One was Cai Chang. She came from a revolutionary family; her brother was a prominent revolutionary in the early years. They went to France in the work-study program, as did Zhou Enlai, Deng Xiaoping, and many others. Cai Chang supported herself by working as a house painter. She had a strong, firm will; in the soviet area she was a member of the Provincial Party Committee and in Shaanxi was an inspector of party discipline. During the Long March she traveled with Liu Ying, whom we saw yesterday. She had a horse but usually walked. Was "loved and respected by all her comrades." Now, sadly, she is blind.

Madame Li Bozhao said Zhou Enlai's wife, Deng Yingchao, was sick on the Long March. Kang Keqing, Zhu De's wife, was the daughter of a fisherman. She joined the Red Army in the Youth League when she was very young. She was a good marksman, an accurate shot. Before her marriage she led a detachment as a soldier. After marrying Zhu De she became a political instructor.

Li Jianzhen worked among the peasants and villagers, and also within the army. She was one of the most capable of the women comrades, and is now a provincial party secretary in Guangdong. They were remarkable women, she said, strong and versatile; could do many kinds of work as professionals.

Harrison asked her about Kang Keqing's saying the Long March was just like taking a walk every day. She replied that walking was not too difficult. "We were young and full of vigor whether it was rain or shine." But the enemy bombing was bad.

She didn't say a word about the Cultural Revolution and her experiences, and we didn't ask her. We know that she was "under supervision" and was forced to clean halls and toilets; that she suffered from hypertension; that she developed a blood clot in her leg and still feels the ill effects. We know that her husband was in jail for thirteen years; for nine she didn't even know where he was or if he were alive or dead.

It is hard to reconcile this neat, poised, friendly little woman with what we know her life has been. Her treatment is a dagger in the heart of civilized mankind. [Madame Li Bozhao died in April 1985].

Huang Hua, former foreign minister and now a member of the Standing Committee, and his wife, He Liliang, gave a dinner for us, the Services, and Dr. E. Grey Dimond (an American cardiologist who has visited China every year since 1971). The dinner was held at a guest house in the big area on the outskirts of Beijing where government people entertain and foreign bigshots stay. It is also where Jiang Qing chose to live when she was at the height of her power. We have been to Diaoyutai, which means "Fishing Terrace," several times before to different houses, but we had never seen this especially lovely place. We walked on a little bridge over a stream and into a garden where all the guests were gathered. Guests included all of us, Dr. Hatem and his wife Su Fei, General Qin, and several others. The Chinese don't drink before dinner the way many people do. When a meeting precedes a meal, they sit down and drink tea. At the table when food is served, maotai, wine, beer, orange pop, and mineral water are offered.

We dined at a long table in an adjoining open room—it was almost like dining in the garden. Harrison and Jack sat on either side of our hostess, Dr. Dimond and I on either side of our host. The dinner was slightly Western and served by waitresses in the same kind of red dress worn by the waitresses at Hu Yaobang's dinner at Zhongnanhai. The menus were printed on similar forms. There is a government catering outfit at Diaoyutai that provides meals and service to the powers that be, and they must have taken lessons from the French at Maxim's.

It was a wonderful friendly evening with lots of toasts to the most recent survivors of the Long March. I drank one to my four men companions, "without whom I never could have made it." I kept thinking of the equally friendly dinner our hosts gave us before we took off on the big trip, and how relieved I am it is over and behind us. There can't be any more remote places for Harrison to dream up to visit. But the other day someone suggested he retrace the Ho Chi Minh trail in Vietnam.

SATURDAY, JUNE 16
Interview With Xue Ming, Widow of He Long, Again at the International Club

Madame Xue is younger (she was born in 1916) and more sturdy than other ladies we have seen and talked to, but she uses a cane. She wore a white shirt and greenish trousers and her black hair was done in a bun. She was accompanied by a pretty daughter, who, Jack said, looked very much like He Long, and a man she introduced as "my colleague." She said, "I understand you are going to write a book on the Long March. Everyone is looking forward to it. As you know, I was not a participant, but He Long told me some things about it."

She was born into a poor family; her father died when she was young, and her mother was a dressmaker. Her mother had no support except herself, was discriminated against because she had no husband. Many people, even relatives, would not see her. Amazing that this sort of feudal thinking existed so recently. It's just like the movie we saw in March about a young widow who is shunned and regarded as a whore if she even speaks to a man.

Because her mother could not feed her younger sister and her, Madame Xue lived for a long time with her grandparents. She attended school, worked hard and helped with housework. All she thought about when she was growing up was how she wished she had been a boy. She longed for equality with men but knew it didn't exist.

She went to the March Eighth women's school in Tientsin, and there her eyes were opened to the harsh realities of life. She saw the foreign concessions riding hard over Chinese people. Many university graduates

176

couldn't find jobs, and a number committed suicide. Others became beggars. She thought she had better do something and so became a revolutionary. In 1935 she was a member of the student movement in the underground in Beijing.

She mentioned Lin Biao's wife, Ye Qun, who was in the student movement, and said her performance was "very bad." She had dubious connections with Kuomintang officials, which the party didn't know about until later. Madame Xue thought she may have been a Kuomintang agent when she went to Yan'an.

She herself went to Yan'an in August or September of 1938. She had known about He Long; he was one of her heroes. She said he was tall, big, handsome, spoke in a loud voice, made a very positive impression on her. She was full of admiration for him.

She was assigned to work near him and said, "I confess, I already had a deep affection for him." But she was a lot younger and people advised her, "Schoolgirls don't marry men so much older." There was a saying, "Old comrades are fine, but they are not good lovers."

What she didn't tell us, and what we have heard, is that He Long's previous wife was a very beautiful woman and the sister of Xiao Ke's wife. She was on the Long March with him, was one of the women who had a baby. After they got to Yan'an, He Long was off fighting the Japanese a great deal of the time and his wife took up with a much younger lover. In this case, a man filled the vacancy.

It was a big blow to He Long and he tried to persuade her to give up her lover. But she refused, and the party sent her to Moscow. While there she reconsidered, realized He Long was the man she wanted, and came back only to find herself divorced and her husband married to the lady we saw today.

Xue Ming said that in spite of different careers, fighting and working so hard for the revolution, they had a "wonderful married life." They had a boy and two girls, and she added, "After marriage we were so happy."

She told us some facts about him. He was born in 1896 in Hunan Province to poor peasants. He was number four in the family, had three older sisters, two younger, and a younger brother. His father was a tailor; they had very little land. His oldest sister was commander of a guerilla force in the area. He Long went to primary school, then turned to farming but could not make any money. So he set up a caravansary catering to travelers in the Hunan, Hubei, Sichuan, and Guizhou border areas. He was always wondering how life could be made better, thought people must have guns. In 1916 he led an uprising using cooking knives as weapons. A salt office was destroyed, and some guns captured. He was able to organize a force and by 1920 was known for killing the rich and helping the poor. Warlords were afraid of him. He became aware of socialism and the Soviet Union and Communism, and began to believe that was the way for China.

Harrison said he wanted to talk about the Cultural Revolution. She said, "We were not mentally prepared for what happened." Mao was convinced there were many capitalist roaders in the party, and Lin Biao and Jiang Qing found this theory useful to them. Many were accused. He Long would have been an insurmountable obstacle because of his power in the army, so he was framed by Lin Biao. Zhou Enlai warned them to stay away from their house and they went to the western hills. But later even Zhou became powerless to combat Lin Biao. This was when it was decided He Long was too difficult to be struggled with and a "medical approach" would be more effective.

I have written about their being kept in a courtyard house, closely watched, not allowed to even go out into the yard, not given any water to drink. He Long had diabetes, needed water and insulin. He was denied both and given glucose, which killed him. She was kept in prison for six years after he died. After that, she was sent to Guizhou to do forced labor. Her youngest daughter went with her. The other children were evicted from their home and put in jail.

While in Guizhou no one knew who she was. She was made to use different names, was called a mysterious old woman of the mountains. After Lin Biao crashed in 1971, her life of exile ended, but it took Zhou Enlai some time to locate her.

SUNDAY, JUNE 17

We have no more interviews; I have nearly finished sorting and packing; Harrison is still typing; we leave day after tomorrow. But the time seems to drag. Will the moment ever come?

MONDAY, JUNE 18

This is our last night in China. We leave tomorrow at 10:00 A.M. and get home about twenty hours later. It is crazy to fly all the way without a break. I would prefer to spend the night in Tokyo. But we are anxious to get home, so I guess we can stand it.

We had a wonderful farewell dinner with the Services and Zhang and his wife, in the restaurant in the "dating" park. When we arrived, many people were eating outside in the courtyard. Lanterns were strung up over the tables and it looked very festive. But we were led through a tangle of wires and pipes to a dreadful inside room, all smelly with incense, awful paper decorations, and a huge table big enough for fourteen people. It was like a funeral parlor. We had a hard time convincing the manager that we didn't want to sit in that stuffy room when it was so lovely out. To him it was what he thought worthiest for VIPs. Sitting outdoors is for lesser people. But finally, though he clearly didn't approve, he set a table for us in the courtyard.

Because we had made a reservation, we had to have a fancy dinner—much too much, too many dishes of shrimp in different forms, and no rice until we asked for it.

But it was fun and a pleasant occasion to mark the end of our trip. The park looked lovely with trees in leaf and flowers blooming. Just before we finished, it started to rain, and by the time we got back here to the hotel a violent thunderstorm was crashing around Beijing. I almost felt I was back in Jiangxi.

TUESDAY, JUNE 19
On the Plane Leaving Beijing

No matter how much we want to get home, it was hard to say good-bye to our companions of the past nearly four months. We have lived so closely, been so bound together by our great adventure, by the search for facts and truth. The Services waved us off from the hotel; our Chinese friends came to the airport. And here we are. Our Long March is behind us and we have survived. We will be home at 10:30 P.M. today, though it will be tomorrow morning for us.

AFTERTHOUGHTS

Now that the trip is over, we're home, we're all right, we survived, how do I feel?

I am glad I went, gratified I was able to have such adventures—adventures in history, in learning, in friendship. I never would have believed I could say this, but I enjoyed myself on our Long March. Granted, seventy days bumping around in some of the most remote areas in China doesn't sound like fun, and some of it wasn't, but by and large I had a good time. The only really bad time was when Harrison was sick, and even that experience was rewarding. We got along well with our companions, became close because of our common pursuit. I don't remember anyone being cross, disagreeable, unpleasant, or even out of sorts. Everyone (except me) was sick at one time or another, yet no one asked for special treatment or burdened the rest of us with his feelings. We were a cheerful group, passionately interested in what we were doing. It was quite extraordinary, as I think back on it.

I learned firsthand what China used to be like, the inequalities and hopelessness of the feudal system, what it took to throw it over and start anew. I learned about the courage, bravery, and perseverance of the soldiers and other people we met who suffered so much in the Cultural Revolution and survived that ordeal. Decent, patriotic men and women, dedicated to their country, changing it when they were young; and now that they are old, working to keep the gains and not let it get out of control again.

The meaning of the Long March came home to me as it never could have without retracing the route, seeing the meeting places, the battle-grounds, the mountains, the Grasslands, the rivers that were crossed, and talking to survivors. I understand now how it inspires the younger generation of Chinese, how they want to live up to those heroes, keep their spirit alive. It was a sorting out of the good and the bad; of the people who wanted to help their country and those who wanted only power.

The women who had been on the Long March were especially touching. What a weird experience that must have been, what a strange way to live for so many months, fighting alongside their husbands, having babies in fields and bogs in the middle of battles. Most of the women we met had suffered with their husbands in the Cultural Revolution and now are dedicating the rest of their lives to the memory of those brave men. Their loyalties to China, to the revolution, and to their men are bound up together.

Their children, too, seem bent on straightening out the events of the Cultural Revolution, clarifying what happened, honoring their parents for their trials, and making sure such an upheaval won't recur.

I learned a lot about Mao. Without him there would not have been liberation from the landlord system, at least not for many more years. I think he was the only man who could affect, influence, and teach the poor people of China at that time. He understood the peasants, knew their potential strength, knew how to organize and cultivate it. As I have said, I can now easily understand all the slogans about Mao's wisdom, his love for the people, his willingness to endure any hardship to bring about the change that had to be. If only he had left the scene before the late 1950s, before the Great Leap Forward, before initiating the commune system, before unleashing the Cultural Revolution. Obviously he lost his way, and in the end was the tool of his last wife and others whose craze for power turned China into a nightmare of persecution and degradation as terrible as the system they had once overthrown.

The most nagging thoughts are about Zhou Enlai. We heard very little about him in our talks and interviews along our march. People talked about Mao, Zhu De, Li De, Zhang Guotao, and others, but never made more than a passing reference to Zhou. We know he was Mao's chief of staff from Zunyi to the end; we know that he tried to help victims of harassment at the beginning of the Cultural Revolution, but then, as someone told us, "He became powerless to help." Yet he was the man who, to the world, was the sophisticated spokesman of Mao's China. He had been in at the start, from the uprisings in the twenties through the Long March, the days at Yan'an, the Japanese war, the civil war. He was Mao's right-hand man. How could he not have known about the terrible crimes being perpetrated in the name of the revolution? Did he feel he could do more good by staying in? At the end of his life he, too, was assailed by the Gang of Four and even denied the music he wanted to hear when he was dying in the hospital. Will we ever know the truth about Zhou Enlai? To me this is the most important unresolved question.

181

INDEX

183

114, 142, 147, 154, 160, 165, 166; communist base in, 64, 81

Jiaopingdu, crossing at, 100, 102, 103

Jingpo, 89

Jinping, 77

Jinshi scholar, 91

Kafka, Franz, works of, 172

Kang Keqing, 32, 97, 142, 175

Khrushchev, Nikita, 71, 72

The King and I, 8

Korean War, 38, 79

Kunming, 96–97, 98, 99, 100

Kuomintang, 44, 53, 58, 59, 62, 67, 78, 99, 106, 111, 134, 135, 136, 144, 155, 163, 165; at Baizhang, 113; defeat of, 156; defections from, 170; He Long's involvement with, 147; at Luding Bridge, 116; treatment of peasants, 42, 72, 81, 108, 117, 143; treatment of women, 32, 66; U.S. support of, 79; and Western expedition, 173

Lahu, 89

Lama (religion), 131

Lamaseries, 121–122

Lanzhou, 145, 146; reforestation of, 144

Laoshan, battle of, 163

Lazikou, battle at, 136, 137

Lenin, Vladimir, 57

Lhasa, 115, 118, 123

Lin Biao, 13, 21, 24, 85, 164; as commander of First Army group, 22, 98; and cultural revolution, 45, 100, 166, 178. *See also* Cultural revolution; Gang of Four

Li De, 38, 61, 80, 82, 83, 64, 70, 165; decline of, 70, 97–98; sent by Russian Cominterm, 9–10

Li Bozhao, 32, 173; *The Long March*, 46; *We Must Win Victory*, 174; *Going North*, 46

Li Jianzhen, 175

Li Yimang, 29–30, 32

Li Ziannian, 19, 165, 172–173

Liberation, War for, 56, 91, 122, 125, 128, 144, 147

Lijiang, 90, 91, 94, 97

Lion's Head, 101, 103–104

Liping Meeting, 70, 76

Liu Bocheng, 22, 25

Liu Lizhen, 162–163, 164

Liu Ying, 166–168, 175

Liu Zhidan, 153, 155, 156, 162, 163–164

Longxi, 139–140

Loushen Pass, 83, 86

Lower Depths, The, 174

Luce family, 63

Luding Bridge, crossing at, 20, 21, 31, 115–116, 117, 134

Luo Fu, 166, 167, 168–169

Lushan, meeting at, 168

Ma Brothers, 173

Maerkang, 119, 120, 121, 124, 126, 154, 171

Manchu, 40, 108

Manchuria, 153

Mao Zedong, 3, 20, 21, 24, 29, 46, 55, 63, 64, 66, 85, 86, 97–98, 100, 102, 124, 129, 140, 152–157; and Autumn Harvest Uprising, 52–53, 168; and concept of Peasant Revolution, 15–16, 27, 81; conflict with Zhang Guotao, 112, 121, 132, 173, 174; leadership of Communist Party, 70, 80, 82, 83; on Long March, 4, 20, 22, 23, 30, 41, 59, 61, 71, 108, 131, 153, 167; marriages of, 44, 97, 168; relations with U.S., 27, 79; and Rus-

sian Comintern, 9–10, 163; teachings of, 57, 125, 147
Maoping, 53
Maotai (drink), 20, 43
Maotai (town), 28, 85, 86
Marx, Karl, 57
Maxim's, 17, 176
McCarthy era, 3
Meitan River, 82
Miao, 69, 73, 89, 108, 109, 120, 136
Ming Dynasty, 135
Minxian, 138
Missionaries, 24, 62, 83. *See also* Catholicism
Mongolian horses, 133

Nanchang, 47, 49, 60, 63, 65, 89
Nanchang Uprising, 53, 147
Nashi, 89, 92
Nationalists, 10, 12, 19, 27, 42, 43, 49, 53, 62, 67, 157. *See also* Kuomintang
Nepal, 115, 118
New York Times, 36, 37
Nine Hundred Days, the, 8
Nine Dragon Gorge, 135
Nineteenth Army, 11
Ningdu, 60, 62, 63, 67
Ninth Army, 41
Nixon, Richard M., 172
North Vietnam, 11
North Korea, 11
Nuoergai, 127–131
Nutcracker, The, 73

Old Marshall, 153
Old Silk Route, 4
Opium, 76, 85, 86, 94, 114, 122
Ordination Terrace Temple, 44–45

Pagoda, 95–96
Party Central Committee, 168
Pei, I.M., 16, 39

People's Liberation Army, 49
People's Provincial Congress, 135
Peking Hotel, 6, 7, 9, 37, 47
Peking Hospital, 12
Peking Opera, 40, 156, 157
Peking University, 23, 28, 24
Peng Dehuai, 97
Percy, Walker, 31
Pinyin System, 37–38
Polo, Marco, 62
Portuguese, in Macao, 53. *See* Catholicism
Provincial Museum, 111–112

Qian Xinzhang, 26, 40–41
Qian Zhongfei, 174
Qiang, 120, 127
Qin Shi Huang, 150–151
Qin Xinzhong, 26
Qing Dynasty, 95, 128
Qinggangpo, battle of, 85, 108

Reagan, Ronald, 39, 56, 86, 150, 169
Rectification program, 27
Red Army, 10, 16, 21, 22, 23, 25, 27, 53, 54, 62, 63, 64, 65, 67, 70, 72, 77, 78, 82, 83, 87, 92, 96, 97, 99, 111, 114, 121, 122, 124, 128, 141, 142, 143, 145, 146, 154, 160, 170, 175; attacked by warlords, 71; at battle of Lazikou, 136; crossing Luding Bridge, 115–116; at Jiaopingdu, 100–101; memorial to, 115; and peasants, 42, 44, 81, 94; at Qinggangpo, 85–86; reception of at Lijiang, 91; in Yi country, 24
Red Badge of Courage, The, 49
Red Bandits, 67, 99
Red Guards, 33, 36, 53, 59, 150, 155
Red River. *See* Chishui
Red Star Over China, 23, 156

Tong'an, 100–101
Tongzi, 84
Tonkin, 99
Truman, Harry S., 79
Two King's Temple, 113

United Nations, 34, 38, 46
United States, 27, 79, 86
Uprising Museum, 49–50

Viet Nam, 176

Wade Giles, 37–38
Wang Bin, 170
Wang Ming, 9, 16, 155
Wang Yanjian, *An Ordinary La-borer,* 9–10, 20
Wang Yunlong, 54
Wang Zuo, 54
Wang River, 145
Wanzai County, 142
Warlords, 24, 81, 84, 86, 91, 94, 97, 102, 177. *See also* Feudal system
Wei (River), 149
Wei Xiuying, Mrs., 65–66
Weimar Republic, 38
Western Expedition, 173
Whampoa Military Academy, 9, 155
White Dragon River, 134, 135
White River, 128
World War II, 28, 43, 146, 161, 153
Wren, Christopher, 16, 18, 39
Wren, Jacqueline, 16, 18, 39
Wu (river), 82
Wu Jiqing, 66–67
Wu Seng, 145–146, 147
Wu Xiuquan, 37–38
Wuqi, 152, 155, 156, 157, 163

Xiaguan, 89, 90
Xi'an, 5, 15, 31, 33, 86, 115, 145, 146, 148, 149, 150, 151, 158–159, 160, 161, 163, 164

Xiang River, crossing at, 10
Xiang Qing, 23
Xiao Hua, *The Red Army Fears No Hardship on the Long March,* 24
Xiaojin, 121
Xichang, 104–105
Xingguo, 56, 58
Xiao, Ke, 12–13, 33, 70, 90, 91, 97, 147
Xiao Yedan, 25
Xiaquan, 94
Xiao Mao, 66
Xiao You, 97
Xishui, 83, 85
Xue Ming, Mme., 176–177

Yan'an, 14, 15, 26, 27, 28, 31, 32, 33, 66, 90, 97, 113, 146, 151; home of Red Army, 152–153, 157–158
Yang family, 135
Yang Chengwu, *Reflections on the Long March,* 21–23
Yang Kaihui, 168
Yang Shangkun, 32, 45–47, 174
Yangtse River, 85, 99, 100, 129; upper, 91. *See also* Golden Sands River
Ye Qun, 177
Ye Yingli, 160–161
Yellow Emperor, 152
Yellow River, 128, 129, 145, 147
Yenching University, 23–24
Yi, 37, 24, 25, 89, 108, 154; customs and dress of, 90, 106
Young Communist Central Committee, 166–167, 170
Young Marshall, 15, 153
Yuan Wencai, 54
Yuan Yaoxiu, 156
Yudu, 64, 160, 167
Yugoslavia, 38
Yunnan, 85–86, 98, 99, 101, 134; warlords of, 91

Zhang Guotai, 30, 46, 122, 130, 143, 153, 154–155; conflict with Mao, 47, 112; defeat at Baizhang, 113
Zhang Quan, 163
Zhang Qinqiu, 32
Zhang Renshi, 145, 146, 147
Zhang Shengji, 147
Zhang Wentien, 166. *See also* Luo Fu
Zhidan, 154; reforestation near, 153–154
Zho Enlai, 6, 9–10, 22, 32, 38, 44, 70, 80, 100, 112, 121, 137; Gang of Four treatment of, 24; on Long March, 20, 23, 30, 170; in Uprising of 1927, 49
Zhongnanhai, 169
Zhoukeji, 123, 171
Zhu De, 10, 22, 32, 49, 53, 63, 80, 97, 111, 121, 130, 134; at battle of Qinggangpo, 86, 108; struggle with Zhang Guotai, 46, 112, 161
Zidaldi, 114, 115
Zunyi, 80, 83, 85, 86, 87, 108; conference at, 11, 70, 82, 97, 112, 165, 167